Books by Eda J. LeShan

THE WONDERFUL CRISIS OF MIDDLE AGE, *McKay 1973*
ON "HOW DO YOUR CHILDREN GROW?" *McKay 1972*
WHAT MAKES ME FEEL THIS WAY? *Macmillan 1972*
SEX AND YOUR TEEN-AGER, *McKay 1970*
NATURAL PARENTHOOD, *Signet 1970*
THE CONSPIRACY AGAINST CHILDHOOD, *Atheneum 1967*
HOW TO SURVIVE PARENTHOOD, *Random House 1965*

THE
WONDERFUL
CRISIS OF
MIDDLE AGE

* * * * * *

Some

Personal

Reflections

BY

EDA J. LeSHAN

DAVID McKAY COMPANY, INC.

New York

THE WONDERFUL CRISIS OF MIDDLE AGE

Selection from *The Prophet* by Kahlil Gibran, reprinted with permission of the publisher, Alfred A. Knopf, Inc. Copyright 1923 by Kahlil Gibran. Renewal Copyright 1951 by Administrators C.T.A. of Kahlil Gibran Estate and Mary G. Gibran.

ISBN: 0-679-50398-6
LIBRARY OF CONGRESS CATALOG CARD NUMBER: 72-95159
MANUFACTURED IN THE UNITED STATES OF AMERICA

*This book is dedicated in most loving memory
to a great teacher and friend,* DR. ABRAHAM MASLOW,
*who taught me the word and lived the spirit of
what I wanted most to be: Self-actualized*

Contents

*

WHAT'S SO WONDERFUL?

Chapter 1

As I begin to write this book, I am forty-eight years old—just about as middle-aged as you can get, with fifteen years of it gone and another twenty to go, if I'm lucky, before I begin to be old.

I can't drink coffee after three in the afternoon if I want to sleep at night; a pastrami sandwich at midnight would have me bilious at dawn; I haven't been able to eat onions or green peppers for five years—the reaction of my lower colon is too sordid to discuss; the "liver spots," the less-than-firm chin line, the gray hairs I notice before each "touch up," the creaking joints when I first get up in the morning—all are upon me and hardly need further definition for anyone old enough to have picked up this book!

Why, then, do I call it "the *wonderful* crisis"? Am I about to perpetrate a first-class hoax, or am I so hung up about aging that I plan to write a whole book denying its existence? Well, in addition to the stiffening joints and the other signs of gradual decay, these facts are also true: I wrote my first book when I was forty-three, and this is number seven. I began to appear regularly on a TV program when I was forty-six, and at forty-eight had my own program on educational television—a program that was the sum and substance of twenty-five years of meeting and talking with parents and to which I struggled to bring whatever I had learned about myself and about the human condition; it was, in other words, an experience of creative fulfillment. I have come to understand and enjoy motherhood far better and I find myself loving my daughter more deeply these last five years than during her first fifteen, and the dimensions of wifehood seem to become more fascinating, complex and profound each day. I have learned more about who I am and what I want to be in life, since the age of forty, than in all the years before. I feel more truly myself than I have ever felt before; I work harder at self-discovery, and, I think, bring more courage to that struggle today than ever before in my life.

I have been thinking about writing a book on middle age for several years, but I could not think of the right title for it—one that would reflect the underlying theme I was trying to define. The title came to me in a moment of bleak despair some months ago, when it seemed to me I had hit the blackest depths of personal upheaval and misery. Was the inspiration of this title an attempt at denying the problems of life? I think not—for even in that moment of feeling overwhelming sadness and defeat, I knew that what I was in for was more growing, more awareness, more discovery of what it means to be human.

And this is the wonder of the crisis of middle age: *its challenges are the greatest opportunity one has ever had to become most truly alive and oneself.*

A friend recently told me of a Saturday afternoon's shopping expedition with her sixteen-year-old daughter. Lynn was wearing new shoes, and with all the walking her feet were soon badly blistered. Mother suggested that Lynn take off her shoes and just wear a pair of loose-fitting rain boots she happened to have in her bag, but Lynn was horrified by the idea and said, "But everybody will *look* at me and think I'm crazy!" Her mother told me, "Wear her shoes she would—and even with the Bandaids and tissues we put on her poor heels, she was a bloody mess by the time we got home. I was really horrified by the amount of pain she would endure because of what other people might have thought— especially since *I* was wearing a pair of those 'space shoes,' which look so ugly and feel so good!"

That story symbolizes the difference between the first period of growing up—adolescence—and the second opportunity that comes with middle age. Psychiatrist Dr. Carl Jung describes this as a time in which some people, usually in their forties or fifties, turn away from concern with other people's opinions of them, to concern with the growth of the self—or, to put it another way, with their good opinion of themselves.

When one is a young child, the need for dependence on others is literally a matter of life or death; you just can't survive unless grownups take care of you. You need to be loved and nurtured more than anything else in the world. Each of us made a thousand unconscious choices during those early years of our lives—choices between living out what was unique and special in our natures, or satisfying the dreams and expectations of our parents and all the other adults who cared for us. It is rare, indeed, that a child is born into the world who is able to please himself (*be* himself) and also please those he needs. In most cases, and to varying degrees, each of us sold out when we were children; we tried desperately to become what we felt others wanted us to be. And because we were young and our brains were neurologically immature, we often misinterpreted what others wanted from us and frequently sold out when we didn't need to. Grownups were pleased when we were "good," and unhappy when we were "bad." We therefore assumed that all our energies must be focused on being the one and never the other—as if that were ever really possible. Our view of what adults wanted from us in the way of accomplishments often had nothing to do with reality. A parent might say, for example, "I don't know why you still need that night light—you're really too big," and we would make an assumption that really wasn't even there: "To be a good and strong person, I have to be braver than I feel." The parent may have had no such thought in mind—and might be shocked to know the weight of those words—but young children think rigidly and concretely and invest adults with wisdom and power no adult really has or even wants.

To be good, *we felt* we had to be quiet; to be loved, *we felt* we could not be angry; to be approved of, *we felt* we had to learn to swim while we were still too scared, and to read and write, add and subtract at a time when *we felt* that a teacher could never really love us if we didn't always know the right answers.

We came into adolescence with confused and misleading perceptions about what it meant to be oneself and what it was possible to feel as a human being. During those often stormy and rebellious years of adolescence, we needed to shake off attitudes and ideas that were deeply ingrained. We needed to begin to come to terms with the inaccuracies of our lofty perceptions about human perfectibility and we needed to begin to try to solve the problem of our dependency, so that we could start the long, tough struggle toward autonomy and personal responsibility for our lives. We came into adolescence with inflexible and unrealistic expectations for ourselves and everyone else. During adolescence our personalities "softened" so that we could move toward a reorganization, so that we could discover anew what we were and could become human in the true meaning of the word.

The first adolescence is never a complete reorganization of one's identity. Even with all the "emancipation acrobatics" that go with it, we are still so young and in need of approval and support that we never quite break loose from all the "shoulds" we have learned in childhood. We are at least still partly preoccupied with pleasing others rather than ourselves; in moving away from parental values and expectations, we need the support and approval of our peers—who often turn out to be more demanding than our parents were. And so we turned for comfort to other adolescents and in our mutually shared uncertainties and lack of self-confidence, we sold out all over again, trying to fit our images of ourselves into whatever pattern seemed most valued at the time we were growing up. The poorly coordinated intellectual tried desperately to become the athlete; the introvert, the life of the party; the shy, quietly serious student, the clown. Being still only partly grown—naked and vulnerable in our struggle for our identity—we still needed to make the choice of being concerned with what others wanted us, expected us, to be.

Eventually, we felt secure enough to make important personal choices; we *did* break away from real or imagined parental and peer-group standards and expectations; we chose our work, our marriage partners, our life-styles; we had children of our own, and chose our methods of childraising, we chose our homes, our hobbies, our friends, our ideals and goals. But the first decades of being grown up were so active and busy that we rarely found time to sit down and really take stock, to question what we were doing with our lives or why.

It may seem strange, but I believe deeply that for those of us who are middle-aged, the most profound growing still lies ahead of us. We are a generation which has been brainwashed into believing that genuine growing is something that takes place only during one's childhood. In the admittedly fascinating preoccupation of recent years with the "ages and stages" of childhood, we have all but ignored the fact that growing and learning and changing are never (not even mostly) the prerogative of childhood; quite the contrary— what happens to us *after* the age of twenty-one is just as significant, just as dramatic, as anything that has happened before.

The impact of psychoanalysis, with its explorations and insights into "the formative years," has tended to distort our vision, to lead us down the primrose path of absolute determinism. Many of us, raised on the psychiatric revolution of the past half-century, have tended to arrive at the foolish conclusion that just because it *is* true that many of our basic attitudes and values are deeply rooted in our childhood experiences, we cease to make real and meaningful choices as adults.

Nothing could be further from the truth. For those of us who make the free and conscious choice to go on growing, middle age is the time when we can become most deeply and truly ourselves. At this time of life, when we have much less need or desire for dependence on others, when we have more autonomy than we have ever had before, or will have again, to discover and assert our own unique and fundamental nature, it is possible to become more oneself than ever before. There is no longer the need to sell out for love and approval, and we have at our disposal, for the task of reassessment, all the strength and maturity and wisdom we have accumulated in *a lot of living*.

Of course we bring with us some burdensome baggage of childhood, and if we have really lost touch with what was unique and special in us when we were children, we may have to embark on a treasure hunt in search of who we really are, with someone who can guide the way (more of that later). For now, I'd like to mention just one major obstacle to the kind of adventure-in-growing that I know is possible, and that is the idea we bring with us from early childhood that life is orderly and "makes sense." It comes under the heading of "Good Behavior Will Be Rewarded."

It was the most impossible and yet most universal promise of childhood. We *should* be kind because then people will be kind to us; we *should* study hard because then we will be successful; we *should* always tell the truth because then we would be rewarded with love and approval; all families *should* love each other. We learn to make claims on life, we begin to believe in bargains where none really exist.

Kind people sometimes get beaten up; some people who have the most money and power, studied the least; sometimes family members really don't like each other at all; sometimes telling the truth can get you into more trouble than you can handle.

In fact there is nothing the least bit orderly or predictable about the course our lives take, and we find ourselves entrapped by attitudes that make us feel bitter and angry much of the time. If we carry this residue of childhood into middle age, we are in trouble. On the other hand, if we can take a sharp and candid look at the "shoulds" we have been burdened with, we have a chance to shake off this heavy weight. We feel we *should* be happy because we have led a hard and selfless life—but there is no such law of the universe, and if we refuse to give up this claim on life we are doomed to eternal disappointment. A father says, "I can't understand it; we gave Ronnie every opportunity, he had the best of care, the best of schools, the best of everything—he should appreciate all that and stay at college." The "should" in that last sentence has nothing to do with reality: Ronnie sees all kinds of reasons why "the best of everything" has nothing to do with going to college—and so his parents are bitter and angry. A middle-aged woman says, "I've worked for other people all my life. I should have some pleasure now, instead of being crippled with arthritis." Or a retired teacher comments, "I hated teaching, but I did it, and I gave the children all that I could; now it should be my turn to have others do things for me."

Children learn to believe in such powerful rules of justice because the most important people in their lives tell them it is so. But when we live with such "shoulds," such claims on life that it be orderly or fair, we burden ourselves with impossible hopes and inevitable disillusionment.

Middle age is an opportunity to reassess the claims we each have made—and to give them up. It's an *enormous* relief —until the fear of hedonism overtakes us. "After all," we think to ourselves, from the roots of early training, "if there *is* no order in life, then why would anyone try to achieve anything, or ever try to be a good person?" Perhaps this was the biggest hoax of childhood—that only the belief in an orderly universe could drive us to doing the best we could in achieving personal goals or in feeling concern for others. There *is* an alternative! And that is to attempt to be all the best one can be, simply for the pleasure, for the joy, for the pride in oneself that is a by-product of the struggle itself: to "do good" because it makes one feel good; to give one's best because nothing is more pleasurable; to show compassion for others because such behavior gives one good feelings about oneself—without any promises, without any rewards provided by others. It is, indeed, the difference between doing something because it pleases our parents or doing something because it pleases us. And it is almost unbelievable the degree to which we can live into middle age, without realizing that it is still our parents we are trying to please rather than ourselves—even if they are no longer alive!

The wonderful opportunity of middle age is that once and for all, we can begin, with the wisdom and maturity and perspective of our experiences in living, the tough job of sorting out whom we want to please—and in this quest, we discover that until we learn to please ourselves, free of the "shoulds," we can give little genuine pleasure to anybody else.

To move creatively and courageously into a second adolescence—a "middlescence"—is to invoke the exultant cry of Martin Luther King on a never-to-be-forgotten moment of affirmation on the steps of the Lincoln Memorial in Washington: "Free at last! Great God Almighty, free at last!" If ever there is to be a moment that belongs to us, it is now, in our middle years. In addition to our greater independence and autonomy, what seems to me to move us toward the experience of "middlescence" is that middle age brings into sharp and poignant focus the incredible and all but unbearable fact of our mortality. No one under the age of thirty-five or forty ever really believes that time-for-living is not "forever"!

Suddenly—and oh, how suddenly it does come upon us!—we are forty or forty-five years old. Suddenly we find ourselves taking stock: Who are we? What have we done with our lives? We become painfully aware of our mortality, and life is no longer limitless. I think my first awareness of middle age was that I would never read all the books I wanted to read, never see all the places I wanted to visit, that time was running out. Few of us come to this moment of truth without misgivings and regrets; most of us find ourselves often feeling quite overwhelmed with the "might-have-beens" of life. We are more than likely to begin to experience some of those old familiar feelings of adolescence—the fear that life might be meaningless, a sense of despair about our limitations, a hopelessness about our future. What we need to remember is the other equally real and valid part of adolescence—feelings of excitement and wonder, curiosity, the joy of uncovering latent strengths, the exultancy in being alive, with so many adventures to anticipate.

"Middlescence" is the opportunity for going on with the identity crisis of the first adolescence. It is our second chance to find out what it really means to "do your own thing," to sing your own song, to be deeply and truly yourself. It is a time for finding *one's own* truths at last, and thereby to become free to discover one's real identity. No matter how many people still depend on us, no matter how many mistakes we may have made, we can now take another look— and this time around we can bring to our decisionmaking the greater flexibility of our independence, more honesty and courage. Because we have such a sensitized awareness of how precious time is, we can appreciate the urgency and importance of our quest, for if we don't take this opportunity—if we don't really search for ourselves, now—we may never do it.

The chips are down; the years ahead are not numberless, as we thought at fifteen or twenty-five. If we sell out now, it matters as it never did before. And if I have learned anything in my forty-eight years, it is simply this: in order for life to have the most profound meaning, in order for one to be glad to be alive, one must try to find oneself. A woman with terminal cancer was weeping quietly when her doctor came into her hospital room. He tried to reassure her, but she interrupted him. "I'm not crying because I'm *dying*," she said, "I'm crying because I have never *lived*." The only thing that seems to relieve the anxiety of getting older, the terror of dying, is the feeling that one has made the most of what one can be. Jack London put it most poignantly when he wrote:

> I would rather be ashes than dust.
> I would rather my spark should burn in a brilliant blaze
>   than it should be stifled in dry-rot.
> I would rather be a superb meteor,
>   every atom of me in magnificent glow,
>   than a sleepy and permanent planet.
> Man's chief purpose is to live, not to exist.
> I shall not waste my days trying to prolong them.
>   I shall use my time.*

If I were to suggest that I have any easy answers for the excruciatingly difficult task of becoming most alive, I would

* Quoted by permission of Irving Shepherd and the Estate of Jack London.

be a liar and a propagandist, a con artist with something to sell, some formula for a happy life that isn't true. Oversimplifying the complexities of the human experience seems to me to diminish people, to suggest that they do not have the courage and the wisdom to face the challenges of life. The expert with the easy answers seems to me to be encouraging people to expect the very least from themselves. Books that provide lesson plans for fighting or making up in marriage, for disciplining children, for how to be more sexy, are an insult to the intelligence—for no matter how we may be seduced into longing for the simple solution, we know it never works.

In his book, *Toward a Psychology of Being,* Abraham Maslow wrote:

> . . . If grief and pain are sometimes necessary for growth of the person, then we must learn not to protect people from them automatically as if they were always bad. Sometimes they may be good and desirable. . . . Not allowing people to go through their pain, and protecting them from it, may turn out to be a kind of overprotection, which in turn implies a certain lack of respect for the integrity and the intrinsic nature and the future development of the individual.

Happiness, in my experience, is not a "goal" to consciously work toward; happiness comes in precious and rare moments of piercing joy as a by-product of the struggle to be most alive, to surrender oneself most openly to all one's experiences, and it comes as a kind of counterpoint to accepting and understanding the tragic and the painful in the human condition.

In *The Prophet,* Kahlil Gibran writes: "Your pain is the breaking of the shell that encloses your understanding." If one is to search for deeper understanding, pain seems to me to be inevitable. We are and will be confused, uncertain, sad, depressed, hopeless, furious, and frustrated a good part of the time—and the more so if we are really alive. All I can offer is the companionship of my own groping, and for whatever it may be worth, the absolute conviction that the struggle to be most oneself is really all we've got; the quest for one's own deepening humanity is what life is all about. Growing hurts a lot of the time—it hurts like hell; it leaves one raw and open—sensitized to one's deepest feelings.

In order to make the most of this new crisis of self-discovery in middle age, one has, in a sense, to become a lobster— only *knowing* the danger, which I presume the lobster is happily free from experiencing! In order to fit into his shell as he grows bigger, the lobster goes through periodic sheddings of his shell. During these times he is naked and vulnerable and in terrible danger of being eaten by his enemies in the sea. And yet, in the inexorability of nature, he must go through this crisis of dangerous exposure, or not grow. So with middle age, it is possible to remain stationary, to accept life as one has lived it and to settle for more of what has been, good, bad, and indifferent. One says, in effect, "Here I am, with my middle-aged shell; I know myself quite well, where I am right now; life has its ups and downs, but I think I'll settle for what I know. It's the safe way, and I feel ready to be safe."

That is not the sort of lobster I can be, or that I can recommend to you. I know all the dangers of that unshelled state—I have already been there many times. Each time it is an agony of self-doubt, of confusion, of terror of the unknown self that lies ahead. Each time I come close to that existential nakedness, I wonder how I could be such an idiot as to go through it again. And then the new and bigger shell begins to form, with more life-space in it, with new opportunities for understanding and fulfillment. For a while there is an exultant sense of new horizons opening up, increased sensitivity and awareness, deep new insights into myself and others, new creative forces bursting into life. And then, slowly, inexorably, the shell begins to feel uncomfortable again, I begin to feel the constrictions of a plateau in growing, of becoming ready to understand more and to become more—and then I know it is time to find the safest and quietest place I can through meditation and introspection, through trying to get more in touch with my feelings and dreams, or through a return to psychotherapy, where I can shed my shell and begin new growing. It is a dangerous life, but I do you the honor of asking you to join me!

It takes no courage at all to do something if you are unaware of danger. The real test of one's courage is to risk all when the danger is known. If I could say, "Here is a prescription for a happy life," and if you were foolish enough to believe me, there would be no courage needed to follow my plan. What I say instead is that middle age can offer the greatest risks of all, but if you have the courage to take the necessary leap into faith, the adventure can be the most important and wonderful one that you can ever experience.

I would like to use my personal experiences to reveal whatever I can about what life is really like—to allow the reader to bring his own perceptions and judgments into a mutually shared examination of what each of our realities seems to be like, and what we can learn from it. By disclosing myself, I hope to enlarge the reader's experience just a little, in the hope that the more we can be open to each other in our experiences and feelings, the more we will find the inner strength and wisdom to find our own ways of Being and Becoming. Not in search of final solutions to problems, but rather, in search of the courage we need to live with the insurmountable problems we are bound to encounter and to use both the joys and the tragedies of living for our own further growth.

I hope that you will come along for the ride, in friendship and mutual trust, and perhaps come away from my experiencing of life with some feeling of comradeship and encouragement.

CAUGHT IN THE MIDDLE

*
*
*
*
*
*

Chapter 2

Middle life is exactly that: mid-life,
Halfway between young and old,
Between young girls and old ladies,
Between budding and wrinkled breasts,
Between my mother and my daughter.
Jealous of the daughter's youth,
Afraid of the mother's age,
I'm in a run down
Caught between two bases:
My mother and my daughter,
About to be tagged out of the game
By either one.

Carol Dinklage *

Having started on an upbeat note, it seems only fair to add that this is a very rough time in which to be middle-aged. For those of us who remember Uncle Don, open streetcars, double-decker Fifth Avenue buses, icemen and milk wagons, breadlines and fireside chats, there is a sense of having been hurtled through space at a breakneck speed. We are *tired!* It's all been too much—living through more change in our lifespan than occurred in the last five hundred years. We are

* Quoted by permission of the author.

not only middle-aged, but we feel caught in the middle of our past and our present. What is perhaps most special about us is that we have always been in the middle! We were raised to have respect for our elders, and to see it as a central focus of our lives to please our parents; we are still trying to do this. But we also came to resent this role, and to feel cheated. Sometimes we sacrificed far too much in this homage; sometimes we even sold our souls for parental approval and satisfaction. We were the first parents in the era of the child-centered family; when we became parents, our children tended to come first; *we* worked hard at pleasing *them!* We were the first crop of parents to take our children's failures and limitations as an indication of *our* inadequacy, not theirs; the first to believe, even briefly, that one could aspire to being a perfect parent. We found ourselves in the middle, trying to please both an older and a younger generation.

One mother summed this feeling up succinctly: "I worked like a slave at college—even choosing the career my parents thought best for me. It never occurred to me to defy their edict on the subject of virginity at marriage. When I dared to defy them in marrying someone of a different religion, we tried to please both sets of parents by being married twice in each of their religions; neither ceremony really meant anything to us—and I've regretted it for thirty years. Now my daughter is getting married. She quit college twice, never *ever* consulted our opinion about a career, had three or four love affairs before marrying, and is now marrying a man whose background is totally different from ours. My mother, whom I almost never dared to defy and tried too hard to please, isn't saying a word; she really likes and respects my daughter more than she did me; she's learned to hold her tongue and she's intrigued with how her grandchildren obviously love her, but don't consult her about anything, and expect her to accept *their* ways. I look at my daughter and think, "You lucky little devil—how I wish I'd had the chance and the guts to make my life my own!"

We are caught in the middle of a sexual revolution as well. When I was a growing and impressionable girl, I could not conceive of anything more romantic or passionate than seeing Leslie Howard kiss the palm of a girl's hand. Today I feel a vague sense of guilt because I'm not dying to try fifty-seven new varieties of sexual activities and positions. I was brought up to believe that nice girls were virgins when they got married (which gives you a rough idea of my gullibility) and I have had to adjust in my middle age to attitudes about sexual relations and marriage that have made me embarrassed and ashamed of the "prehistoric romanticism" of my youth. Most of us who were raised to believe that the world would surely come to an end if sex and marriage didn't go together are ricocheting from wall to wall as we try to accept and acknowledge the evidence of our eyes and our instincts that many of our children are having important, meaningful, responsible relationships without marriage, and that it takes a lot of digging to find a married couple, however devoted to each other they may be, who remain faithful straight through the middle years we are now experiencing. It boggles the poor mind that was formed in the 1920s.

The same sense of trying to survive in a world we can never fully understand or feel at ease in occurs in almost every sphere of life. We feel as alienated and confused as we might be if we landed on Mars. Another example of this is in the realm of race relations in this country. From the point of view of the militant young black today, life is terrible, and change is excruciatingly slow—and he's right. And yet, for the middle-aged the changes since our youth seem enormous, and we feel betrayed because no one seems to appreciate us at all; on the contrary, we feel hated and this hurts our feelings.

I can remember when the country held its breath and

thought it was on the verge of revolution when Mrs. Roosevelt began to behave (in public!) as if there were Negroes who were her social equal! And having said that currently dirty word, it reminds me that most of us middle-aged thought "Negro" was a beautiful word as we tried to get "Nigger" out of the American vocabulary.

In my youthful idealism, I *know*, I *remember*, that I thought I could help to change the world and that brotherhood in America depended on my trying to integrate Nedick's and Macy's. And what a struggle that was; it didn't come easily. The first black saleswoman in Macy's was a major victory for the civic organizations working to change employment practices. Those of us who were involved in the early efforts at integration really thought this country would make it; that white people could be persuaded to change and that black people would sort of melt quietly into the general scheme of things.

Looking back now, we know that the anger of black people was deeply repressed for the purpose of survival, but that once it became *possible* (although still dangerous) for it to be expressed both blacks and whites were in for the shock of discovering the depth of hatred and despair that bubbled to the surface. The white middle-aged—at least a lot of us— thought, when we were young, that we would be the first generation in America to have genuine friendships with black people; and for a while we did—at least *we* thought they were genuine. From about 1955 on, all hell broke loose in this country, and we could see for the first time the oozing pus of centuries of horror. We feel utterly caught in the middle between the "good works" we felt we were doing—our overly romanticized ideals—and the stark, terrifying hatred we feel surrounded by, now.

We know that many of the things we set in motion in the 30s and 40s bear very directly on what became possible in the 50s and 60s, but we feel angry and dismayed that nobody appreciates us. We listen to the fury (and we know its roots are real and just) and we find ourselves reacting with anger; after all, from where we began, it all looks pretty good. Practically everything that we thought was daring and almost impossible to attain has happened. Nobody under the age of forty or forty-five can understand how we feel when we see a lawyer portrayed by a black person on TV; nobody too young to remember Steppinfetchit can understand our sense of accomplishment because there is a black general, and black sheriffs in the South. To us it seems a miracle, when we remember that blacks were kept in segregated divisions in the army when they were offering their very lives to the United States all over the world in the Second World War.

We are caught in the middle between the idealism of what we have tried to do all our lives, and the feelings of despair that we failed. The same is true of so many other social issues. A lot of us believed that strong unions, social security, and unemployment insurance would wipe out poverty; there are more poor and their plight is more terrible today. We believed that science would work for the betterment of man's life on earth—all we had to do was learn, discover, invent; and so we have the atomic bomb, the pollution of our air and water, and concrete highways slowly but surely replacing every tree, every blade of grass. We believed that the new insights that were coming to us through psychoanalysis and psychiatry would make it possible to raise children in such a way that there would be no more neuroses or psychoses. We could be accurately described as the Hopeful Generation when we were young.

A great many of us are also the children or grandchildren of immigrants who came to this country with one great dream: an opportunity for one's children and grandchildren to get an education and to become prosperous. I cannot recall in my own childhood and adolescence ever doubting for one moment that it was necessary for me to go to college and to settle on a career; that was the road to fulfillment, security, social prestige, and for making an important contribution to the society that had allowed me this opportunity. We were the children of our parents' and grandparents' dreams; we were the generation who made it—*really* made it. We are the generation of affluence; what would our grandfathers or great-grandfathers have thought of our suburban homes, our two-car garages, our swimming pools? Here we are—just where our ancestors hoped we would be—and everything they worked for and dreamed of has turned to ashes in our mouths. We live in fear, we are often bored and feel life has no meaning, and our children are completely turned off by our materialism. Caught in the middle again—between the aspirations of our forebears and the disillusion of our children, who have made us take a good hard look at the fundamental self-centeredness of our goals, the meaninglessness of the search for personal security, and the high cost of this to the social good. We worked hard, made money, and bought things—and we are called "the polluters." Our parents worked hard for us, and we believed in what they gave us; we are caught in the middle because we worked hard too, but our children do not believe in what we gave them; and deep-down we know they are right.

When I was in elementary school, we used to read books about "Children of Other Lands." It was between the two world wars, and I really believed that people would not fight with each other anymore. Since that time there has never been one half-hour period when there wasn't a war going on somewhere—and we are the generation who experienced the greatest holocaust of them all. We thought we were the children of the age of enlightenment—and six million died; we believed in rational man—that the development of the intellect would make us behave decently to one another—and we learned about the doctors who experimented on pregnant women. The values, the hopes, of our growing years have become the lost dreams, the shame and despair of our aging years.

We are also a generation in which many were attracted by socialism in the 1930s. In general that was a time of belief in "the common man." All we had to do to reach a utopian life was give power to the people. In high school, I used to join marching strikers, sing union songs, and I really believed that once the working man had some power he would bring about good race relations, he would see that housing projects were built, he would bring about socialized medicine. If our children are turned off by the "hard hats," how can *we* feel, who helped them to achieve the powerful union they've got? We see many unions misusing power in exactly the same way the "capitalist devils" of our youth misused it. We see many unions fighting and screaming all the way to integration; we see them moving ever more certainly toward representing the most conservative and selfish interests in the country. It's another blow. We are caught in the middle again.

We are a generation who believed in steady progress, in the perfectibility of our institutions, our corporate life. It has been a terrible shock to discover that our dreams for a better world have not come true. Despair comes hard to us, for it was unfamiliar in our growing. We are a generation born to hope.

When we went to school, all we were taught were the wonders of America, all the good and noble things in our history and traditions. I cannot recall, even though I went to a progressive, liberal school, ever having a real sense of some of the horrors in our history; slavery was bad, and we should befriend the Indians—but never in my growing up did I have any understanding of the degree of perfidy in our history or the clear pattern of a predilection for violence which young people perceive so clearly today or that has been documented with such horrifying clarity in the Kerner Report.

Now we are facing up to the horrors, and we find our children going to the opposite extreme—denying that there was ever anything good in the history of this country. We overlooked whatever was uncomfortable; the younger generation assumes everything was and is terrible. Somewhere in between there must be some truths about human nature; that in every period of history and in every country there have been forces for good and forces for evil, and we have not cornered the market on the latter. But the climate of self-hatred sweeps us, drowns us in deep sadness—for we are the ones with the lost illusions.

So many things look and feel strange to me. I would rather travel three hours longer on back country roads than on thruways, which seem ugly and frightening to me. I look in horrified wonder at a city I once loved so much, and found so exciting and beautiful, and which now seems to me to be a dirty, crowded, noisy insane asylum. If I see an old car with a rumble seat, the world seems real to me again, while a 747 makes me feel that by some awful accident of fate I've landed on Mars. The sight of a full moon and the moonpath on a still night on a lake fills me with wonder and delight—while the televised scene of a landing on the moon fills me with great uneasiness.

I am too young to give up and retreat; I must stay in the world and try to be part of it—but I am too old to feel at home in it.

When we reached the childraising phase of our lives, things were changing radically. We were greatly influenced by the revolution in psychology; we were becoming aware, through the new techniques of psychotherapy, that wanting to please your parents more than yourself can have crippling effects on our newly discovered psyches. We would do a different thing with our children; we would understand and respect their feelings and try to help them realize their own deepest needs and goals. We did a good job! Do any of us have children who want to please *us?* Don't misunderstand me; I think they are deeply kind and caring, and hate to hurt us, but when the chips are down, they almost always choose what is meaningful and relevant to them, not what would please us or make us feel comfortable or proud. In our better moments, knowing what it often cost us to be good, obsequious children, we are glad; but we also have moments of panic and fury because again we are caught in the middle.

There is a wonderful Yiddish word which personifies what I am talking about: *nachus*, which means "giving pleasure," "making someone proud." We are a generation who tried (still try!) to give it to our parents, and who have raised a generation of children who would feel they had failed to become genuine persons, if they gave it to us! Our fathers could say, "My son, the doctor"; we hardly feel inclined to say, with *nachus*, "My son, the guitar player" or "My son, the organic farmer." Grandpa was the peasant in Eastern Europe who made it into the American sweatshop so his grandson could wear a tie and a white shirt and work in an office— and there he is, that prodigal grandson, living on a commune, a farmer again, after all that sweat and tears!

The trouble is that *nobody* wants to please *us!* One mother told me, "Every other weekend Sam and I travel eighty miles to visit his mother in a nursing home. She's eighty-seven, senile, it's absurd—but we both understand why we do it; that's how we were raised. We visit relatives we can't stand, we have big Thanksgiving dinners for people who bore us to death, we are always available for weddings, funerals, christenings, and confirmations. We have a great sense of *duty* and we are constantly doing things, seeing people, going places we don't want to. Our children grew up knowing perfectly well how we felt, and they learned from us how hypocritical and soul-killing these kinds of relationships can sometimes be; they will have none of it. But, because we never demanded dutiful behavior, because we were so open with them about our feelings for our relations, because we spoke out for freedom and honesty in human relationships, they took us at our word and behave the way we wish we could have. We remain caught in the middle, between our guilt as imperfect children and our guilt as imperfect parents."

We are caught in the middle between the hypocrisy of our relations with our elders and the brutal and painful honesty of our children. A fifty-four-year-old friend wanted to come and visit me at the seashore. We were close friends, and it had been four or five years since we had spent any time together. We really needed each other, since we were both living through painful crises in our lives. The complicated shenanigans that she had to go through to keep her mother from knowing she was visiting me were unbelievable—because her mother's jealousy would be so great, and she would get told off in no uncertain terms: "It seems you have time for everyone but me." It is shocking how often many of us have to lie in order to avoid hurting other people's feelings, to protect our privacy, to give us any freedom of movement. We know that in a like situation, our children will say, "Sorry, Mom, I need to see my friend right now, not you," and part of us is overjoyed at this necessary and good change in family relations—but we are caught in the middle between guilt at hurting our parents and anxiety about the fact that there *must* be something wrong about the honesty we experience with our children.

We seem to have freed our children to like us or not, as they please. So naturally most of them are crazy about us, and want to spend time with us of their own free will! A father told me, "When Alice got married we thought, Oh, how great—we're really alone at last. Two weeks later she called and said she missed us, and could they come for the weekend. Then it got to be two or three weekends a month, just at a time in our lives when we had expected to have some time alone together. What can you do when your children love you so much? " We are caught, inexorably between the demands of our elders and the freely given devotion, of our children. It shakes us up!

Of course, despite their good taste in liking us, our children are far from perfect, and we blame ourselves for that. We are the first generation to blame ourselves for everything that ever went wrong with our children. We are the generation that were told we were responsible for the mental health— or lack of it—in our children. Our children know what nonsense this is, and will accordingly have a lot more fun with their kids than we did. It wasn't until our children were well into their teens that a note of sanity seemed to return to theories about childraising. We were the victims of the "nurture theory." Our parents—and all parents before them —assumed that if a child turned out peculiarly, it was a freak of nature; somewhere along the line he must have inherited some "bad blood" from an in-law! It was a time of faith in the relatively new discovery of genes and chromosomes. Our ancestors were never burdened with the horrible idea that their attitudes, their childraising procedures, were in any way responsible for how their children turned out.

If Junior heard voices that weren't there, it wasn't anybody's fault—he must have inherited that from his Uncle Simon, who had to spend most of his adult life locked up in the attic. Freud changed all that; if Junior heard voices, it was a sure thing his parents were making him sick because of their terrible childraising practices. We are the generation of parents who blamed ourselves for shyness, bedwetting, stuttering, nightmares, selfishness, rivalry, and every other normal problem of growing up. The fact that many of these were necessary in the process of growing did not daunt us in our guilt; nor do I ever remember thinking it strange that while I blamed myself with passion for every fall from grace, I never took the slightest credit for all the lovely, good, and wonderful things about my child.

By the time they were teenagers, and we had flogged ourselves mentally at least once a day for our failures, child experts began to suggest that maybe nature had at least as much to do with personality development as nurture; it was just barely possible we shouldn't throw out the genes and chromosomes completely. In the past five or ten years there have been fascinating studies which make it quite clear that children are born with very definite predispositions, and that the climate of their lives merely modifies these tendencies, depending on how parents react and handle the innate forces at work in their children. But it's too late for us. We were caught in the middle of the nature-nurture battle, and it is almost impossible for us to learn to forgive ourselves, even for imagined failings.

Many of us also feel guilty for the unfulfilled dreams of our parents; it's ridiculous but childhood experiences die hard, and we can't help ourselves. Somehow there was always that feeling that if a parent was sad, disappointed, frustrated, it was our fault, even if we had nothing to do with it. We see our parents growing older, and feel their sense of discontent at never having really fulfilled themselves—for they were under even greater pressure than we to please others rather than themselves. One woman told me about a recent visit of her parents: "I was shocked—at feeling nothing, anymore. My father *is* his medicines, his illnesses—there is really nothing left of the man. He and my mother are full of demands and empty of living. It scared me—does old age have to be like that? Will we be like that? One thing is certain; I know absolutely that my three kids won't endure what I do, in guilt and frustration."

The discontent we sense among our older relatives for the unfulfilled dreams of their youth is an ironic counterpoint to what our children are doing with their young lives. A couple of years ago we went to Miami with our daughter for the Christmas vacation to visit relatives. There were many "hippie-type" grandchildren there, and the hostility between them and many of their grandparents was electric. On the one hand, here were people in their seventies and eighties who had often had hard and unrewarding lives. Nobody had ever asked them, when they were fifteen or twenty, what *they* wanted to do with *their* lives. They did what their parents told them to do; the boys went into "Poppa's business" or into an approved profession; the girls married the person chosen by their parents. Life was assumed to be a vale of tears, with pain and worries. The idea that one could take the time to "try to find out the true meaning of being alive," and "search for one's own identity so that life could be fulfilling and creative"—these are thoughts that can flourish only in a time of affluence; when you work to stay alive, you have no time for such luxuries. So many of the elderly feel they have been shunted aside; they worked so hard, and for what? They were once important—now who listens to them? They have lost the status of their work, which was often the only thing their work gave them. Few have the inner resources to find new patterns; it is really too late for the elderly to have the identity crisis, the second adolescence that is still possible for the middle-aged. But we are caught in the middle between our elders who are filled with anger and resentment against our children who are the first generation ever to say, "My life is for *me*, not for you, and I will please myself." How jealous some grandparents are—and how angry this makes them! And there we are, trying to explain the hard and unhappy lives of our elders while at the same time apologizing to these older people for the long hair and bare feet and the self-concern and gratification demands of the young. We understand them both, and have one foot in each attitude. It makes us feel guilty to want to pursue our own interests, needs, talents—and yet we know our children are right; doing just that, when one is young—and even middle-aged—must surely be the only way to avoid the sour miseries we observe in the older generation.

However there is a strange irony in the fact that sometimes, while we sit smack in the middle of the biggest generation gap ever imagined doing our damnedest to help our parents and children to bridge it, they do just that, leaving us
out altogether! One grandmother assured her son she would
drop dead of a heart attack when he informed her that her
granddaughter was living with a young man without benefit
of marriage. Grandma threatened to disown her granddaughter, never to speak to her again, and assured her son and
daughter-in-law that they had failed completely as parents.
The battle went on for more than a year, with the middle-
aged parents feeling ashamed and guilty one minute, and de-
fiant and ready to argue the merits of the case the next.
Slowly but surely, through long hours of discussion,
Grandma at least became willing to see her prodigal granddaughter and the sinful young man. After a week's visit, during which Grandma had the courage and the wit to face
what she saw—two warm, loving, kind, good kids, with
their own very real sense of values—she wrote to her son,
"I still think you were terrible parents, but I have to admit
that Nina is a lovely young woman; it's all due to Jonathan,
whom I have decided is very good for her."

Part of the relationships with our parents and children is
financial; we are also the generation caught in the middle between what grown children have always accepted—
responsibility for at least some part of the care of elderly
parents—and the entirely new idea that parents can or
should also offer financial aid to their grown children. It used
to be that the middle-aged began to face up to the financial
needs of their parents at a time when their own children were
on their own and earning their own living; the giving was
only in one direction. A father of fifty-two says, "My mother
is a well-to-do widow, so we are not worried there. But my
wife's parents are both sick and have no resources after my
father-in-law retires, except social security, and maybe $20,-

ooo of other assets. I have two boys in college, whom I support completely—their expenses come to about $8000 a year. One of them will certainly want to go to graduate school. My daughter quit college and is living with her boy friend on an island off the coast of Maine. They earn a little money making and selling jewelry and leather belts, and they don't ask for any money—but I send my daughter money every month, even though I disapprove completely of what she's doing. How can I not, when I worry about her health and safety, and we own our home, have two cars, take trips to Europe, lead a comfortable life? But the truth is, I am in a panic; I wonder how much longer I can earn as much as I do now. I have nothing saved for my old age, and no expectation my children will feel any duty toward me, because I never wanted them to feel that way. Everything I earn is going out, and I feel as if it will never end. I'm scared to death of what would happen if I got sick. My wife and I used to think this would be the time of life we could really save for our old age—instead our expenses for others are higher than they've ever been before."

Having been raised in tightly knit families, we feel anxious about changing patterns of family life. Most of us grew up at a time when we believed that only the really depraved got divorces; in our current milieu, it seems to be happening to half the people we know, if not directly to ourselves; certainly the *thought* of divorce is no stranger to us. When I was a child, you just assumed that at least 90 percent of your relatives and close family friends lived near enough to each other so that you saw each other at Sunday dinners almost every week, and certainly for every birthday and anniversary. The mobility of families is now so great that almost all the children of those relations are now spread over the entire country. I have a cousin that I saw every week as a child, whom I now haven't seen for twenty-five years; chances are we may never meet, except perhaps at a funeral, which seems to be the one remaining gathering place of relatives. We grew up, for the most part, in close touch with most of our relatives, and now we find ourselves so scattered that it is hard to have any sense of family. Because this was a familiar part of our childhood, we experience waves of sadness and aloneness, despite the fact that some of our relatives are not people we are really dying to see very frequently; it is just a sense of something vague being the matter, when contacts become diffused or even lost.

A friend of mine was having an argument with her teenage daughter and was complaining bitterly about this young lady's lack of manners, sloppiness, etc. The daughter finally burst out, "I have a right to be an adolescent!" Without a moment's hesitation, mother replied, "And I have a right to be a menopausal mother!" Middle-age tends to arrive at the same time as the adolescence of our children. We find ourselves caught in the middle between the defiance and rebellion of a fourteen-year-old, and the anxiety that accompanies the first awareness that we are getting gray, get winded after one game of tennis, and can't leap into the ocean anymore. At the same time that we are out of our minds with worry about whether or not our children "have started," and if they have, what are they doing about birth control, we may also be worrying about the possibility of a gradual diminishment in our sex lives—the sudden awareness that it's been three weeks and we hadn't even noticed! We are only too well aware that our children are on the threshold of the hungry, passionate, unappeasable time of sex, while there is that frightened, shameful inner knowledge that for us it's sometimes a toss-up between sex and the late late movie—and often the movie wins. While our children have all their choices before them, and can make what they will of their lives, we are facing the unfulfilled dreams of our lives, the mistaken decisions and choices, the things left undone, probably never to be done, we feel. The whole of life is opening to our children just at the very same moment when we are having our first terrors that life is closing off for us. Where our parents may be bitter about the unfinished business of their lives, we are frightened by the thought that we may be moving in the same direction; is there time, we wonder, for another chance for us?

We were taught the virtues of hard work and delayed gratification of our wishes. It "built character," if we had to wait to get married because it was during the depression and we had no money. It built character if you hated certain subjects in school and had to work five times as hard to pass courses in them. There was this thing about character; you got it only if you suffered enough! A couple who were engaged for three years, while they helped to pay for their younger brothers' and sisters' education developed much more character and were "better people" than a couple who could get married after a two-month engagement. With this sort of upbringing, we get a little hung up on the assumption of our children that if something will give them pleasure, there isn't any reason in the world why they should postpone gratification. From a world in which self-sacrifice and self-denial were just about the highest values one could attain, we find ourselves spinning madly in a hedonistic world in which the economy depends upon our gratifying every silly impulse for nonessentials, and our children demonstrate by their pleasure in living that there is much to be said for doing your own thing when you want to.

We are a very *tired* generation. We have been through too much, have been called upon to change too much, too fast. Our parents tell us that it has been even worse for them, but I don't really think so, because if they can't or won't change, they can get away with it; we have *had* to change—or lose our jobs, our contact with our children, our sense of participation in the life of our communities.

We are caught between a world that valued age and one

that values youth. We were brought up to respect older people, to believe that they had much to teach us out of the wisdom of their experience. We now live in an age that values only youth. It used to be that to have white hair, a lined face, a bent body, was to be respected, even venerated—for a life of hard work. The highest compliment we can be paid today is to be told we don't look our age. Men and women spend millions of dollars every year on trying to remain youthful and glamorous—untouched by life and aging. Change has been so rapid, science and technology have brought such an avalanche of information, that it is no longer true that older people can teach younger people; the young know more. They may be immature, lacking in experience —but their information and understanding of the world they live in is often far greater than ours.

On the face of it, being caught in the middle sounds depressing and hopeless, doesn't it? Not for me, anymore; just getting it all off my chest has helped a lot! I mean that quite seriously—and not just for myself. The solution to most human problems seems to me to start with acknowledging what the reality is and facing our feelings about it. There is no doubt that this current place in the middle is not an easy or comfortable place to be—but is it hopeless? Not at all. It is certainly possible to resign ourselves to the thought that we cannot have any control over the social forces which buffet us, so that we might as well give in and give up—but we don't have to do that. The alternative is to accept the challenge and creatively search for the loopholes, maybe even the stimuli which can move us to new opportunities, new growing.

Recognizing, for example, that we feel bitter and unappreciated by a younger generation that feels we did too little and too late is the first step to truly empathizing with what that anger is all about. I find that I have gone through quite a change, myself, in the past few years. At first, if someone young or black expressed their resentment and fury, their sense that nothing had been accomplished by my generation, I got just as mad as they did, and seethed for days after a confrontation. Now I tell myself that they cannot possibly know how little we understood, how hard we thought we were trying, how much we hoped for. It just isn't their experience; from where they sit, injustice is just plain terrible, and I agree with them that nothing has changed fast enough. I try now to *join* their anger instead of being its target. I tell myself that I am truly not responsible for the failures, and that I will feel much better if I simply refuse the blame but join the anger. It makes me feel young again! There are some ways in which I am still set apart; you can't get to middle age, if you are really growing up at all, and still believe in the good guys and the bad guys! The evidence of your lifetime has to be acknowledged, and the ally and the enemy are never all in one camp or another. I have some friends who have remained Communists through all the last thirty years, and I must admit that when I hear them talk in all the same old clichés, as if nothing has happened since the Spanish Civil War, I marvel—and I even envy the simplicity, the childlike naïveté in which they have kept themselves encased. That far I cannot go; some Panthers are genuine idealists, some are just opportunistic or paranoid; some members of the Young Lords tear my heart out in their loving longing for a better life for Puerto Ricans, others strike me as dangerously megalomanic. There are beautiful people among the black and the white, and probably just about an equal number of both colors whose self-interest and stupidity is absolutely maddening.

But if I can join in the fury about the *issues*, I become revitalized. Instead of wasting my time and my energy feeling left out or misunderstood, I have tried to recall my own youthful idealism and vitality, and to agree that things are just plain awful in the country right now, and all of us have got to do something about it. If one answers fury with understanding and compassion, one finds oneself in the ballgame again—and it's a good feeling.

I try very hard to make a friend of change; I don't always succeed, but I do often enough to know it's worth the effort. For example, a few years ago a lovely outdoor café appeared in Central Park near a lake and a fountain. The sight of the brightly colored umbrellas, the rowers on the lake, the sound of the fountain gushing, all reminded me of the Bois de Boulogne in Paris, and I felt so delighted that in my city there was some care being given to the aesthetic side of life. In the past year or two this area around the Belvedere Fountain has become a gathering place for young people. And what with the natural consequences of the population explosion, and the colorful and noisy aspects of our young people, the place has changed from what might well have been taken for a park scene in the late 1800s to the wildest and hippiest scene in America today.

One day recently my husband and I walked over to the fountain. We hadn't been there for a long time, and the shock almost killed me; there were literally thousands of young people crowded together in a very small area around the fountain; there were so many boats in the lake that they could hardly maneuver; the noise from transistor radios, drums, and guitars was deafening; the litter was considerable. The costumes and hairdos were so far out that I suddenly felt estranged and angry; how dare these mobs invade my park! My husband was elated; he tried to help me to see the changes through his eyes—which, fortunately for me, seem never to have even approached middle age! He was excited, stimulated by the vitality of the scene, the rich variation, the freedom and individuality, the feeling that everybody was doing his own thing, and respecting the rights of others to do likewise. Instead of feeling strange, he felt entertained and refreshed.

I really worked at it; I took a good hard look at my nostalgia; yes, I had liked the quiet, picturesque world of my childhood and growing; I was partial to the genteel, pretty world of that fountain area a few years ago. Okay. But it was gone. I could spend the rest of my life mourning for what had been, or I could hug my memories and appreciate my past—and then, go on from there and try my damnedest to become part of this world, *now*. I had a choice to make—to be an angry bystander or to try to look with new, fresh eyes at *what was*.

I am grateful to my husband; I don't think I could have done it alone—but I was ashamed of being left behind. I began to really look. I saw such freedom and flamboyance in the clothes; I saw hope and love and kindness in the midst of the crowded miseries of modern city life; I saw a kind of passion for experiencing the moment, with no claims made on the murky and terrifying future. I saw the struggle, the pain, the uncertainty and also the courage of young people to connect with each other, to express joy through the freedom of their clothes and language and in the ways they touched each other. . . . I feel younger and I feel connected to them.

Another way in which we can take control of our own lives is to acknowledge that we are caught in the middle between pleasing our parents and pleasing our children, but that we can decide we are sick and tired of this arrangement, and don't plan to give into it as much as we have. A lot of us are learning that we really don't have to put up with all the things some of our children hold us accountable for! A friend told me that one day she was looking at a picture of her son, aged twenty-three, and she showed it to him, next to a picture of his father at the same age. It was really almost impossible to tell who was who, and she commented, "You and Daddy are so much alike—and how he adores you!" Her son replied, "I know; that's one of my problems." On the face of it, our generation understands that comment very well. We know that sometimes being loved too much can make it hard to try one's wings, to separate from childhood. On the other hand, it seems to me we also have a right to answer such a comment with, "That should be the worst problem you ever have to face!"

A woman I know was facing the loss of a business that she had started and run successfully for twenty-five years; her husband had had an accident and would be partially crippled for the rest of his life; she was facing some surgery that had frightening possibilities. In the midst of this, her daughter, on a visit from college, began to tell her all the terrible, damaging things that had been done to her during her childhood. This daughter had been in therapy for some time, and whatever the sins of omission or commission, she had been loved and supported in every way that her parents could manage. Her mother said, "What could I say, what could I say? The whole world was coming down on my head, I just stood there and listened and then went away and cried." I found myself saying, "You should have told her to buzz off, to get off your back; it's her choice now—whether to make something of her life, or waste it in self-pity and dependence."

We simply cannot carry the burden of guilt; guilt for the unspoken demands of our parents or the criticisms of our children. We did our best and that will have to do. A friend was telling me of a visit she'd had with her aging parents, after which she'd gone home and wept for hours. "All my life," she said, "I tried to feed them with my life; I would say what they wanted to hear, I played the role that pleased them. I could never make their life what it wasn't and yet I felt responsible. Now I saw them, fretful, angry, using each other to blame their miseries on—and I knew I couldn't do a damn thing about it. I loved them, I felt deeply sorry for their disappointments and discomforts, but I knew I could not carry their burdens or change their experience and I felt angry and guilty and desperate."

We will sometimes have to set limits for both the older and the younger generations in ways we have not had the courage to do before. If we feel we have played the role of culpable villain too often, then we may have to say, "Everybody off!" If we do it in anger we will feel too guilty, but we can begin to try to insist that others see *our* needs, and we may have to fight for time for our lives, for our fulfillments. To love those before us and after us, we *must* love ourselves, we must begin to be loving, nurturing parents to ourselves. Otherwise we can only bring our frustration and anger to our relationships. By insisting on the right to nourish our own lives, we will find the strength to meet those reality demands that are unavoidable. We cannot always be available only to the emotional freight of others; there has to be time to deal with the real and urgent needs of our own middle years.

One comfort I offer myself is that I don't really have to adjust to *everything* in order to participate in life. I have a right to allow myself a few resistances. It won't really hurt anybody else if I can't get used to watching naked people romp across a stage; if I can't appreciate or enjoy what is available to me so easily today by way of sexual freedom, well, let people see that as my loss—and let them leave me alone with my old-fashioned feelings. If the glass and concrete get to be more than I can handle, I can find myself some escape hatches, at least part of the time; I can escape to the woods or the shore, find some place left where the carbon monoxide in the air isn't in larger proportion than the oxygen that I find myself still partial to. Despite sometimes feeling that I can be easily replaced by a computer, I can still write furious letters threatening to mutilate my bills, I can take comfort in friends who share my middle-aged hang-ups, I can take refuge as so many of us are, in nature, and cherish what's left of it in ways I never have before. And by conscious effort, I might even allow myself the luxury of getting older, and looking older, without living in terror that my years and my living show.

I want to go on caring and loving; I feel compassion and empathy for the struggles of those who are older and younger—but I am also thinking more and more of what *I* need for my own sense of being most alive and growing. I have the right to spend some of my time and energy on concern for my life—and I intend to do so. Middle age has its own special needs and challenges, and each of us has the right to a certain amount of preoccupation with what we want to make of this time of our lives.

THE *

FEMININE *

Chapter 3

MISTAKE *

*

Today seemed to me to be the appropriate moment to start writing about the problems of women—liberated or enslaved, if that's the choice at hand—for I have just come from watching Melina Mercouri in the film *Promise at Dawn*. Having been ruminating for many months on what I might say about the Women's Liberation Movement, I found myself wondering, as I left the theater, whom would I choose as a symbol of what it means to be a woman —Melina Mercouri or Germaine Greer? I experienced no conflict whatever over this question!

Since I know neither of these ladies personally, all I can deal with is the public image, and on those terms, there is really no contest as far as I am concerned. Miss Mercouri leaves me glowing with pride and joy at the happy circumstance of our belonging to the same sex, while Ms. Greer sends me, a lifetime-liberated woman, running, not walking, to the nearest kitchen to bake a cake—something I dislike doing intensely—to reassure myself that I do not have to share her frenetic feminism.

In the middle-aged struggle for selfhood, it is no easy matter to find ourselves faced with not only our internal conflicts about our sex roles, but also embroiled in the midst of a social revolution concerned with this issue. There we are, trying to face what menopause, or the empty nest, or retirement, will mean to our sense of ourselves as women, and we are caught in the midst of a battle about what it means to be a woman from birth to death! For those of us who have been turning inward to try to discover our own feelings, it sometimes seems almost more than we can bear to be constantly reminded of the larger issues. Especially since we are inclined to feel that whatever happens in the current upheaval will all be too late to influence our lives.

I don't feel this is true at all; it seems to be that the struggle for women's rights can give us just the shot in the arm we may need in order to do some necessary soul-searching—when there is still *plenty* of time to make very good use of whatever we may discover about ourselves.

There are many middle-aged women who can be greatly helped to reassess the meaning and purpose in their lives, if they feel they are too close for comfort to the stereotyped image painted by the lady liberators, of the brainwashed and enslaved housewife who has never fulfilled herself. One cannot argue with the reality that many women *have* been made to feel like second-class citizens, *do* have unfulfilled dreams for themselves, and *can* take advantage of the militant climate of our times to begin to explore a wider realm of possibilities for themselves. Such women find that perhaps for the first time they are becoming consciously aware of having always felt hemmed-in by restrictions imposed by parents, husbands, or society in general. They begin to discover a responsive chord as they listen to the discontent and anger of women's rights groups and begin to experience feelings of deep dissatisfaction at all the unused pieces of themselves as persons. A friend told me, "Last spring I just couldn't decide whether or not to join the Women's March. I was so annoyed by some of the stupid, childish things these groups were saying—but I must admit, something drew me to 42nd Street at the right moment, and I did join the march. I felt a great sense of exhilaration, and a new determination to develop myself as a person. I always thought I had resolved any major conflicts about what I was doing with my life, but there was something in the air that day. All those young women demanding freedom and equality *did* churn something up in me—and I needed it."

For the middle-aged woman who was taught as a child that some jobs and activities were womanly and some were not; for the woman who was restricted in her choices of goals as a child, who saw her brothers fulfill ambitions that she was not allowed to voice—for such women, the current revolution can be a source of inspiration and direction in searching out one's anger and despair, and discovering the unfinished business of fulfillment. Middle age is *not* too late to try one's wings, to challenge oneself with new tasks.

One middle-aged lady who lives on Cape Cod has become a secretary at the Woods Hole Oceanographic Laboratories, and has taken up sailing. She told me, "I grew up on the Cape and I remember as a child wanting to become a sea captain. It was a terrible blow to find out there were no more whaling boats, and that my father thought it would be a good idea for me to study typing and shorthand in high school! I became a reluctant secretary and a not-at-all reluctant wife and mother, but when the children were in high school, I decided that from that point on, I was going to save as much money as I could to buy a boat, and when I did, the kids taught me sailing. When they left home to lead their own lives, I decided that I might as well use my skills in a place where I could also feel connected to the sea. My job fascinates me; I'm still typing, but I feel part of a team that is doing marvelous research about the dangers of pollution in the ocean. I've never been happier."

Another woman told me, "In my family, any woman who wanted a career was expected to become a teacher. I lived up to these expectations, and I don't really regret the decision —I taught sixth grade for twenty-five years, and I was good at it. But in the back of my mind, from the time I was a little girl, I had a great longing to travel, to meet people who were very different from myself. If I were starting over now, I think I would become an anthropologist. At any rate, when I retired from teaching two years ago, I joined Vista and taught in a school in Appalachia for a year. Now I am about to leave for Guatemala, to do teacher-training. My wanderlust is being satisfied at last."

There are other middle-aged women who find the atmosphere of unrest and discontent among women a direct and personal attack on their own lives. They are deeply disturbed by the strident note of disapproval, they feel profoundly humiliated by an attack on the activities and roles they feel they have found so satisfying. Typically, a grandmother comments, "The happiest days of my life were when the house was full of children; there was really no part of it that discouraged me—not even the dirty diapers, the runny noses, or the terrible report cards. I always felt I was doing just exactly the work that God meant me to do in this world, and I had enough energy for any three people. I hated to go to sleep and loved waking up—my world was filled with such pleasure. Now I listen to these young women, and they make me feel I must have been crazy or stupid."

It can be deeply disturbing to be told that one has wasted one's life, especially when that seems most untrue. To denigrate the mothering, nurturing, nesting instincts of so many, many women is just as unjust, evil, and dangerous as making the assumption that women have no other potentialities. It is hard to keep one's perspective when so many piercingly vocal women are so angry at the tasks that one has found most enriching.

There are psychologists who would say that if a middle-aged homemaker finds herself feeling threatened, saddened, angered, or depressed by members of Women's Liberation, this is an indication that deep-down, she too feels deprived, but has built up walls of defense against such feelings. Like all such sweeping generalities, there can be some truth in it for some women, but the problem is far more complex than that. For the woman who has truly found the central core of her creativity in homemaking, middle age is bound at best to be a time of challenge and fear, for she sees these tasks diminishing and wonders if her life can be useful, meaningful, rewarding, when her children are grown. If she is bombarded with the notion that even her *past* has been less than she thought it was, she becomes paralyzed in her quest to find new and different ways of continuing to be that nurturing, mothering person she has been. The truth of the matter is that many women *do* find exultancy and joy in the traditional tasks of womanhood, and they need the encouragement and the self-respect which will lead them to finding new outlets for perfectly respectable talents. There never was a time when the *whole world's children* needed mothering more, and the woman who sees this quality as good and worthwhile is more open to finding new avenues for nurturing and caring for the young—in hospitals, in day-care centers, in becoming a foster parent, in becoming a teaching aide, in finding ways to struggle against the heartbreaking decay and dehumanization of our inner cities.

We need to make the most of the current controversy— to use it for self-examination, for coming to grips with the choices we have already made, and as a stimulus to thinking about the years ahead. Whatever our experience or point of view, we who are now the middle-aged, have a great deal to contribute to the process of redefining who and what women are. Rather than allowing our ideas to be swept aside, we need to assert our right to be part of the revolution and to demand that our voices be heard, that we be permitted the opportunity to make the valid contribution of our experience and maturity.

This brings me to the middle-aged woman who has been

"liberated" all her life, among whose number I find myself and most of my friends. Whenever one hears a heated discussion about the pros and cons of the women's rights movement, sooner or later a militant woman will say, "Our greatest problem is not men, but other women; we were all so brainwashed as children, that women are their own worst enemy in this struggle; they are so used to second-class citizenship, they have so deeply repressed their own drives, that they fight us harder than the men." This may be true for some; for others it may be a lot of baloney. The truth of the matter is that a lot of us middle-aged liberated ladies *know the real dangers* of our experiencing of liberation, and the militants would do well to hear us out. It never surprises me, when there is a panel discussion on this issue on some TV talk show, that it is the older women, who are the acknowledged leaders in their various professions, who try to strike a note of caution about women's liberation, while the younger women, who still have most of their career lives ahead of them, are so absolutely certain that they have found The Truth and that it shall make them free. Little do they know!

A dynamic and creative career woman of great and glorious talents was recently asked by her son, "Hey, Mom, are you into this Women's Lib thing?" She replied, "Look, I don't know what to do with all the freedom *I've got now!*"

I think I am eminently qualified to make some judgments about the price one may pay for liberation. My mother was a liberated woman, long before that term was used; so were most of my other female relations. I grew up in a milieu in which all the important men and women in my life assumed that I could and should do "far more important things" with my life than "only" stay at home and take care of babies and a household. Of course, one great difference between that first generation of middle-class liberated women and my time or the present, is that my mother's generation had full-time sleep-in maid service. That fact is not to be taken lightly. I recall some woman of my generation, caught between her child's chickenpox, no babysitters, and a commitment to give a speech in another city, saying, "It was all very well for Eleanor Roosevelt to become the President's Ambassador to the world; she had a houseful of servants at home, holding down the fort!"

With this not-to-be-overlooked asset, most of the women who served as the models of my childhood had interesting jobs and were successful at them. Their husbands were just as "Gung Ho" about women using their brains as were the women themselves. During my adolescence and early adulthood I was as smug, superior, and intolerant of women-as-homemakers-only as any of today's revolutionaries. Such a fate would never be mine. I was, and have remained, a working wife and mother all through my adult life—and looking back on it, there are a helluva lot of things I would like to have changed.

I am delighted that I was encouraged to use whatever capacities I had, and I'm deeply grateful for the fact that I *did* live and work in a time when I could fulfill myself as a person. My regrets have to do with what I did *not* do: that in my struggle to achieve, to be an intellectual, I often lost touch with the woman in me. When my daughter was a baby, I spent so much time worrying about the possible atrophying of my brilliant mind while changing diapers that I rarely allowed myself the privilege and the joy of *just plain reveling* in motherhood. When we went to the playground, instead of permitting myself to enjoy the wonders of growing, allowing myself to experience the miracle of looking at the world through her eyes, all new and fresh and full of curiosity, I would bury myself in the latest child psychology book. Instead of building sand castles, or walking in puddles or smelling a flower with her, I made notes for my next lecture or article on raising children. Instead of really listening to the growing sounds of her, and joyously responding to what she had to teach me about just *Being,* just watching and looking and listening to life happening, I was agitating about wasting my time. I was an idiot, and I deeply regret the times I missed out on quiet moments of loving.

In order to focus so much of my attention on my career, I became the world's best manager—always planning, organizing, running things. I was so efficient that it never occurred to me then, as it does now, that my chronic backaches at that time had more to do with trying to carry too many burdens, too many roles, than with any organic or anatomical difficulties. In recent years I have been discovering that I paid a price for my efficiency, that in the process of directing the traffic of my life so well I lost touch with myself and with the people I loved the most.

I was not a neglectful mother. If anything, I hovered too much in my guilt about working, for in spite of my background I was constantly exposed to all the "expert" warnings that practically every mental aberration of childhood was due to the evils of working mothers! There were, of course, many times when I did allow myself to enjoy the growing and the loving, but I could never have been described as a relaxed mother, able fully to experience the moment. Too much of the time I felt harassed, driven, short-tempered and preoccupied.

I worked too hard at being a wife and a mother, mostly I think because my concept of achievement was that one always had to be *doing* something or *changing* something. I could not be contented with what was. I think now that it would have been good for me if my husband and daughter had said, "Let be, let be," but even if they had, I would not have understood them. Rather than being brainwashed into thinking I could have only certain circumscribed feminine functions, I was in constant overdrive, and it seems to me now that *this* is what can rob a woman of experiencing her femininity in the most profoundly satisfying ways.

I have a close relative who grew up with me, but whose father was far more militant about the rights (and obligations) of women than mine. To her father it was unthinkable for a woman to lower herself to doing housework. She recalls her father's rages when her mother had to prepare dinner on the maid's day off. In reminiscing recently, Helen said, "He used to say, 'Help your mother, help your mother!' in a tone of voice that made me think she was suffering some terrible, horrendous burden in having to wash the dishes!'"

When Helen was married and about to become a mother, her father was shocked and outraged by her plan to stay home for a few years; all her education, her well-trained mind would be lost in this inferior functioning. Helen was wiser than I: she paid no attention, stayed home to have three children, enjoyed it thoroughly, and felt she got more out of it than she gave, and then, about ten years ago, when her brood was well on the way to independent lives of their own, she went back to school herself and is now happily fulfilling herself as one of those great, "born teachers," working in one of the toughest and saddest ghettos in the country. I envy her those years at home; I envy the unhurried, contented time of full-time mothering. Not romanticizing it—of course she had days of despair and disaster, like every other mother—but she also was allowing life to happen, was nourishing the young and savoring it. And I confess to seeing this as profoundly feminine.

During those early years, I don't think either my husband or I were aware of any deprivation. On the contrary, he was the source of all the inspiration and encouragement a working wife could possibly need or want. He seemed not to be at all threatened by my talents, and he was ready to meet the domestic crises that inevitably occur when both husband and wife have careers; the mornings he was late to work because my car wouldn't start; the nights when he (despite having to study for doctoral exams) took dishwashing and bedtime detail so I could go to give a lecture, the times when he went to the school play because I had a commitment I couldn't get out of, the late and lousy dinners he ate when I came home too tired to cook. I had all the help any man could have been expected to give a working wife at that time, although I suppose today many younger women would feel that he should have carried half the work of cooking, cleaning, shopping and childraising—something that never entered my mind, or that I feel I could have chosen.

As I look back over those years of marriage and motherhood, I can hear my husband's voice saying, "Go, girl, go!" with genuine pleasure in my accomplishments. I am almost afraid to say that I take a somewhat jaundiced view of today's women liberators. I had so much going for me that it sounds ungrateful and irrational to voice my regrets and misgivings, but they exist. Without wishing to denigrate my good fortune in being encouraged to become whatever I wanted to be, it seems to me now that ambition and drive drowned out something quieter, something softer, deep inside me.

I never felt discriminated against in my work, and in all honesty, I must acknowledge that that was another part of my good fortune. Whenever I was paid less than a man for the same work, it was because I chose those jobs in which I could feel free to serve my family's needs first; it was a bargain I made with each employer: less money for more flexibility. So I never had the experience of feeling that my work was less valued simply because I was a woman.

And nothing terrible happened; my marriage is still more important to me than anything else in my life, and my daughter is the loveliest young woman I know, and I adore her; I have had a very successful career. Why then, do I find myself so often cringing when I listen to those who are now fighting for women's rights?

Mostly, I guess, because it seems to me that they don't really know very much about the liberated woman of my generation. I have been greatly privileged in knowing many leaders among my contemporaries—women who have truly made their mark in a wide variety of professions, many of the most talented and creative women around. Without exception, the ones who seem to be the most fulfilled as human beings are those who have enjoyed a considerable dependency on their husbands, and who seem to experience the most enjoyment in the tasks that are traditionally associated with homemaking; they tend to be gourmet cooks, they thought baby-nursing was a miracle, and they thrive on being cuddled! A woman holding a high government position once told me, "The fact that most of us often feel shy and scared, and weak and soft, is the best-kept secret of our century. Our coworkers often see us as overbearing, aggressive, terribly ambitious—and I suppose we are, some of the time. But little do they know now much we need reassurance that we are women, how much we want to be taken care of, how much we want our husbands to be in control. I may go into an important conference like a 'white tornado,' fighting for something I believe in—but nobody knows that all last night I shivered and shook with terror, and had to be patted and kissed and reassured in all sorts of ravishingly interesting ways in order to have the courage to do my job."

This is not to suggest that men don't want and need to play many roles as well. The career women of my acquaintance seem to feel this very strongly, that men need to be dependent and helpless sometimes, too, and that there is nothing demeaning or frightening for women in sometimes playing the stronger role. But I have almost never met a professional woman contemporary, who seemed to be enjoying her life, who didn't admit that when the chips were down—in any real crisis—she wanted to feel that her husband was "in charge." I know younger women feel quite differently, but that's how my generation felt. In my own experience and observations, I have never known a successful, happy, able career woman who was not more deeply committed to her family than to her job. This does not mean that there weren't periods of time when husbands took over more of the burdens of homemaking. A friend told me, "While I was writing my Ph.D thesis, Jerry did all the grocery shopping." When wives work, there surely must be a greater sharing of the domestic realities. But no matter how glamorous and important the work of the women I've known personally, the most essential and central source of their joy in living still seemed to come from being somebody's wife and somebody's mother.

There are, of course, many women who don't want husbands and babies—and it should certainly be their right to have such freedom of choice, with no value judgments attached. For such women, equal opportunities and equal pay are absolutely essential in a democratic society. But what intrigues me, as I try to examine my own liberated life, and that of my friends, is that we enjoyed our work only in the context of womanly fulfillments. A friend who is a successful magazine editor once told me, "I'd give up my vote if I had to choose between that and having somebody warm my cold feet on a winter's night!" Fortunately she doesn't have to make such a choice; but what she was saying was that in all the years of professional achievement, she had never found anything as important to her as being loved and cherished by her husband. I think it is a not irrelevant fact that younger militants ought to look at: that we, who have had the best of both worlds for many years, would hate like hell to have to make such a choice, but there is little doubt in our minds about which comes first in the order of our needs.

If the women who have had the most opportunity for personal growth and freedom, who have realized their potentialities the most, still tend to value the roles they play as wives and mothers as the essential core of their lives, doesn't this at least suggest, that there are some special and delightful and natural differences in the very nature of being a man or a

woman? In our discussions among ourselves, my friends and I
seem to be in general agreement that we want our husbands
to be the main wage-earners; his work must be given priority
over ours; we move where his jobs take him. Most of us have
no desire to have our husbands share equally in the housework (although we all want to feel we can count on as much
help as we need). In the last analysis we also expect our husbands to make the major moral decisions for the family, such
as do we or don't we go to a peace demonstration where people might be arrested, or do we or don't we try to find a
black family for the house next door in our lily-white neighborhood? A lot of us admit we might chicken out, that we
are too concerned with the safety of those we love, and expect our husbands to keep us towing the moral line. We seem
to have partnership marriages in which there is great flexibility of shifting roles, where there is trust and friendship—
but where differences in our roles strike us as essential and
good and we seldom, if ever, find ourselves concerned with
the question of absolute equality.

And that seems to be the heart of the matter: What do we
mean by *equality?* What I fear most is that the word "equal"
often seems to be used as synonymous with "the same." That
men and women, that human beings, are equal in their value,
their dignity, their right to the greatest personal fulfillment
should go without saying. But does that kind of equality
mean that women need to feel free to become construction
workers, or deprive men of their own luncheon club? This
seems absurd to me.

It is one thing to insist that women have equal human
rights, but quite another to suggest that such equality vitiates
differences. I am very fearful that too much of the current
cry for liberation carries this implication, and I am convinced
that in the process of minimizing differences women will lose
touch with the deepest and most important resources within
themselves. We need to differentiate between women's *rights*

and women's *liberation*. The first seems just and necessary, but the second seems too often to be associated with a rejection of the enjoyment of being female.

Every human being cries out to the world, "See *me*, here I am—special and unique and not like anybody else—just myself." Each of us wants to be acknowledged for our own needs, talents, strengths, and weaknesses—our own unique possibilities. When others whom we trust and care about help us to see ourselves as different, life opens up to us: we can begin to have our own goals and hopes for ourselves as persons; we begin to feel the glow of our own incandescent identity in ways that can never be experienced by the denial of differences in the name of equality.

I find the comparison between women's rights and the black struggle for equality dangerous. Of course economic and social disfranchisement are their common problems, but there is not a comparable struggle for equality. As a group, black people have only one difference from white people— the color of their skin—and that is not grounds for discrimination because it is not a difference that makes them truly different in their human needs. In order to fulfill his best possibilities a black man needs the same kinds of freedom of opportunity as the white man. All men and women of all races have a right to equal opportunities for the development of their individual differences. In that sense, black or white is the same. But women are *not* the same as men—the difference goes far deeper than skin color. On purely physiological grounds we are different in every cell of our bodies, the difference in the chromosome combination being basic to the development of maleness and femaleness. Besides the function of menstruation which involves glandular activity that produces differences in feelings and behavior, women have larger stomachs, kidneys and livers, and smaller lungs. Their breathing power and basal metabolism are lower, their blood contains more water, they tire more easily in the short range but have more constitutional vitality over the long haul. Men have 50 percent more physical strength, but women outlive them. And then there are all those perfectly obvious and delightful sexual differences which confirm what seems absolutely clear to me: we are meant by nature to be different and to complement each other. I believe in this evidence of my eyes, and the deeper knowledge of my experience—we look different and we have different natural purposes and we feel differently because of this. It is very unpopular these days to believe in instincts, but I do. The fact that we don't really understand what we *mean* by that word doesn't, in my judgment, mean that we haven't *got* them! I simply cannot believe that our biological sexual differences—the female equipment for the gestation of our young, and the consequent cyclic nature of our hormonal system—can have no bearing on how we act or feel.

One of the dangers I sense in the Women's Liberation Movement, is a subtle, sometimes almost unconscious process of dehumanization. It seems to me that the request for twenty-four-hour-a-day nurseries comes close to the scientist's Machiavellian search for gestation of babies outside the uterus; that wanting the opportunity to work on construction crews, the right to do anything and everything men now do, can become, sooner or later, a denial of the special, instinctual, absolute differences between the male and the female anatomy, physiology—and psychology.

What this technological age seems to have brought with it is a kind of self-destructive compulsion to prove that we are creatures who are capable of living in glass and concrete, with no access whatever to the natural world, and that we will survive. It would seem that only *after* we have cut down every tree in the world and replaced them with concrete highways will we finally face the fact that nature meant us to get oxygen from living plants, not from air-conditioners. In our worship of the machine, it seems that we are hell-bent on

proving that Man is nothing more than just another complicated computer—and perhaps we will neutralize our sexual
differences to such a point that we will begin to wonder why
we want to live at all, much less reproduce our species.

I am not suggesting that the human experience can't be
modified or changed. We have survived as a species only because of modification and adaptation through the ages. Whatever "instincts" may be, they are not static. Where it may
have been "instinctive" for Neanderthal man to reproduce
himself as frequently as possible, in order for his race to survive, we had better learn to curb what procreative instincts
still remain, or overpopulation will be our *non*survival. It
seems to me that one can have a deep sense of what it is to
feel one's natural humanity, and still make sensible and realistic modifications. For example, I find one new attitude of
many young married couples quite lovely; they are planning
to have two children, at the most, and then to adopt several of
the world's unwanted and rejected children. A friend told me
recently, "I think it's great; Bob and Nan have told us we are
going to have two grandchildren with our genes—our
immortality—and several others of varying colors and unknown backgrounds, in our family!" What impresses me
about this is that it acknowledges the *human* craving for re-
producing ourselves in the interesting and satisfying way provided by nature, but takes into account the realities of modern life, and the flexible possibilities for nurturing the young
of the world in new and different ways.

There is, I think, a very significant connection between
some of the angry demands of militant women for equality
without differences, and a more generalized climate of con-
tempt for nature. A case in point is the strident attitude of so
many in the Women's Liberation Movement that all the
claims about the deep psychological gratification in bearing a
child are pure mythology. It surely isn't the road to fulfillment for everyone, but to deny the miracle is a kind of insan-

ity. We seem to want to reject the most basic of our human feelings in the quest of some mysterious rational freedom. It sounds hollow and empty and unhuman to me. Another expression of this is our current impatience with childhood— our preoccupation with seeing how fast and how much we can teach children in the first five years of life. We simply cannot bear, it seems to me, to allow life to unfold, to trust growing. We have university laboratories searching for new horizons of brain power in infancy; we have some insane notion that if a kid can read and write by the age of three, this will somehow make the other ninety years of his life more purposeful. There is an unwillingness, today, to *look* at children, to perceive the natural tasks of the growing years, and to respect the miracle of growing, which brings every child who is growing normally, in an optimum atmosphere of loving stimulation, to a natural and appropriate *inner* moment for learning and understanding the necessary tools and skills needed for further growing. Any child who feels loved and approved of, who is surrounded by learning, curious people, who is given opportunities for adventures in playing, who is offered an environment rich in stimulation will learn to read by the time he is seven or eight at the latest. But we cannot bear to wait or to provide that atmosphere, and I have a feeling that this is in some way connected with how women feel about being women. If one cannot accept or enjoy the womanly quality of being receptive to life, of nurturing the young for the simple natural pleasure it can bring, then one becomes impatient and dissatisfied and feels compelled to improve on nature's ways. The pressure on young children to grow too fast seems to me somehow related to the discontent of women in being the nurturers of the young.

Another example of what strikes me as the dehumanization of life through the denial of differences is the sex research of the past twenty-five years. It seems to me that the focus on the facts about sex and the emphasis on sexual techniques has the effect of mechanizing the feminine experiencing of sex. A technological approach to anything that has so much to do with *feelings*, seems to me to be antifeminine. An example of what I mean is the earthshaking discovery by the sex-scientists that there is only one kind of orgasm, that it is a clitoral orgasm, and the notion of the "vaginal orgasm" is pure mythology, because *it cannot be observed in the laboratory.* None of the hardware of sex research has been able to demonstrate any such distinction. I would not argue that there is such a thing as a "vaginal orgasm" in any literal sense; the physiological accuracy of the fact of clitoral excitability only seems clear. What I am suggesting is that whatever one may call it, there are different *feelings* that go far beyond what physiology can teach us, and that intuitive experiencing is as valid a source of information as anything we can discover through the scientific methodology of the laboratory.

If women want to learn more about women-and-sex, I suggest they read every book of Doris Lessing's they can get their hands on, instead of poring over the published reports on the Kinsey/Masters-and-Johnson research. When the dramatic report appeared that vaginal orgasms were a fictional plot of sentimental women and Freudian psychotherapists, I remembered something I had read many years ago in Doris Lessing's *The Golden Notebook* *:

> . . . for women . . . sex is best when not thought about, not analysed. . . . They get irritable when men talk technically. . . . they want to preserve the spontaneous emotion that is essential for their satisfaction. . . .
>
> . . . a vaginal orgasm is emotional and nothing else, felt as emotion and expressed in sensations that are indistinguishable from emotion. The vaginal orgasm is a dissolving in a vague, dark generalized sensation like being swirled in a warm whirlpool. There are several different sorts of clitoral orgasms, and

---

* London: Penguin Books; p. 212. Quoted by permission of Simon and Schuster, Inc.

they are powerful. . . . there can be a thousand thrills, sensations, etc., but there is only one real female orgasm and that is when a man, from the whole of his need and desire takes a woman and wants all of her response.

The intuitive introspection of a creative woman gets to the heart of the truth more wisely and well than hooking ladies up to electrical gadgets. It is part of the natural, instinctive, anatomical, hormonal specialness of being a woman that leads her to feel more in a sexual experience in which physical sensations may be secondary to feelings of loving. That is what women have meant by the "vaginal orgasm"—that there are qualities, in the human nature of women, for sex to be far more related to the experiencing of a relationship, and that for the woman who allows herself to feel her feelings and is deeply in love, sexual satisfaction is far less dependent on technical skills—the vast armamentarium of activities— that her partner can learn. Technically, expert sex play can indeed produce clitoral orgasms—a woman can do *that* for herself, for heaven's sake! What women in love mean by the "vaginal orgasm" is that what they experience simply is not localized, that they feel a great sense of openness, a melting, a mystical sense of becoming part of the total universe. Psychologist Dr. Abraham Maslow called this a "Peak Experience"; the Yoga teachers might call it "the moment of enlightenment." In Christianity it is described as being in a State of Grace. It is indeed a "religious" experience in the sense that one becomes part of the "All," one feels profoundly at home in the larger universe. And it is produced by love, by poetry, by passionate music as much if not more than by the techniques of clitoral stimulation so far devised by man or machine. It is an *emotion*, which simply never appears inside a scientific laboratory and cannot be tested with electrical appliances.

The Women's Liberation groups have made much of the sex research, emphasizing women's capacities for great quantities and varieties of clitoral orgasms, and a plank of the women's rights movement seems to be the right to make men assure them of these gratifications. Boy, are we going to be in trouble! Not only will we tend to ignore the possibility of achieving that more mystical state that can be the most miraculous, indescribable, and profound of female sexual possibilities, but it ought to be eminently clear to women that *ordering* men to be sexual—in any way—is a guarantee of a lost partnership.

There may well be a connection between the increase in impotence and homosexuality and women becoming freer and asserting their rights. In the denial of male-female differences, women have *everything* to lose, if they are not careful. Men cannot have sex relations, no matter what the heart and head say, as women can. They are dependent on there being a happy connection between brain and genitals, and in the absence of a joyous message from one to the other, they become helpless to perform. *That is a difference* and it seems to me that the new radical woman is out of her cotton-picking head, when she does anything which makes men feel diminished or threatened.

For the middle-aged woman the current preoccupation with sexual techniques rather than feelings and relationships is especially unsettling. A charming lady of sixty-three told me, "I read *The Sensual Woman* and I knew I was a complete bust as a woman. Never mind that my husband and I have been married for thirty-five years, and love each other more than ever. We are obviously failures, because I'd rather *die* than do most of the things in that book!"

At a time in our lives when we are in doubt about our attractiveness and desirability, it is frightening to be made to feel that our ways of loving are old-fashioned, unimaginative, and square. But it might give us a lift to look at new ideas, and maybe even try a few. What better antidote to middle-aged doldrums! However, we need not relinquish our sense of concern at what appears to be an entirely too mechanical, unromantic, dehumanized approach to sex relationships— because that is very much part of the current scene, and we are fortunate in knowing better than to fall for it.

By suggesting that the denial of differences is dehumanizing, I do not want to imply that I am not concerned with injustice; that is another matter entirely. With our differences quite intact, we still *do* have human rights! Injustice is evil wherever and whenever it occurs. I am outraged by the fact that women are discriminated against in employment and wages. Of course there ought to be greater opportunities for women to fulfill themselves. The facts are outrageous; half of the women who work earn less than $3,700 per year. They are paid 40 percent less than men doing the same work. There is only one woman senator after fifty years of woman suffrage. Only one-fifth of all college faculty are women and this ratio hasn't changed in sixty years. Only 9 percent of our doctors are women. We must surely face our rage on this kind of injustice without separating ourselves from men and without rejecting the absolute and essential differences in being female.

Nor can we assume that because women have not had their full rights, giving them those rights will change the world. It won't. At present in the United States, more than 50 percent of the eligible voters are women, and we still keep electing presidents and congressmen who see some moral justification for that obscene and endless war we are carrying on in Asia. I see no discernible progress in American society since women's suffrage. It is not because women will improve our lot in life, that they should have justice; it is simply because anything less diminishes—even destroys—the meaning of democracy. When militant women talk of their goals and hopes as a way of saving the world, I am reminded of my adolescent years, when I believed that *unions* would save the world! All we needed to do, we young idealists of the 1930s thought, was to allow the working man some power, and he would end social injustice. Union men turned out to be just like all other men; some noble and good and wise, some with a vision of a better society—and some who are evil, stupid, mean, and selfish—just like any other group of people. So too in the current struggle of women; some women are good, even great—and some are idiots. The thought of "woman power" expressing itself through the likes of Martha Mitchell, does *not* reassure me about the world's future.

I suppose one problem for me is that I am so uncomfortable with almost *any* brand of revolutionary/radical. I can recall so well my own first experiences with radicalism in the 1930s, and the lovely simplicity of dividing the whole world into the good guys and the bad guys. The only thing that has changed in the past thirty or forty years is the designation of the good guys and the bad guys: now all white people are racist, self-serving, and evil and all black people true and noble brothers; and women who are homemakers are finks while women revolutionists are going to save the world. Or women are peace-loving, responsible, and intelligent and men are chauvinist pigs.

I am deeply troubled by the anger at women who won't participate in the revolution. But what bothers me most of all is that the unspoken fact of much of the vitriol is a hatred of men. We certainly need a social revolution through which women will have free options to do what they want to with their lives—the same options they like to think men have, but which men also often do not have. But with the rigidity, the oversimplification of issues and personalities that seems to me to represent so much of the movement, I find it hard to see how something truly constructive and realistic can come from it. There are no simple issues, no simple answers, and people are a complex, mysterious combination of good and evil, selfishness and altruism.

I have just been listening to Betty Friedan on a TV talk-

show, where she announced the "political wave of the future" in which women would work for women candidates
and change the face of politics. That is exactly what is wrong
with the whole movement; it won't change a damn thing.
Some women will make a wonderful contribution to the welfare of society and others will be bigots and tyrants and easily
corrupted by power, just like men. Some *human beings* are
wonderful and some are terrible—and *that's* where it's at.

It is wrong for anybody to be discriminated against on the
basis of class or sex or color or age. All rules which judge
groups of people rather than individual ability are immoral.
The argument comes with whether or not it is helpful to
make the issue *women's* rights, or whether we ought to stick
to the tougher and more complex struggle for *human* rights.
There is a fanaticism about separating women from human
beings in general. When we do that, we are burdening ourselves with a hidden agenda of bitterness, resentment, and
anger. We are really saying, "I am so *furious* at the way *I*
have been treated that I cannot now look at the larger picture."

The responsible leaders of the women's movement insist
that it is only a minute lunatic fringe who hate men. That
may very well be true, but even the steadiest and most articulate spokeswomen impress me as women who feel they can
achieve their goals only by separating themselves from men
—it *is* "Women's Lib," not "Human Lib"—and in doing
that, they are denying, at some very deep level, their femininity and therefore their humanity. I see so little softness, receptivity, need to nurture all human life, and so rarely any genuine exultation in being born female. Even worse—because I
see this as a fundamental requirement for true humanity—
they are utterly and completely humorless.

It seems to me that if one feels inclined to take up the ban-
ner of women's rights, one ought at least to spend some time
reflecting on the fact that we never yet have known every-

thing about anything; we have never yet found a simple answer for a complicated problem; never in human history has
any social movement ever discovered A Final Truth. Just a
little genuine humility, just a little indication that there are
more questions than answers on the part of Women's Liberation groups would go a long way to gain my sympathy for
the movement.

I would very much like to see women liberated from the
brainwashing they've had at the hands of Madison Avenue
and too many experts on childraising. It may well be that the
current put-downs about femininity, homemaking, and childraising are a result of the terrible struggle for perfection and
the resultant ceaseless, exhausting, paralyzing guilt when of
course it turns out to be impossible to have a kitchen floor in
which you can see your reflection (and you're not a gorgeous
size 9 blonde in high heels) or a problem-free child.

It seems to me that I have spent twenty-eight years of married life trying to overcome the influence of the wax and de-
tergent people. And yet I *still* feel disappointed and guilty
when my sheets are a nice, comfortable, old, yellowish color
instead of blue-white. What in *hell* is so magical about white,
I ask myself? And I reply with courage and self-righteous-
ness, "If they'd told you for over forty years that yellowish-
white was the most beautiful color in the world, you would
be proud of your wash instead of ashamed." Sometimes I lose
control; I go on a wild cleaning spree—closets, the inside
of the stove in the places you can't reach, I even pick up by
hand the dust the vacuum can't get at in corners. And then,
by enormous effort, I bring myself back to sanity. It is utterly
absurd to try to turn our homes into hospital surgical units. It
is not only possible but exhilarating to give it all up, to look
with fierce fury at the TV commercials and say, "Not me,
brother, you're talking to the wrong girl." The first year I
was married I stopped ironing dish towels. (They were always ironed when I was a child and there was a sleep-in

maid.) The second year I stopped ironing sheets, towels, pil-
lowcases and underwear, and each year since, the decrease
has continued. Just this past year I decided to see what would
happen if I didn't empty the closets, and move all the winter
things out, spraying them with camphor. I left everything
as-is, and put one hanging can of camphor in each closet. The
friend whose advice I'm following says that in New York
City she has never done any mothproofing. Well, we shall
see; I'm still nervous. At any rate, one thing I'm sure about:
closets get emptied and washed-down when I am convinced
that decay and pestilence are the only alternative.

When I look around and see the general chaos—books
and papers unfiled, photographs never put in albums, letters I
can't bear to throw away, piles of clothes not yet sent to
some charity—I begin to get the nervous itch. Most of the
time I manage not to give in to it. I talk to myself a lot; I say,
"Eda, remember what's important; a clean and neat house or
your work; time to talk to your husband, or order in the immediate universe; people or things."

It takes time and diligent practice to look with any kind of
objectivity on the pressure of advertising and to recognize
that you cannot allow even the most charming and creative
advertising man to decide what you want to do with your
home. First of all, he can't deliver, knows he can't and
doesn't care. And second, even if he could, would it really
improve your family's life to live in a plastic vacuum?

I can also understand why many young women might feel
it incumbent upon them to refuse to be pretty! While advertising makes it perfectly clear that any woman worthy of her
sex must spend eighteen hours a day scrubbing, polishing and
germ-fighting, she must also look like Brigitte Bardot. All the
time and at any age. It is perfectly true that the cosmetic industry has terrorized us about what it means to be sexy and
attractive to men, and that if they had their way we would
all be Barbie Dolls. It surely *is* high time that we insisted on

what we know, somewhere deep-down, below the TV-level of consciousness, that beautiful, sensuous, feminine women come in all shapes, sizes, ages, hair color and skin tones, and that what makes them that way is not false eyelashes, dyed hair, corsets, lanolized skin, but something deep inside which exults in being female. However, I can't believe that the way to fight the pitchmen who make us feel unfeminine is to wear dirty clothes and not shave our armpits.

We also need to be freed from the guilt of not having perfect children. The child experts have had their way with most of us, and I'm less hopeful that I can overcome the feeling I've had for twenty-one years that I was personally responsible for every sad moment, failure, and frustration my daughter experienced in growing up—and the fact that she is now a lovely and beautiful young woman whom I admire enormously was just a lucky accident!

I look with genuine envy on the many young mothers I see today, *enjoying* their children, obviously feeling free to do what comes naturally. They are the beneficiaries of all the useful, meaningful, very important information on child nature that was beginning to be available to us—but it is no longer new, it's no longer the final answer or a panacea; we have come back to a sense of balance. We know that neither parents nor their children can avoid (or should ever want to) the normal vicissitudes, the pain in growing and that no one can take responsibility for everything a child feels or does.

If Women's Lib can help to free women from "the White Tornado" and the expectations of Dr. Ginott that mothers can have the perfect dialogue memorized for every occasion, it will be a lot more fun to be a woman and a mother.

The task for the middle-aged woman—or rather, the opportunity—is to be stimulated by all the controversy and to use it as one dimension of a search for individual answers within oneself. When *The Feminine Mystique* was first published, I just got angry; since then, as I have tried to grow and become more introspective and closer to my own deepest needs and feelings, I have found that Women's Liberation has played some part in prodding me into trying harder to search out the truth of who I am and what I want to be. I mentioned earlier that I had some regrets about the liberated life I once was leading; much of that awareness has come about only as I have found myself changing and making new and different choices.

I have always been a city girl. I liked to get away on vacations, but it never occurred to me until two or three years ago that I could live in the country. I was never able to make plants grow; someone would give me a plant that was as hardy and indestructible as crabgrass, and within a few weeks the poor thing would be withering and dying, no matter what I did. I cannot recall ever doing *nothing at all* until a few years ago. Much to my amazement, I have become a birdwatcher lately. I am a happy and successful gardener; nothing delights me more than to find a scraggly rose bush at the supermarket on a summer day, and watch it become an absolutely luscious, gorgeous bush under my watchful and adoring eye. I don't really know any more about fertilizers or optimum watering conditions than I knew before my Green Thumb days, but I *care* now! I am an absolute believer in the idea that all growing things thrive with love and wither from indifference.

I have learned a great deal in watching plants grow. Someone gave us an amaryllis this year, a flower I don't recall ever seeing before. I had no idea at all what it would look like when it bloomed. As the weeks passed, and we watched the stem grow and the bud get ready to burst, and then the unbelievable, voluptuous beauty of the flower, I had a renewed sense of the miracle of *unfolding*. All the possibility of this gorgeous thing was already there, inside that dumb and drab-looking bulb. All I had to do was put it in soil, water it, and watch it—and all this beauty came out of it, from inside. It was all there, to be born into life.

I think there is a connection between the emancipation of women and the changes I have experienced. All my life I was taught that if I wanted to achieve something, I had to struggle for it. That's the way we raise our children, teaching from the outside, pinning facts on them; not trusting what can flower from within, what is already there, to come into fruition. It's the same with sex and being a woman; all the possibilities are deep inside us, only waiting to be born. The task of living fully is to *elicit what is inside* and *allow it to happen*, not to invent something or build something outside of ourselves.

There has always been a kind of desperate stridency in my creativity, a struggle, a demand, a stressful search. I am learning that there are reservoirs of energy and creativity already inside me, and if I watch and look and listen, and only provide some psychological soil, air, and water, the flowering will come. I don't have to struggle, and grasp and exhaust myself; I can simply be open to what comes.

Until recently, I had no patience for listening to music; I thought operas were absurd. A few years ago I discovered that the reason people loved the opera was not because it made sense, but because it filled one's soul with beautiful sights and sounds; that I could sit in a great hall, and hear sounds and see color that seemed to open up my brain and melt my head. I later discovered that I didn't have to *know* anything about music to let it fill me, to gradually come to understand that if I really allowed myself to be open and receptive, from head to toe, I could be swept away by the sounds coming into me.

I discovered a hunger for the sea, a deep need to do absolutely nothing at all but watch the swell of the waves, and the lights and shadows of the spray, and hear the thundering surf.

I discovered that the moments of greatest happiness were those in which I was just *being*, not *doing*.

For a lady who was scheduled by the minute for more than twenty-five years, it seems astonishing to me that I now find that the most important event of a happy day can be watching the birds on the lagoon behind our cottage at the seashore. In April and May I watch the wild ducks begin their homebuilding. I listen to the squabbles among the males, I watch the preening and the fussing as they try to advertise their virtues, and the calm, dignified way in which the females settle down to the practical realities of life. I am fascinated by the preparations made for family life—and I am like a nutty grandmother, reveling in the joy of birth, when a proud mama duck brings her new brood into the lagoon for my inspection, quietly waiting for the children to have their fill of saltines or rye bread, or whatever other largesse I can quickly gather up.

I mentioned at the beginning of this chapter that I deeply regret not having spent more time enjoying my daughter's childhood, nourishing my own soul with her curiosity and wonder and joy. Just this past year she has joined me in my delight in the wild ducks. Every time she telephones me at the shore, she wants a rundown on how many came for dinner, how many I've discovered nesting, how "Charlotte the Harlot" is getting along (she's a highly individualistic duck who has a wonderful time with the ganders while all the other lady ducks are nesting). We planted a vegetable garden last summer—the first of my lifetime. And when she babysits in Central Park, I sometimes join her and sit on the edge of the sandbox reveling in her warmth and beauty and lovingness with her charge. I'm making up for what my "liberation" made me lose.

Each summer the gulls and the redwinged blackbirds— (and whatever other species may have managed to survive the DDT, and the bay-dredging with which we kill them off)—remind me of the miracles of life. How do they know when to come and when to go? How are they so quick to sense danger? What drives them to such industry, such concentrated purposes? There is an order in the universe, and as I watch I feel a part of it—a sister to whatever lives.

I don't want to be a lady duck, limited to such a small area of instinct. I'm glad I was born a woman, with larger scope and purposes and less imprisoned by limitations of nature or society. But something in me wants now to remember and to be at home in watching and looking and listening to some primeval rhythms. I have been too long and too much the doer, the achiever, the organizer, the changer. I was always in there, teaching, advising, telling—trying to improve myself, my husband, my child. I could never let life just happen to me; I was always analyzing and examining and trying to articulate everything I felt. I think that in my active, achieving state I said too much, managed others too often—and in the process drove those who were closest to me to develop an emotional distance from me, to protect themselves from my too many words, my ideas and expectations, my ambitions for them and for myself. To some degree they learned to withdraw into secret places, to escape me.

But I think I have been learning, and what I have learned is that I shut myself off from myself, too, that I made too little use of some available femininity when I became the liberated woman. I paid too high a price for my efficiency, my well-organized life and expectations, my capacity to push and shove and demand that the world mold itself to my wishes. I find myself searching for a deep inner core of passivity and receptivity, an openness to life—the part of me that yields and watches and is *just there* for living, that participates without having to run things.

I seem to have less desire to tell people what to do, and what I now enjoy more is watching and listening and letting them know how much I am enjoying *their* growing. When my daughter was growing up, I constantly had the feeling that I had to do things to change and improve her life, to teach, to advise, to direct, to help her accomplish more. Now I find that I want to watch her own emergence as a self. I am always available to help and give comfort when I can, but I am the observer of her unfolding, not the director of it. I want love and compassion and tenderness to be available, in me, without any bargains or demands. To be a woman most completely, one needs to become a vessel of life, a catalyst, a nurturer—not always an arranger.

Passivity and receptivity seem to have become dirty words, as though they meant being weak and colorless—subservient. At the shore I also find myself entranced by the inexorability of the ebb and flow of the ocean, finding something deeply feminine in the lack of claims or demands, in the simple inevitability of the waves; they ask for nothing, they plan nothing, they just *are*. Not lifeless in receptivity at all —full of dynamic vitality and power.

As a liberated woman I have been too busy with the world's work. Now I find myself turning inward, yielding to my feelings without having to express them, sensing the growing of others without having to drive them, cultivating experiences from the inside out instead of the other way around.

A real hazard for the "liberated" woman is that in accentuating her right to and potential for intellectual development, she may lose touch with her own body. In all my years of being so busy, my head and my body seemed to have become separated. I was using my head too much and not connecting it to the rest of me. One of the luckiest chance circumstances for me has been the emergence of great interest and concern among psychologists, psychiatrists, and others with expressing oneself through one's body—of connecting one's feelings and thoughts to an awareness of one's physiology. For the past few years I have been taking occasional classes in Body Awareness Techniques—trying to relearn connectedness with myself as others have discovered these important experiences in Yoga classes, in Esalen-type workshops which deal with physical well-being and centeredness.

Watching a small baby move, or the way a cat walks and stretches and rests, gives one a sense of the miracle of nature's synthesis. The trials and tensions of the "civilized life" tend to fragment us, and the symptoms of this come to us through fatigue, tension, sleeplessness, backaches and—for me— pains in my arms and shoulders when sitting at a typewriter for many hours of the day. By trying to recapture what is natural and normal in early childhood—a wholeness of breathing and moving, and sensing one's body from head to toe—I am helped to move toward what our young people call "getting your head together." I feel sure that at least some part of the intrigue of mind-expanding drugs, the concern about touching and skin contact, and the renewed interest in meditation, are the hunger of twentieth-century man in search of a less cerebralized and narrowed experiencing of oneself as a totality.

I am struggling to find a quiet, inner repose, a yielding, an ability to be an enhancer rather than a seeker. It seems to me that what has happened to me in this identity crisis of middle age is that I have been in search of the softer side of myself and have discovered that it speaks to me with profound meaning and importance. Each of us must find his own way in this; for others I know it must be an entirely different adventure. Surely one thing is certain: femininity is not what you are *doing;* it is what you *are,* whatever you are doing. I realize that for many middle-aged women who feel they have never been all that they could be in areas of work or achievement, answers will be very different from my own. Perhaps each of us is really in search of a new balance, a filling-in of what has been missing.

On one issue the Women's Liberation Movement and I are

in complete agreement, and that is the right of individuals to choose their own roles and assess their own needs. If some young couples find their salvation in equally sharing the functions of childraising and domesticity, if some young women make the conscious choice not to marry, if some couples find fulfillment in the various new life-styles of communal living, if some men discover that they want to be homemakers— fine; the most important thing our children have been teaching us is that nothing can be better for oneself or for society than for people to find and do "their own thing." But in searching out these new ways, we have to be careful that we don't encourage a new dogmatism, a new set of extreme restrictions. The little girl who is made to feel, by a militant mother, that she *must* be a career woman, is just as likely to be damaged in her self-esteem, if that is not "where she is at" as a human being, as the little girl who was brought up to believe that her only natural place was in the kitchen.

I suspect that within the next few years we will begin to see just as much discontent among the newly liberated ladies as among the old-style hemmed-in housewives, and the reason will be that we always go to extremes. Nothing is ever right for everybody, and I am sure there are many young women deciding not to get married, not to have children, or to have absolutely egalitarian marriages, who, deep-down inside want to bake bread and sew draperies and nurse babies—just as in the past there have been thousands of miserable housewives who felt imprisoned by their homes and wanted to be out in the world doing other things. Discontent is always the result when we don't search out who *we* are, what we as individuals really want to use ourselves for, in life.

An equally dangerous extreme is the woman who acts as if the biological fact of womanhood is somehow enough, the woman who self-righteously insists that she wants nothing for herself but a home and family. For many such women, the denial of selfhood leads to discontent, and the compulsive need to control and direct the lives of others. She stays home and kindles the hearth, but boy, does she ever have ambitions for her husband and children! The driven husbands and children of the world, those who sell their own souls for achievements that have nothing to do with their own real needs, bear witness to the fact of the unlived ambitions of many stay-at-home women.

The essential issue is not so much the activities and roles that we choose as women, but what we do with them. One can spend one's life cooking, cleaning, and raising children and not be much of a real woman, while a woman who may choose to be single may be the most feminine of creatures in her love relationships and profession. Some of the most nurturing and loving woman I've known have been unmarried and childless, but have brought a shimmering and lovely femininity to their work and their friendship relationships.

There never was a time when women needed more courage, for the task of searching one's own soul and finding one's own answers to what one will do with the possibilities of being alive and human are enormously painful and difficult. All of us are being challenged to find our own individual answers, and there has never been a more terrifying or more marvelous challenge.

The problem is a human one for both men and women, and that is where I find my deepest resistance to the women's revolution. Our problems cannot be solved if we make this unnatural division. Men have been as brainwashed and as damaged by rigid and inflexible rules-about-roles as women. They have been equally imprisoned by such dangerous stereotyping as that "real men" never cry, never show weakness, are never frightened, and must never be gentle. To be angry at men, to see them as an enemy is lunacy; and when such anger is expressed, I find myself wondering if it may not really be an expression of a woman's deep sense of loneliness, caught in the awful dangers of today's world. Could it be that such women want most desperately to be taken care of by men, but have no hopes of this? If there is to be a genuine revolution it must be for *human* rights—for the right of each person to seek his own meaning and his own expression of himself, using his sex and his mind and his creativity in the fullest way possible, for in the act of self-discovery and self-fulfillment we bring the best that we are to all the others in our lives. It is that revolution to which I am joined; the common struggle of men and women to find the wellsprings of their own identity and purposes, and to enjoy the freedom and the right to that discovery. If we separate ourselves from each other, we all lose. It is only in the total celebration of ourselves as human persons *with all the glory of our differences* that we can begin to change the world and make it better.

*

THE   *

OPPRESSION   *   *Chapter* **4**

OF MEN   *

—BY THEMSELVES   *

*

Since I have tried to focus on my own experiences and feelings almost entirely in this book, it seemed presumptuous to include a chapter about middle-aged men. But as I tentatively explored the possibilities, certain very strong impressions rose to the surface and seemed worth mentioning, since I'd hoped to write a book for the middle-aged, without discrimination as to sex, and since men interest me greatly, I'm happy to report.

After some preliminary conversations with men, I thought the title of this chapter ought to be, "I Don't Know Much about Middle-Aged Men—But Neither Do They." There was a startling difference between talking to men about how they were experiencing middle age and talking to women. I can't recall a single woman who was reluctant to tell me how she felt; quite the contrary—most women seemed to be only too eager to talk about their experiences and feelings and were strikingly articulate and impassioned. Almost without exception the men whom I approached were uncomfortable, ill at ease, and many were frankly annoyed. I did not have the feeling that the primary issue at hand was my being female, for their discomfort was immediate, before we could possibly have got into any truly personal issues.

For example, I was having lunch with a charming, attractive man who must have been somewhere between forty-five and fifty. We'd had a lovely time together, discussing some work we were both doing, and as we left the restaurant, I said, "Gee—I forgot all about interviewing you on middle age." He looked startled, then half-embarrassed and angry, and said sarcastically, "Thanks *a lot!*" There was no missing the implication, that his initial startled reaction was how dare I assume he was middle-aged.

It happened again and again, at dinner parties, in offices, in private conversations. Men did not want to think about middle age; if they were going through the traumas that seemed so characteristic of middle-aged women, the large majority did not want to talk about it and indicated it was a subject they did not think about, consciously at least.

Although my conversations were necessarily relatively superficial, and there were many issues I did not try to explore, I was so startled by my overall observations that it seemed valid to include them.

The main impression I got was that men are far more unhappy about middle age than women are, and are much less in touch with these feelings; that there is something about the way society operates today which has shifted things around. Few women seemed to feel "the best" was necessarily over; the majority of men I spoke to did!

I began, after a while, to have the feeling that men are more oppressed in our society than women—and not by anyone else, but by themselves. Of course that's an oversimplification; any kind of oppression is a complicated web of many factors: it was, of course, the culture we grew up in which taught men not to cry, to feel totally responsible for the security of wives and children, and not to express their loving feelings too openly. There was a marked and pervasive feeling of gloom—even despair—once men began to discuss how they felt about this stage of their lives.

In the absence of economic or social necessity for proving one's brawn and bravery, most middle-aged men really believe, deep-down, that enthusiasm for hunting, fishing, boxing, and football still take the measure of a "real man." It is appropriate, they were taught, to be tender to women and children, under certain circumstances, but never to show such feelings toward other men. They tend to have accepted, at some deep level, the stereotype of the successful male as the one who knows the most dirty jokes, has seduced the most women, and secretly goes to pornographic movies.

I had the strong feeling that today's middle-aged man is the last of his kind. He is usually a man who is working at an ever-and-ever-faster pace to provide his family with more and more things no human being really needs. He is too often desperate and despairing, born too soon for his son's wiser world. His son can cry, can ask for help, and isn't going to kill himself for material possessions, or lie about his sexual prowess, or play games with women; he is going to be himself, in partnership with women, sharing the burdens and the joys of life, with less hypocrisy, less fear of not being a man —and therefore likely to be more of one.

A man I knew died a few months ago. He was fifty-four years old, and everybody said he died because he worked too hard, and was overweight and had high blood pressure. I think that what he really died of was knowing he would never have the courage to live. Frank was the "good son and husband and father" who worked hard, so hard in fact, that he became more successful than he probably ever really wanted to be, made a lot of money and got to be a lawyer. I always had the feeling he would have liked to own a diner in a small town. Instead he lived in the city, and went to see his old mother every single day, and never yelled at his wife, and took on all his relatives as free clients, and worked six days a week, and many evenings, and was too tired and busy to get to talk to his sons very much.

There are tens of thousands of such men, who live short and unlived lives of pleasing other people's perceptions of who and what they are. We are too easily inclined to think that the worst crime a man can commit is to kill another man. It seems to me that it is just as evil for a man to kill himself by gradual stages through living a tense and anxious and meaningless life in which there is hardly ever a sense of exultancy or joy in being the man he might have been.

It may well be that men get paid better salaries, and are not discriminated against by colleges and employers, as women too often are, but I must admit I've come to see their lives as even more oppressed than women's. Women tend to be more aware of themselves and their problems; they talk and talk and talk—and feelings flow freely. They feel sorry for themselves, they feel their fears and their angers very openly, and they are constantly examining and reassessing their lives.

My conversations with men have led me to the conclusion that men are less flexible, have less insight, are far more defended against experiencing their feelings. There are all kinds of "oppression." It may well be that women are taught to think of themselves as second-class citizens; but somewhere along the line—I have no idea if it is an instinctive and biological factor or some socially developed techniques—they have learned to cope, to be survivors, and this is at least in part that they have learned to experience themselves, to acknowledge their feelings and be able to communicate with others about what they are experiencing. Most of the women I talked to seemed to be at home in the world of "facing things head-on," while most of the men seemed to respond instinctively with avoidance reactions.

However, after the initial reluctance, many men did share with me some of their feelings about middle age—and their observations explained and justified their hesitancy to do so! They are not a happy lot. Not at all atypical was the response of one man who said, "If you call this chapter 'I'm

Not the Man I Used to Be—And I Probably Never Was,' that will cover everything!'"

High on the list of concerns and special sensitivities was the matter of remaining sexually attractive to women. One man told me: "When I used to pass a pretty young woman on the street, there was a sort of electricity between us—a message that I found her very attractive, and that the feeling might be reciprocated. Lately I've noticed that this happens less and less often. *I'm* still responding to them, but now, the younger women especially, don't even acknowledge my existence. For the first time I can really understand why men my age leave their wives for younger women. It's to reassure themselves and tell the world they've still got 'it'— whatever 'it' is."

The subject that was brought up most frequently (probably because it was easiest to talk about with a woman) was how men felt about their work. A friend told me on the phone, when I asked about his reactions to middle age, "About ten years ago I was in a really deep depression for several months. I had no idea what was happening until my fortieth birthday arrived, and I suddenly realized the depression was related to facing that day. All of a sudden I said to myself, 'Ted, you have gone as far as you can go. So what?' The rest of my life would merely be more of the same if I was lucky; downhill if I was not."

In a similar vein, another man told me that he felt middle-aged "when I knew the only place I was 'going' was toward the cemetery!" He went on to explain, "Up to that time I always believed that if I didn't really like what I was doing, I could just pick myself up and do something else. I was very much in demand in my twenties and thirties and knew that I had a choice of a lot of very good jobs. One day, while shaving, I saw myself in a sudden sharp flash of *un*recognition— you know, like the man in the mirror was a total stranger I'd never seen before. What started it was noticing how gray my hair was getting around my ears, and then I noticed how puffy I was under the eyes, and then I saw how lined my forehead was—and then I saw my whole face, and it was a terrible shock. I wasn't going to be changing jobs ever again; I'd be lucky if some bright young thing fresh out of Harvard Business School didn't come along and replace me."

The vice president of an investment firm told me, "I'm fifty-two years old now, and I became a vice president when I was forty-four. That was considered quite young at the time. I felt very successful and secure. Two weeks ago a twenty-seven-year-old kid became a vice president of the firm! He's sharp and bright and 'with it.' He speaks in the idiom of the young; he brings with him all the contemporary thinking of his college professors. The top executives are aware of how rapidly the world is changing, and they know that to be successful they have to be contemporary and able to change. I agree, but I get a hollow feeling of terror in the pit of my stomach; if vice presidents are made at twenty-seven, when am I going to be obsolete?"

Many middle-aged men feel that their usefulness is waning; they feel they are being replaced by younger men who are more at home with rapid change. One man said, "Just to keep up with the computer technology of the last *five years* and its effect on banking, stones me out of my mind. It isn't the way I learned, and no matter how willing I may be to learn new ways, I still feel a stranger in my own time."

Men who looked forward to the fifties and sixties as a time of power, success, and financial security now find themselves full of fear and foreboding. There is that first faint but terrifying sense that maturity and the wisdom of experience are commodities that nobody values any more.

Another man told me, "I think we know we are middle-aged when we feel there are fewer options open to us. We have kids in college, we are earning as much as we ever will, but saving nothing; we've got all the things we've been collecting all through the children's growing up—the cars, the house, the cleaning lady, the antiques, the four Princess telephones, the electric-powered lawn mower, the basement stereo system—and we've got to maintain this empire; we're wondering why in hell we ever wanted it, and every evening the main 'acquisition,' the middle-aged wife, tells us her life has no meaning and she's got to find herself, and you wonder what in hell you've got to look forward to, except more of the same. I haven't got there yet, but believe me, I understand the men who drink too much and play around with other women; at least those are open options."

I was surprised to discover as I met and talked with more and more men, how many of them were holding down several jobs. The insurance company bookkeeper who was also working as a part-time tax consultant; the high school math teacher who tended bar three nights a week; the lawyer who goes on the lecture circuit part of each year, advising on wills and estates. Part of the reason for this was, of course, anxiety about money, living above one's means and concern about the future, but many men said that taking on a second job in the middle years was really a way of saying, "I hate what I've been doing, but there's no way out, so I'll do what I like after hours." A statistician for a large corporation said, "By teaching night classes, I get all kinds of extra satisfactions. I like being with other people, which isn't possible on my regular job, and I have a legitimate excuse to get away from my wife. I feel well liked and interesting to others—and of course, it eases the money troubles we all have."

It used to be that women thought that their major work was over when children grew up and left home; nowadays it is as often—or maybe even more often—the man who feels that the work status of his life is waning or finished by the time he is nearing 50. One man told me, "You have no idea how many women are successfully entering the labor market as their children reach high school and college age.

The woman who even ten or twenty years ago felt that her life was really over when her children left home is becoming a faint memory! Even in a time of considerable unemployment, they are finding that employers appreciate their maturity and reliability. Today the middle-aged woman feels confident that she can be trained for a job if necessary, that she has many working years ahead of her, at the very same time that society seems to be increasing her husband's anxiety about his future."

The anxiety about losing one's job in middle age is not without basis in fact; we are all only too well aware of the fact that men who have had responsible and important jobs, often for ten to twenty years, are suddenly finding themselves unemployed. To a large degree this is due to the undeclared Depression of the past few years. Today's middle-aged man is still very much the victim of a society that sees men as the main breadwinners, and the man who loses this function as a failure. Our children will be luckier; a man's measure is not judged by them in terms of whether or not he is a good provider. But our generation is stuck with the myth that men control their economic destinies and even if a company makes it clear that they must fire 20 percent of the staff or go out of business, the fired man's reaction, especially if he is over forty, is almost certain to be a sense of personal failure.

Another aspect of unemployment for men of middle age is the long-ago memory of a father who may have experienced a similar time of feeling personally devastated during the acknowledged Depression of the 30s. We were the children of that time, and many of us have spent much of our adulthood getting rich enough to forget it; we were sure it could never happen to us or to our children. We really could not imagine another time when teachers and engineers would be driving taxis and selling vacuum cleaners door-to-door. But it is happening, and it arouses all the old and buried fears—the memories, perhaps, of a father's frustrated rage when a mother went to work, and he hid in museums and parks, to keep people from knowing he was out of work.

A man who had recently been fired from an executive position (and a salary of $40,000 a year) told me, "A memory came back of something that happened to me when I was eight or nine years old, I guess—and I find I am obsessed by it. One morning I walked into my parents' bedroom without knocking, to say goodbye before I left for school, and my father was sitting on the bed, sobbing, while my mother cradled his head in her arms. I ran all the way to school that day, and spent the night at a friend's house. The next day my mother told me that it was really nothing—my father was just upset about some bills he couldn't pay right now—but it had a permanent effect on me. I'm sure my own drive and ambition have been at least partly a reflection of that experience. Being fired brought it all back so clearly, and I find that I've lost all my confidence in myself. I expected to succeed until I lost this job. I seem to expect to fail now. You can imagine what effect this has on my job interviews!"

In some families, being fired has turned out to be a blessing in disguise. One wife told me, "Jack and I didn't have the guts to do it on our own. I knew he hated working for that drug company, but—I admit it—I was scared to death of his giving up the wonderful income he had, and so was he. Then it was forced on us. We're living on my salary as an assistant school librarian (some trick!) and Jack is back in school. Underneath our worrying about the accumulating debts, I think we are both relieved."

A vice president of an advertising firm was suddenly and summarily fired. He was shocked; he said he'd had no inkling that such a thing might happen. For several years the president of the company had been playing one faction of his staff against another, encouraging a great deal of rivalry and subtle playing for power. Frank was sure he'd been "playing the game" with great success. Suddenly, without warning, those he was associated with were out; thirteen years of hard work and loyal devotion gone. He felt utterly betrayed and rejected. He became immobilized, unable to do anything. His wife and friends kept making suggestions about letters of introduction, ads to put in papers and professional meetings that might produce contacts. Frank did write some letters, but they were pompous and grandiose.

He was out of work for over a year, unwilling to acknowledge the fact that he was really suffering from a deep depression. Finally, when all his resources were gone and his wife was threatening to leave him unless he got some help, he went with great reluctance to a counseling service for unemployed executives. "I kept insisting that I would only take a job that was similar to the one I'd had. I had lost so much self-esteem that it seemed as if I were clinging to what was left of it by refusing to consider any other kind of work. A friend called and told me there was an opening to teach a course in advertising at a local college. I was highly insulted and turned him down. The counselor at the center mildly suggested that it might not be a bad idea to just keep busy a couple of days a week, while I was waiting for the right job to come along—why didn't I try to get the teaching position, just for fun? I got the job, and it was like falling in love for the first time—wham! I knew the minute I started that I was home free. Imagine—forty-three years old, and *no idea* that I was a born teacher! I was so good at it that the inevitable happened: I've been hired full-time. My salary is one-fourth of what I was earning before, but when I wake up in the morning now and realize I'm going to college to be with kids all day, I think I must still be dreaming!" Losing a job can be a new beginning.

There is another kind of being fired that has little to do with the state of the economy. A man told me, "When you lose two jobs in three years, after steady employment for twenty years, and the reason isn't an economy drive, then you have to begin to ask yourself if maybe you really *want* to get fired! It was the most painful day of my life when I lost that second job—I came as close as I guess I ever will to suicide. And I mean that quite literally. On the way home with the news, I smashed my car up and ended in the hospital with a concussion and a broken leg. It gave me time to think, and I couldn't escape my wife's insistence that we talk things over. Usually I'd run when she would say we needed to communicate better! There I was, in bed, and after a while I got sick of her doing all the communicating, so I began to talk about myself and how I felt. One day she looked me straight in the eye and said I was a coward—that if I'd always hated being a salesman why in hell didn't I try some other field, for God's sake! When I was well enough to get around, I decided to go back to school. I took evening classes in accounting, which had been the field I majored in in college. I'm a bookkeeper for a men's knitwear company, now, and so relieved not to be under all that pressure anymore. Getting myself fired was the healthiest thing that I'd ever done!"

One of the most interesting things I discovered in my pursuit of information about men in middle age was how lucky the "late bloomers" were! In all my conversations, I never found a middle-aged man who was in trouble with himself or his life who had "found himself" after the age of thirty or thirty-five. The men who seemed most optimistic and at ease about getting older were people who had developed talents and interests slowly and steadily, without peaking early. They were men who, at forty or fifty, still felt that their best work was ahead of them. They had found work they loved, often after many different tries. One man of fifty-one said, "The actuarial tables tell me I have another twenty-two years to live—and here I am, with a hundred and ten more years of work to do! I have no time to think about getting older!"

The crisis of middle age seemed to be hardest on those who started too early; the most tragic of all were the burned-out boy-wonders. The man who is in a terrible hurry to get to the top as fast as possible seems to burn himself out, unless he has deliberately planned to change professions midstream or to work for fun after earning enough to live on for the rest of his life. The man who deliberately plans to retire *into* life at forty-five or fifty succeeds as well as the late bloomers. But it is the rare exception who can do this. One man made up his mind at twenty to be a millionaire by forty and to then spend the rest of his life becoming an archeologist and traveling to various digs as a volunteer. He did it too! But such planning is unrealistic for the large majority who need other options.

Many of the men who seem to be in trouble in middle age are those who have had some sense of quiet desperation about their work, and as they get older they realize that "this is it." There isn't going to be a chance to try some other kind of work. If we are truly concerned about helping each human being achieve his greatest potential, we need to find ways in which both men and women can have a chance to shift gears in middle life. We need special loan programs, college scholarships, part-time jobs and on-the-job training programs.

We need to make it possible for both men and women in middle age and older to relinquish their jobs without loss of self-esteem and financial security. Too many people hold on to jobs they no longer enjoy, or are no longer suited for. Many of the roles we enjoy and do well in our twenties and thirties may not suit us at all later on. Boredom, too much of a vested interest, a stuck-in-a-rut attitude are not at all surprising if you've been doing the same thing too long.

If society would offer better incentives, the middle-aged man might have a very different feeling about the need to hold on—to grit his teeth and pray that no one will replace him. In the light of some of the feelings many men seem to be having about the quality of their lives, and the lack of meaning in what they are doing, it seems to me we need the kind of cultural climate in which men can find new roles and opportunities as they get older—roles that are not seen as demeaning, but quite the reverse. Where, for example, a bus driver might become a florist; a lawyer, the owner of a chartered fishing boat; a teacher, a travel agent; or a supermarket manager, a social worker. When a man felt ready to change his work and his pattern of living, there would be all kinds of enticing possibilities. To some degree this kind of thing has been possible under the Peace Corps and Vista programs, where older people with special skills have offered themselves for service. In a community that truly set great store by such dedication, fewer middle-aged men would be so terrified of younger men taking over their jobs; they would feel that they could graduate to other more pleasurable activities or make important contributions to society!

In the absence of the needed social sanctions and aids to such midstream experimentation and reevaluations, much of the burden for such necessary changes must depend on the courage of husbands and wives. I know of a number of families in which middle-aged wives are supporting the family (when the children can pretty much take care of themselves) so that husbands can go back to school. Our children have often been helpful to us in their indifference to the luxuries, the material possessions we thought were so important; they make it possible for many of us to take a second look, and we find that we don't need most of what we've got. We find ourselves wanting to live more simply, get rid of big houses or apartments, expensive furnishings, unnecessary luxuries.

I find, for example, that I keep wanting to give things away, move to cheaper quarters, stop buying clothes; I don't want people to give me things for the house anymore; I've stopped buying, myself. I look at the cracked lamp and the torn couch and the faded drapes and I think to myself, "Hello, old friends, we are going to stick it out until death do us part." Many of my contemporaries seem to be feeling the same way. If we love our husbands, then we want to keep them alive, and we want them to have the chance to find out what they need to be and do.

One of the less constructive techniques for "solving" problems around unsatisfying work is early retirement. The personnel director of a large company told me that he has seen a consistent pattern developing, with more and more executives taking earlier retirement. He told me, "It's a cop-out; these guys are saying 'I'm getting out of here before you make me feel old.' It's also a way of saying, 'Sure I've hated what I'm doing—so now I'm going to have fun.' The only trouble with this is that the frenetic energy spent on figuring out how to have fun all the time gets to be a worse drag than the job was."

For many people the answer may well be to develop new approaches, innovative ideas, for "the same old job." One man told me, "I've always been very competitive and ambitious and when I realized I was probably as close to the top in my profession as I might ever get, I went into a real depression. A therapist told me to try to imagine that I'd got the *top job* in the country in my field; what would I do then? I realized that *any* job can become routinized and boring—a dead end—unless you're constantly changing *yourself. That's* the important variable."

The middle-aged man who finds himself depressed and uneasy in his work and personal relationships is probably caught in the trap of seeing himself in his external measurements; what he does, how he looks, what he produces. Middle age is a time for men to think about what is on the inside rather than the outside. Any job is enhanced when performed by a person who is in the process of his own deepening and growing.

Despite the frequent sounds of gloom, I also heard a counterpoint theme: the middle-aged man has something going for him—and that's the mood and philosophy of younger people. There were signs of hope and rebellion! To some degree

I suppose men of all generations may have had periods of self-examination: a sudden or gradual awareness that it was time to take stock. This generation of middle-aged men have been surrounded by teenagers and young adults who have been explaining—perhaps more and more convincingly—that for life to have any significance, you have to search out what it means to "do your own thing." The inclination to finish unfinished business, to experience before it's too late all that one once dreamed of doing, may be a natural consequence of facing the fact that life is getting shorter all the time. Today this is brought home more sharply than ever before. As one father put it, "Danny thought he was just trying to help me to understand him, with all his proselytizing about finding oneself, and not settling for too little and living life as fully as one can. He convinced me! I began to really take a look at my life—and the result is that much to his own surprise, Danny is now mad as hell at me because his mother and I have separated and I gave up my business! I'm living my life, all right, and I think he's sorry he ever brought the subject up!"

Our generation had more choice about work than our parents and grandparents, but the large majority among us still have jobs that primarily satisfy the need for food, clothing, and shelter rather than feeding the human soul.

I have been especially aware of this because my husband was so much the exception among our peers. He has always done the work he loved; he is a man possessed by his work, and he was never willing to take the safe job in order to be financially secure. If I may say so without undue immodesty, he was also fortunate in having a wife who accepted the fact that he was not being selfish or thoughtless, but was, rather, a man who had a sense of mission in life, and the spirit to insist on its fulfillment!

There are of course, a great many men who do not have any burning ambition, any talent which is "death to hide."

The contented middle-aged men I know are often those who settled, when they were very young, for jobs that earned their keep; they live outside of their work—through watching baseball games, playing golf, painting, mountain climbing, and often a great pleasure in childraising; they love to go camping with the whole family, and they play as big a role in their children's lives as their wives do. Since their work is not clearly related to their sense of meaningfulness, this is not a source of middle-aged stress.

For those who *do* suffer, it is still the rare man in middle age who is able to take his life in his hands and say, *"No more, God damn it, no more!"* Often it is the wife and kiddies who keep him at whatever treadmill he's at—their fear of insecurity and their pleasure in having the good things of life. But that is not as often the case as some men would have us believe.

I asked a number of women this question: "If your husband were to tell you he hated his work and wanted to quit and either go back to school or get a job with much less pay, how would you feel? What would you do?" The majority of women gave this kind of answer: "I guess I'd be scared at first—I would worry—but I would never say 'No.' I'd be willing to change our way of living—and after the first shock, I think a part of me would be relieved and glad."

But a lot of men are too polite and considerate to do it the hard way; some take the easy way out and have an almost fatal heart attack! For example, there was Milton, a friend I had not seen or talked to for almost two years, who agreed to meet me for lunch to discuss middle age. I was startled when he walked into the restaurant; he was thirty pounds lighter and looked ten years younger than the last time I'd seen him. His explanation: "I had a very severe coronary about a year ago—and I've never felt better in my life!"

Milton is a quiet, able, attractive man who succeeded beyond his own wildest expectations in an important job in a big corporation. At the time of the heart attack he was an active board member of five social and educational agencies, president of a professional organization, trustee of his church, and knew that with his immediate superior's imminent retirement he would be the likeliest candidate for the job as head of his department, and would become a vice president at a salary that was staggering to contemplate. He also had a nice wife and three kids in the suburbs, but what with all his do-gooder work, he didn't get to see them very often.

After the coronary, and during a seventy-two-hour vigil in the intensive care unit of the hospital, during which he knew he might die at any moment, he was surprised to find himself writing letters in his head. The letters were to all the people he would now be able to say "No" to; first to the five organizations: "You know how dedicated I am to your cause, and how sincerely I regret having to resign, but naturally, after I recover from this coronary, I will not be able to continue my work. . . ." The letter which began to form in his mind and which surprised him most, was this one: "Dear Bob: I know that you have been talking to the top brass about my inheriting your job when you retire, and I appreciate your confidence in me, but of course I could not possibly carry such a responsibility having had this coronary. I will be happy to continue in my present position."

Milton told me, "I couldn't have been more surprised! Anybody who didn't want that advancement would have to be crazy, but I felt only relief and pleasure at being able to say I couldn't take it on. Well, of course, you know what I learned, I'm sure. I never wanted that much responsibility, I like doing things quietly and slowly in my own way, I don't like competing or trying to stay on top—and I was nearly out of my mind, with the pressure of all those extracurricular and very prestigious positions I'd held. I have never been happier than I am right now. I got to know my kids again, and my wife was able to tell me that she'd been pretty close to leaving me there for a while; I'd been too busy to realize how lonely and fed up she was with my psychological desertion. You know, the essence of what I've experienced is this: I've lived in the same house in the same suburban neighborhood for seventeen years. It was only when my doctor ordered me to walk five miles on every Saturday and Sunday that I began to realize how beautiful the countryside is! I'd never noticed anything—I'd never walked before. The pace I'm living at now, is exactly right for me; I love my work, and I don't have to think of advancement; instead of going to committee meetings three or four nights a week, I come home and read and garden and talk to my family. I was a smalltown boy from a poor family, earning more in a month than my father used to earn in a year, and I really didn't want to be living at that pace; it just sort of got away from me. I never could have had the guts to change my life so dramatically. I think I created a critical episode for myself, unconsciously; maybe it was the only way I could force myself into the existential crisis I needed to go through. My energies were all diverted; now I know I wanted to live inside myself more. I 'peaked out.' I was going too far too fast, and it wasn't my nature to do that. All I have felt ever since is relief and release."

There are other kinds of extreme measures being taken by men who become desperate. For some middle-aged men, who suffer terrible disappointment, copping-out seems the only answer. Greg is—was—a child psychologist and educator of teachers, one of the most sensitive, talented, creative men I've ever known. At one point, about six or seven years ago, he became the administrator of a fantastic poverty program in a large industrial city. At the age of forty-three, he was responsible for the most brilliant, human, compassionate —and successful—anti-poverty program that I have ever heard about, involving a level of human rehabilitation which was tremendously exciting and inspiring. In essence what he did was to create a total community environment in which illiterates, prostitutes, drunks, the physically and psychologically disabled—considered to be permanently unemployable by the employment and welfare departments of his city—became part of a training program of such humanizing proportions that they ended up being nursery school teachers, nursing and social-worker aides to the children of the worst slum ghettos in their city. I have spent about thirty years in very close association with the nursery school field, and when I went to observe and to help to evaluate the program, I saw just about the same proportion of excellent, fair, and terrible professionals as I have seen in any program, including those loaded with graduate degrees.

No educational or social program has ever moved me more deeply. I found myself believing in the possibility of making our cities places where human beings might live and grow and thrive. But too many people in high places became very uneasy with the flamboyance, the unorthodoxy of his ideas. Too many people felt left out, wanted power, wanted in. He was crucified by those who could not endure his freedom and uniqueness, and who wanted his power and resources. With an administrator more interested in people than paper work, it wasn't hard to find ways to scream mismanagement.

Greg was allowed to resign; the program was finished. He tried to teach in a college, feeling that he might still make a contribution by helping teachers teach more humanly. In order to do what he felt was right—helping people find their own ways of growing—he could not, in all conscience, give his students passing and failing marks. He was fired.

At the moment, Greg is in Virginia. He bought about one hundred acres of land and is going to build a log cabin, with the help of his wife and neighbors. He does not plan on having electricity or indoor plumbing, and he wants to live on what he can grow. He hopes to do some writing, to earn what little money he will need. He's copped out of the system. Was he wrong? Could he have continued to have an impact? I don't really know, anymore. But I understand. It is very hard to live with honor and dignity and courage in our society. There are plenty of windmills left to conquer— God knows we need proud brave human beings willing to fight to save the world—but how much frustration and pain is enough?

Another problem for the middle-aged man is that he tends to carry the burden of emotional isolation from other men. He may have dozens of male acquaintances but rarely a real friend—the kind his wife has. Our generation was raised to believe that strong men kept their feelings to themselves and this has made it very difficult for them to have a truly intimate and warm relationship with another man. The jolly bunch who drink together in the commuter club car or who tell dirty stories in the locker room of the country club are exactly what I have in mind. In our generation it is usually the women who are comfortable in intense personal relationships with each other; they feel at ease about hugging and kissing each other without the danger of gaining a reputation as lesbians, they unburden their sorrows and share their joys, and in many cases share a love and loyalty that is often as rewarding and satisfying as their marriage relationships— sometimes more so.

An American who was born and raised in Turkey was given a psychological test by a big corporation which was considering employing him in an important job. He told me, "There was one question on the test, 'Would you ever kiss another man?' Without giving it a second thought, I wrote in, 'Yes, of course.' I did not get the job, and many months later, when I chanced to meet someone from that firm, he told me that that answer had killed my chances of getting the job! When I was growing up, the men in my family always hugged and kissed each other."

I recall an incident a couple of years ago when a friend of ours was being divorced by his second wife; a daughter by his first wife was in serious difficulties at the same time with drugs, and he was concerned about rumors of layoffs in his business. He had not called us for several months, and one night my husband called him and asked if he'd like to meet him somewhere for a cup of coffee. The friend said thanks, but he was too tired and hung up. He called back about ten minutes later and said, "I don't know why I did that; I was so moved by your sympathy, I just couldn't take it. I wish you *would* meet me." My husband told me later that both of them had shyly shared the fact with each other that this was the first time either of them had reached out toward a friend with this degree of intimacy since adolescence.

There are exceptions of course, but my impression is that on the whole men tend to have relatively superficial relationships with other men. Friendships tend to be with the husbands of their wives' friends. Most of the men I talked to looked surprised when I asked if they had any really close men friends, with whom they shared their sorrows, or worries or deeper feelings. Few men feel comfortable about hugging each other, and yet almost all the men I asked about this said they wished they could show affection more openly to other men. One candid fellow said, "You know—I have a feeling that many middle-aged affairs occur because a man is looking for a friend and he doesn't know how to find or be a friend with another man! We've only been trained to be more open with women!"

Which brings me to the matter of middle-aged masculine sexuality, where it seemed to me biology was the determining factor in the difference in feelings of most men and women. The majority of women were only too eager to believe all the contemporary views being revealed by scientific research; when most of us were children, we were taught to believe that while we could become sexually aroused and fulfilled by "the love of a good man," implicit in our learnings was a sense of passivity—a willingness to be dominated by the male whose sexual needs were greater than our own. We find ourselves in middle age being assured that our sexual capacities are staggering to the imagination, and that menopause need have no effect on these potentialities. Whether the middle-aged woman is thrilled or mortified by these tidings, she has a very significant choice in what she does—a choice which is *not* shared by her husband. As one candid lady put it, "I'm really too old and set in my ways to become a sex fiend but *it's very easy to pretend you are one!*"

Women, because they can have intercourse whether or not they are mad with passion, have the option of exploring the new possibilities which have been opening up before them, or faking it, if that seems appropriate or desirable. There need be no threat to her status, sexually—at least overtly. She may, indeed, have inner self-doubts, but she can perform, she can maintain an image if she wants to.

The anxiety among middle-aged men about waning sexuality, the fear of potential impotence, seems inevitable in a society that is so preoccupied with techniques of love-making, and such indifference to love. The tables have surely turned on men since the Victorian era. In those times it was far more likely that the thoroughly repressed wife was relieved by menopause; having done her duty as a good wife and accepted the burden of intercourse, pregnancy, and childbirth, menopause represented the signal for the cessation of unpleasant duties. Her husband—and the more thoughtful and kind he was, the more this was probably true—was now expected to direct his interests elsewhere. Whatever he did about it, his sense of male supremacy was intact.

In our time, as young married couples, we lived through the revolution of change in attitudes about male and female sexuality. Ours was the first generation to feel the full impact of change from Victorian attitudes. Most of us remember with some chagrin the marriage manuals of the 1930s and 1940s and their messages, such as: "The loving husband who wants to increase his wife's sexual pleasure will learn to play her like a violin. . . ." This new demand on the part of women could be a heavy psychological burden for men especially during the period of transition.

It was during our generation that frigidity in women declined and male impotence increased, as society challenged its males to become increasingly sensitive and responsive to women's needs. The myth of male sexual dominance ended during our adulthood and, as in most social revolutions, we went from one extreme to another. Rather than sex becoming a true partnership in which both persons explore and experience new possibilities together, the burden of gratification was placed on men.

A younger generation, now just reaching maturity, may have come to a new and better balance, in which male performance is not the crucial issue; I hope this is the case—but the middle-aged man has had a rough time of it.

The residue of the attitudes and experiences that have been intrinsic to our generation only seem to become more intensified in middle age. Among those generous and brave men who were willing to discuss these issues with me, almost to a man they indicated that many extramarital affairs as well as the middle-aged divorces and remarriages to much younger women were at least in some part related to problems of anxiety about one's masculinity, and urgency to recharge one's battery and reassure oneself.

Women had a lot to say on this subject, too! One woman told me that it was her observation that the more puritanical and chaste a man's life might have been when he was very young, the more he was likely to "go nuts," sexually, in middle age. She said, "Men who have really sown a lot of wild oats in their youth don't seem as inclined to seek for sexual variety in middle age. The men I see who really 'go bananas' are men who were married very young, were faithful for twenty or twenty-five years, and probably had little or no sexual experience before marriage. Everytime they get hot pants they think they're madly in love—they seem to lose all their powers of judgment; I suppose what I'm saying is that a delayed adolescence is a kind of madness!"

A deserted wife told me, "I'd never thought of it before it happened to me, but by the time I went through menopause, I was glad to have it happen. I sure as hell didn't want any more children, and I was delighted to throw away the diaphragm! I really didn't feel old. I thought we had a pretty good marriage—I have since learned what some of the not-so-good things were—but when George left me, when he was fifty-five, and married a young woman of twenty-six, he told me that he hoped to have more children! I was shocked. I thought he was looking forward to being a grandfather, not a father! I think his own anxiety about getting old was all tied up with being a fertile male. I began to understand for the first time why so many men may have as many as three different families in the course of their lives; it's a constant reassurance that they are not getting old."

According to some of the sex-research reports, the incidence of sexual inadequacy in males takes a sharp upturn after the age of fifty. It seems very likely that much—most— of this is due to the *fear* that impotency may be a part of getting older. A man of fifty-four told me, "There's a lot more *talk* about middle-aged men playing around than actually goes on, that you can be sure of. I'm the head of the psychological services and personnel department of a large advertising company. I do counseling with a great many of the executives, so I know what is really happening in their lives. Then I go to sales meetings or conferences of one kind or another and I hear other men talking about the sexual exploits of some of the men I know more intimately than they do—and I'm constantly amazed at the imagined exploits I hear about. Many middle-aged men are scared to death to start fooling around, for fear their worst fears will be realized. It's like the teenage kid who feels he can't stand being a virgin another minute, and yet is afraid to go to a prostitute for fear of being impotent."

The specter of sexual inadequacy as a fear associated with aging seems to diminish to the degree that each man finds his own center—his uniqueness and his *human* potency—in loving and working and living most fully. Sexuality in the context of being as profoundly sensitive and alive and oneself as one can be, removes the mechanistic focus on mere physical performance and shifts to the real issue of relatedness to oneself and to a loved other person.

The degree of toleration of a husband's affairs among middle-aged wives seemed to reflect a compassion for a man's greater anxiety about and need for greater reassurance that his sexual powers were not waning.

There was one other aspect of marriage which seemed to relate very directly to the problem of middle-aged gloom in men, and that had to do with a very deep conviction that it is the responsibility of a husband to make a wife happy. A great many men in our generation were raised in homes in which father was the breadwinner but this function did not make him the dominant partner; it only accentuated the idea that his role was to spend his life's energies on satisfying the real and imagined needs of his wife and children.

"Just take a look at the men and women in their seventies and eighties," a friend suggested. "Whether they are sunning themselves in Florida or ending their days in rundown nursing homes, the women outnumber the men at least two to one, and if the widows are rich, they feel this is only their due, and if they are poor, they feel they have been cheated! Our fathers were a put-upon generation—they made doormats of themselves, focusing all their energies on pleasing their wives, no matter what the cost to themselves. Our husbands were raised by those women, and although there has been some change, there is still a strong sense of obligation."

The more I thought about it, the more it seemed to me that the women who were the most unhappy in middle age were those with passive husbands. I had the strong impression that the happier wives were married to men who had minds and wills of their own. The wives with the most complaints— who struck me as peevish, spoiled, demanding—were married to passive men who seemed to be devoting their lives to trying to make their wives happy.

One man commented, "For all the talk about the enslavement of women, it was our fathers who were enslaved. Their lives were devoted to making our mothers happy—and too many of us are the same way. I never met a really contented woman who was able to control and manipulate her husband."

A marriage counselor told me, "When I treat a middle-aged man, and I find out that he's afraid to really take a look at his life because he might have to hurt or disappoint his wife, I know already that his wife is miserable. There is nothing worse you can do to a woman than to give her the power of life or death in the spiritual sense over her husband. Omnipotence isn't good for anyone. A woman who makes a puppet of her husband can never be happy. When a man tells me that no matter how hard he works, or how much he earns or how much he gives, he can't seem to make his wife happy, I have the overwhelming impulse to tell him, 'I think it's time to punch her in the mouth!' " It is difficult for a husband to extricate himself from the vicious circle of giving too much of the wrong things in an endless and impossible search for the means to make someone else happy.

The middle-aged man needs to understand that no one can make someone else happy. When we are fulfilling our own deepest needs, then we bring a healthy sustenance to those around us—and if they can respond to our sense of fulfillment and go in quest of their own, there can be a mutual exchange of love and joy. But men simply cannot carry the burden of making women happy. It is a burden they have accepted and carried far too long.

"My wife complained about our life almost from the day we got married," one man reported. "For twenty years I believed that her discontent was my fault; that it was up to me to find the secret to her happiness. When I got an ulcer, and went into therapy, I began to learn that the unfulfilled woman uses the men in her life to bring her things she has not been allowed to achieve on her own. I had to discover for myself that I could not carry the burden of her discontent. The day I could really say, 'Don't lay your trip on me,' was the day she began to find out who she was, and to take responsibility for her own life."

The task of the middle-aged man is, first of all, to face his own aging and to begin the hardest challenge he has ever faced—to get in touch with who he is and what he really feels—why he behaves in the way that he does. The second task is to free himself from a sense of obligation to his wife, his coworkers, his children, his parents, etc. If you let yourself be used by others, you only make yourself and everyone else more and more miserable. It takes great conviction and courage to insist on this emancipation proclamation, but it is a necessary step.

There is, however, a subtle and very striking difference between a desperate struggle to make someone else happy and a sense of historical perspective about the "natural" role of men throughout the ages. With some rare exceptions in human history, men have held the primary responsibility for the physical survival of the race. Men have been the protectors, the fighters, the hunters. There are equally impassioned schools of thought in regard to whether this pattern was created by biological instincts or a wide variety of cultural determinants. My own view is that the fact of greater physical strength in men and the dependence of women in the processes of reproduction clearly indicate an instinctual basis for the role of men as the guardians of the survival of the species. If this is so then perhaps another dimension of the discontent, the loss in self-esteem among men, has to do with an underlying sense of becoming obsolete!

The complex technological society in which we now find ourselves no longer requires masculine brawn. Even the farmer has become a historical figure—to say nothing of the knight, the warrior, protecting his women and children from invaders. When doctors tell us that men are dying at an early age, mostly from a lack of physical exercise, it may well be that what we are observing is the dinosaur syndrome! We see an increase in meaningless violence at the same time as we recognize that "muscle" per se has no place to go in the world we live in. The body's capacity for physical strength and aggressiveness has no natural, meaningful outlet.

The middle-aged man of today has one foot in the past and one foot in the future. He recalls, believes in, is familiar with the world in which men take care of women and children, and at the same time he is part of a society in which there are no new territories to conquer unless he's an astronaut!

The current research project jointly undertaken by the Harvard School of Public Health and the School of Medicine of Trinity College in Dublin, strongly suggests that the civilized life of the modern man is his undoing physically as well as psychologically. A nine-year study of 575 paired brothers, one of whom had stayed in Ireland and the other had emigrated to the United States, showed the rate of heart attack to be higher in the United States, and the research sought to discover what differences might account for this. By using brothers, the factors of constitutional differences were minimized. Every possible factor was considered—nutrition, activity, types of work, degree of tension, living arrangements, etc.—and in the report that I read, only one factor had been found to be consistently different, namely, the amount of exercise. The Irish brothers ate more, there were more starches and fats in their diet, but they walked much more and many more of them had the kinds of jobs that involved a great deal of activity. Their American brothers had joined the technological age in which hard physical labor is almost unknown in most fields of endeavor.

One might conjecture, with justification, that men die early of heart attacks because their physical capacities are becoming obsolete; the functions they were meant by nature to perform simply don't exist any more. Can any creature, in all of history, avoid extinction when its very nature no longer suits the environment? One thing is clear: physical action has been replaced by mental tension.

In the absence of such historically "natural" activities as planting, chopping, climbing, pulling, etc., both men and women now require substitute methods for keeping their bodies in good physical condition. It is no accident that there is an increasing emphasis on activities such as jogging, playing golf, or joining a gymnasium. It is not too difficult, once we set our minds to it, to find new forms of physical activities, but that doesn't solve the psychological problem of finding new values for new human endeavors.

What of the psychological needs that were also part of the earlier role of men as explorers, doers, innovators, adventurers, protectors of women and children? I would hope that just as men might substitute bicycling for good physical conditioning as the jungle and the farm become historical memories, so too they might have the imagination and courage to recognize the new social frontiers, the new challenges before us. The lion may no longer be at the mouth of the cave; the corn and wheat fields no longer demand back-breaking labor from dawn to dusk—but what of our cities, our *planet?*

While the physical frontiers may be ended, we now face the greatest challenges that have ever faced mankind. We now have the knowledge and the skills to go either way— we are truly at the final crossroad. We can either destroy life as we know it, or develop the ingenuity and courage to

create a world in which there could be glorious new opportunities for fulfilling the very best of human potentialities.

We could, if we cared enough and had courage enough,
create a climate of life through which human beings could so
change themselves as to be capable of solving the problems
that beset and terrify us. We can, if we want to, move into
an age of *moral* valor, to nurture and protect the human
spirit, now that we have the means for physical survival.

The human person is the greatest wonder of all. It is possible for modern men to set themselves the spiritual task of
protecting and eliciting new dimensions of that human spirit!
It seems to me that the middle-aged men I know who seem
least inclined to die of despair are those who are joined in the
cause of saving the world from naked violence and greed,
who see as the task before them nothing less than searching
out the solutions to the new and terrible dangers of nuclear
warfare, pollution of all our earth and water and air, and
overpopulation.

Is this what our children are searching for? Are they in
quest of that civilized man ready to lay down his life for a
new kind of survival? Is this their implicit meaning when
they say we won't be able to change the insitutions of society until we change ourselves? It would seem to me that
any man who could see his way clearly toward accepting the
task of working to make this planet safe for human beings
would be so busy, so fulfilled, so possessed by this act of faith
that his sense of himself and his purposes could be nothing
less than heroic.

Vachel Lindsay, in his poem *The Leaden-Eyed*, speaks of
the ultimate tragedy:

> . . . not that they die, but that they die
> like sheep, . . .

I think what I heard too often in my talks with middle-
aged men was the bleating of sheep.

WE ARE A GENERATION OF REMARKABLE PARENTS: SO WHY ARE WE HURTING?

*
*
*
*
*
*
*.

Chapter 5

It was about 1965, when my daughter would have been fifteen; my husband and I were on our way to a movie on Broadway when we accidentally bumped into her with a group of her friends. She was wearing a Columbia University nightshirt (red flannel) and was barefooted. It was a sight for a middle-aged mother to behold, for I had been something else again at age fifteen. Cashmere sweaters and pearls, full plaid skirts, saddle shoes, the hated girdle and stockings that one wore everywhere except to bed. The thought that I might ever have walked down Broadway in my bare feet and braless was in the same category as my being the first girl on the moon. But far more than the question of appearance was the underlying theme, that my daughter could dare to be so different, so rebellious, so apparently unconcerned with my feelings, when it seemed to me that so much of *my* life, especially as an adolescent, had been devoted to trying to please my parents, to make them proud of me.

At that moment, to be perfectly candid about it, I was sorry I'd ever bothered with motherhood. I felt that I had been a total flop at the job—and in my case, since my professional life was also concerned with childraising, it seemed that I was a failure in general. How could all the Oleopercomorphum, all that Pablum, those private camps and schools, the sleepless nights wrestling with her nightmares, those consultations with psychiatrists when I felt I'd lost my way, all those Super Colossal toys every Christmas—how could they have produced this peculiar character?

And because I was already middle-aged, I felt devastated and betrayed; at forty-three, I was well into the stage of life where you want desperately to begin to see the fruits of your labors. When you are in your twenties or thirties, it all still seems to be ahead of you; if your kid is a mess, or the job isn't getting you anywhere, or you still haven't been to Europe or bought your own home—well, there's *time*, lots and lots of it. You are oriented toward the future and all things are still possible.

At forty-three, I felt I'd had it as a mother; this was what we'd produced and we were stuck with it; there would be no major changes. Deep gloom barely scratches the surface in describing my state of mind. The only thing that probably saved me from a fast leap out of our eleventh-story apartment window was that practically every one of my friends seemed to be in the same boat.

We had several major problems in looking at our teenage children, and probably the chief of these was that we were the first generation of parents who ever, in all of human history, thought we were going to be able to raise our children scientifically, with guaranteed good results for good behavior. We were the Freudian Generation, the first parents armed with knowledge of unconscious causes of behavior; we were the Mental Health Age parents, the first to study parenthood, the first to see a cause-and-effect relationship between the experiences of childhood and adult adjustment. And believe me, we had really *worked* at it. Could it be possible that all the new theories were wrong? These strange creatures inhabiting our homes seemed to bear no possible resemblance to anything we'd had in mind.

The second problem was an integral part of the first; one of the tenets of the new psychoanalytic theories was that deviance was a sign of pathology. In fact *most* behavior was a sign of pathology! If at four Johnny wallowed in fingerpaints, it was because he'd been toilet-trained too early; if at six he was the only child in his first-grade class who wouldn't sit at a desk, his teacher and the school guidance counselor were more than likely to recommend a Rorschach test; it never occurred to any of us that maybe he was the only kid in the class smart enough to know that six-year-olds shouldn't *be* sitting still, that the teacher was mediocre and the subjects taught irrelevant to a six-year-old's interests. No sireee—that was a sick kid, because he was different. If he was caught looking up a girl's dress at nine, then his Latency Period wasn't functioning properly; if he was funny and clownish with company, it wasn't that he had a good sense of humor, or was sociable, or liked to entertain people—it was a sign of his basic insecurity.

Even as I write this, with some tongue in cheek, I am astounded at what we lived through, and I think we were quite remarkable, because no parent today, who has kept up with psychological research, would go through what we went through. It has become eminently clear that Freud and his followers were naturally preoccupied with pathology, because of their medical orientation, which dictated that by studying disease you begin to learn what the healthy state is all about and how to produce it. We have come to realize— but much too late to do ourselves any good—that deviance from some mythical norm is no measure whatever of psychological disturbance or well-being, and that there are vast reservoirs of emotional health in the large majority of children. It is possible to enjoy fingerpaints just because they are fun; this became clear when we had to face the fact that almost every child loves them, and they couldn't *all* be neurotically fixated at the Anal Stage. It is possible to be restless in a classroom just because you are an active little boy and need a more adventurous life—and why any red-blooded American boy *shouldn't* be interested in what's under a little girl's dress escapes me completely at this point.

Typical of our orientation toward the psychological meaning of our children's behavior was our understanding of any behavior which expressed a child's *problems*—jealousy, fear, anger—and our suspicious disbelief when our children behaved beautifully! If they were kind or brave or cooperative, we wondered "what they were covering up"!

We felt culpable for how our children turned out, and we also were taught to believe that being too different, in any way, was a sign of disturbance, so that I can assure you, a barefoot girl in a nightgown, on Broadway of a summer evening, struck me as someone who proved my failures and was a good candidate for Bellevue Hospital. But there was a third problem affecting my perspective on the situation. In addition to the above Basic Assumptions, there was another one, and that was, "Adolescent Rebellion Is Normal." Maybe all was not lost, after all, for the experts had given us a loophole; a certain amount of deviation (insanity) was to be expected as our children attempted to break away from their dependence on us. What a relief! The only reason my daughter looked like that was because she was rebelling against my authority; it wasn't that she didn't love me or that she'd been traumatized out of her head as a child. I postponed killing myself.

But that was only the beginning; my peers can anticipate what came next, for we all shared such terrifying, mind-destroying challenges during the next few years as Marijuana, school dropouts, sex experimentation, and running away from home and living in a tenement. Whether we experienced these things in our own homes or not, they were all around us and could occur at any moment. We were scared out of our minds. But it did begin to dawn on us that it seemed really very unlikely that *all* of us had been rotten parents; could something else be operating in the lives of our children?

Before we could answer this absolutely essential question, these crazy kids of ours were telling us that the war in Vietnam was an obscene and immoral war, and might well destroy this country as well as Vietnam. They were soon expressing their anguish and their rage on the streets, in the offices of college presidents—and finally, in Grant Park in Chicago—and at that point, something broke and something came together for me in a new way. If I had started to write this book before that Democratic Convention of 1968, I might have started out by saying, "Probably the toughest part of middle age today, is the disappointment we feel about our adolescent children." But the fact that it was perfectly clear that the large majority of American adults did not object—but, in fact, even applauded—the wanton, fiendish, brutal treatment afforded their children by the Chicago police seemed to wake me from a deep sleep. The fact that Americans had chosen *children* to be our first nationally approved scapegoat was an idea so outrageous, so shocking, that it seemed to shake my head clear of all the psychological gobbledygook that had been clouding my vision.

A scapegoat is something sick people need to rationalize away things they don't want to look at in themselves; hating some group in one's society changes the subject and takes your mind off your failures. Scapegoats occur when people are frightened and dare not face what's really frightening them. If we could tolerate the beating up of our children, we must be in a *lot* of trouble. And now, suddenly, things began to fit into place. Instead of looking at my daughter's bare feet and her boyfriend's long hair, I knew I should have been looking at the things that were shaking them up. What was happening to the world they were growing up in? How did they see it?

I was a middle-aged parent in a time of *social revolution!* At first I just couldn't believe it. Other people might get caught in history, but how could that happen to me? Somewhere vaguely in the past, I knew that my father's family had run away from pogroms in Russia; I knew about all the people who had died in gas chambers because of Hitler; I knew that life was tough during the Depression—I remembered men selling apples on the street, but *I'd* never been hungry. And when Joe McCarthy was screaming his ugly accusations, I knew some nice people who lost their jobs, but nothing ever happened to me. Even the enormity of the Second World War had only touched my life in very peripheral ways—all the truly important people in my life had been safe.

Though it had not happened to me, I had always been fascinated by literature and drama which dealt with what happened to people when they were inevitably caught up in history and were forced to make some choices about whether or not to be heroic. From Sidney Carton in *Tale of Two Cities* to Thomas More in *Man of All Seasons,* I was always moved and exhilarated by such larger-than-life heroes as Socrates, Galileo, and Jesus—men who were willing to die for what they believed in. Sometimes I wondered what *I* would do if I ever had to choose between living up to my beliefs as a human being—and perhaps paying for them with my life—or disregarding those beliefs. I remember being intensely preoccupied with a play that appeared every night for one week on the educational TV station in New York, called *The Emperor's Clothes* by George Tabori. It was about the Nazi holocaust, and a not very brave schoolteacher somewhere in Europe who just wanted to be left alone to make a living and take care of his family, but who found himself inextricably drawn into that kind of decisionmaking, as others forced him to begin to choose a path—toward cowardice and safety or toward courage and terrible danger. I remember that I watched the play every night, and was utterly absorbed and overwhelmingly moved by the tragedy of the choosing and the glory of the credit to man's nature in making the "right" decision. I guess I really hoped I'd never be put to the test—but I realized in 1968 that that moment had now come for me.

What an awful shock! I'd been living in the beginnings of a social revolution for years and hadn't really noticed; but our *children* had. If they seemed shook up, if they did not seem primarily concerned with pleasing us, if they were turned off by education and affluence, maybe it was because *they were in mourning for the world.*

As I look back, now, I have the feeling that many of the people who were so angry at young people a few years ago have had a change of heart, and I think the reason is that just about everything our children seemed so upset about—all the doomlike predictions they were making—have come true. Because we were older, and more used to the world we had lived in so long, we had been too myopic to see what they saw with the clarity and honesty of an uncommitted youthfulness— the world, ladies and gentlemen, was *really* going to the dogs.

I am sure there was nothing conscious or planned about the way our children began to look and act as they became teenagers; one doesn't say to oneself, "I think the world is coming to an end, so I might as well stop wearing shoes." But in every human upheaval throughout history, young people have tended to be the first barometer of what is coming. There are historical descriptions of bands of wild children who simply took off on their own during periods of upheaval; there is the story of "The Cathars" and "The Fourth Crusade" in thirteenth-century France when a group of young people were simply wiped out for preaching love in a time of hate, for warning that terrible times were ahead unless some kind of moral regeneration took place.

The radicalization of Eda LeShan in the past few years astonishes me. I have come writhing and screaming into the world of my daughter and her friends, but some of my discoveries have made it one of the most important growth experiences of my life.

My husband was never as myopic as I. A long time ago he urged me to listen—really listen—to what the young were trying to tell us; to somehow get myself beyond the prejudices of my middle-aged sense of aesthetics and hear what was coming out of those faces instead of focusing all my attention on the hole in the seat of the bluejeans. The first thing I found out was that the large majority of the young people I met and talked to were *the kindest, nicest, most warmly loving and decent young people I had ever met in my life.* It simply became impossible to deny the evidence of my eyes and ears; despite their appearance, their immaturity, their hang-ups, these were the most civilized and idealistic children any generation of parents had ever raised. Of course there were many exceptions—the psychically wounded, the destructive; every generation has its share of them—but there was also a core of young people who seemed to me to be changing the very climate of life in this country, irrespective of their numbers or real power, merely by their presence in our lives.

We began to have "dinner parties," the like of which I'd never come across; our guests would arrive when the spirit moved them, without benefit of formal invitation, and at whatever odd times of day or night they felt like visiting. They almost never wore shoes, except in dead of winter, they were usually struggling with heavy instrument cases, and music was almost always part of the experience; they came dressed in everything from farmer's overalls to 1920s skirts,

and they were always ready to provide some nuts and raisins,
or some brown rice and organic vegetables if we were out of
supplies. They sat or lay on the floor, their arms often around
each other, and talked with passion about the problems of
life, the dangers in the world for all of us, and they dreamed
good dreams, while at the same time expressing their despair
and hopelessness. They were deeply kind, not superficially
polite. They were undefended and heartbreakingly vulnerable and open in sharing their real feelings. They were well informed, had broad interests and a deep love of nature and of
all living things.

I began to see the world as they saw it, and as time has
passed, almost everything they talked about has become so
apparent that now most of us can see that our children are
not insane and are not rebelling against us. But one thing we
never thought about when we were trying to help them
grow well, not chained to the emotional diseases of the past,
able to make decisions for themselves, really free to express
love and wanting to live peacefully, was the possibility that
*the world they would find themselves in, as they reached to-
ward adulthood, hadn't any use for people like them.* What
then?

Our children are children of the atomic age; since they
were old enough to talk, they have known that there were
hydrogen bombs in several parts of the world which could
blow up all the major cities in the world. Our children are
the children who were told by an irresponsible governor during their grade school years (if they lived in New York State)
to hide under their desks in case of an atomic war, as if they
could be safe from a holocaust beyond describing. Our children are the children who grew up knowing that in several
parts of the country there were buildings in which germs and
bacteria were being stored for destroying whole populations;
they are the children who saw oil spilled into the oceans, and
nobody stopped it; they are the children who knew that My

Lai would happen and predicted what turned up in *The Pentagon Papers;* they are the children who saw their friends or were themselves in Mississippi jails for upholding the Constitution; they are the children who know that we have poisoned the air and water, to make ourselves rich—and that nobody seems to be able to make us stop; they are the children who grew up in the shadow of the knowledge that men could be so evil they could kill six million in gas ovens in the space of a few years; they are also the inheritors of Hiroshima. In their formative years, they saw the assassinations of men of good will and the murder of innocent young people at Jackson and Kent State.

Nietzsche once said, "Some situations are so bad that to remain sane is to be insane." I have developed a technique for getting some small sampling of how the world looks to our children; I pick a day arbitrarily, and I write down all the news I hear that day, everything I observe that tells me something about where we are at. This is a list of such a sample day, a few years ago, when my own child was about eighteen years old.

1. Report in newspaper, investigation of the death of a soldier in Vietnam. Parents told he died of sun stroke. Was a midwest farm boy and this seemed unlikely. Asked their congressman to investigate. Son died of three bullet wounds while lying in the sun, waiting for a helicopter. (That's how we lower *our* "body count"!)

2. Senator Russell of Georgia, in arguing for the antiballistic missile system, says, into the U.S. Congressional Record, for all posterity: "If we have to start over again with another Adam and Eve, I want them to be Americans, not Russians."

3. Some nerve gas is dumped into the ocean, against the advice of some major American scientists.

4. Report in newspaper, a junior high school in Potomac, Md. decided to experience the impact of segregation, in order to understand it better. With students, teachers, and principal

all back of it, they organized a week during which all bru-
nettes would be the comfortable majority and all blondes
the mistreated minority. Separate bathrooms, separate parts
of the dining room, slurs against the blondes, separate water
fountains, etc. They were really getting the feel of it, and
not thinking it was such a lark—but on the third day the
project was screamed down by a group of parents (mostly
government employees) including a U.S. Senator.

5. The New York City Health Department announced that
hundreds of deaths due to upper respiratory infections could
be directly or indirectly attributed to a recent four-day in-
version of air. No plans for punishing those guilty of fouling
up the air were mentioned.

6. A brilliant observation in a Congressional Committee Report: "Continuity of oil supply in the aftermath of a nuclear
exchange would not be a factor of major significance since
consumption of oil would be sharply curtailed, as would the
capacity to refine oil."

I could go on and on. Several years ago, U Thant, then
U.S. Secretary-General, said we had about ten years left in
which to do something about population, pollution, and international relations—or we were done for as a planet.
Nobel Peace Prize scientists warn us that it is possible we
will have polluted the oceans beyond recall within the next
ten or twenty years. Every day we hear some new evidence
to make it crystal clear that the American people neither
know about nor have any control over the warlike activities
of the Pentagon or the CIA. Any young man, in this time
and place, who is able to concentrate on studying or passing
meaningless multiple-choice examinations, who is preparing
for a career, and marrying and having children, and buying
life insurance, and planning for retirement benefits is just
plain out of his head. I find that most of the "freaked-out"
young people I know who find college a drag, and don't feel
able to decide on a profession, and can't see why you should
get married just because you love someone and want to live

with them, really do not believe in the future. I don't think they expect to ever get to being old. And I have come—painfully, agonizingly—to the point of thinking they are far from crazy.

Whatever the problems may have been during our green years, we always had hope. Most of us felt we could make the world better; we thought we could change the institutions of a society through knowledge in the social sciences, and through technology. Our children's experience has been quite different. If they were adolescents in the 1950s they were apathetic; in the 1960s they were angry; and in the 1970s many seem anguished. They no longer seem to dare to hope.

Why have our children reacted with such sensitivity and pain, to make it impossible for them to go on with the business-as-usual kind of growing up?

I'll tell you why: *because all those newfangled mental-health ideas we were trying out as parents turned out just fine!*

I think that my notions about how childraising methods could change the world were fairly typical of the "liberal, white, urban middle class," especially those of us who were drawn to education and psychology as professions. To over-simplify it considerably, there were two main ideas: the first came from John Dewey and the progressive-education movement: if you wanted to prepare children to live in a democratic society, you had to raise them with democratic discipline; you couldn't make them behave through fear, because in that way they would never have a chance to think for themselves or make wise decisions. You cannot develop your own good judgment if the reason you act as you do is because someone is standing over you with a whip. We wanted our children to be "inner-directed." It seemed logical to us that Fascism and Communism, which were having such an enormous influence on our lives in the thirties and forties,

could not really succeed except in countries where children
were raised in very authoritarian homes, and felt most comfortable when somebody else took control of their lives and
told them what to do.

The idea that all progressive educators believed in laissez-
faire discipline is nonsense; there were some excesses, where
kids seemed to get out of control, but this was the exception.
Democratic discipline meant that you tried to teach by example and experience. If you wanted children to become
thoughtful, reasonable, kind adults, you tried to deal with
them thoughtfully, reasonably, and kindly. As they became
more mature, you also began to give them more and more
opportunities for making choices—and frequently learning
by their own mistakes. You allowed children to participate in
the processes of social organization, rather than inflicting
ready-made rules on them.

Within the framework of such a philosophy there are still
times when a parent gets so angry that he just can't be reasonable or kind. And there are also times when parents and
teachers may misread a child's readiness for some responsibilities. But my generation of parents made the attempt to raise
children who could be good citizens in a democracy. Our
children have minds of their own, and reasons for their convictions. If they believe they are in the right, no authority
(neither Mayor Daly nor Vice President Agnew) can sway
them. They seem to be willing to take their medicine if these
convictions get them into trouble. They seem to be immune
to political propaganda. They have been so thoroughly impressed with looking for their own truths, that they are the
bane of any demagogue, to say nothing of the panic on Madison Avenue as to how you can go on selling junk to a generation who are on to you. Our children seem to have a strong
propensity for respecting each person, allowing everyone to
do their own thing, so long as it doesn't hurt or interfere
with others, and they are in a continual search for their indi-

viduality. They believe in limited rules to protect individual rights, but they are quick to suspect any rules that give preference to one group over another. They did, in fact, come out pretty much the way we told them to. For in addition to the liberal disciplinary methods we used, we also did a lot of talking.

Probably the greatest irony is that our children really listened to what we told them—but we didn't! We told them that war was terrible, and that it had become an absolutely impossible solution to international problems; we told them that we were not interested in how much money a person had, or what he owned, or how he looked on the outside—we believed that what a person was on the inside was the important thing. We wanted them to be color-blind. We wanted them to be concerned about all humanity, not just about Americans. We told them that we wanted them to choose their own way of life, and not be influenced by our preferences.

What surprised most of us more than anything else is how literally our children took us about personal possessions. When we talked against materialism, it never occurred to us that our children would take this to mean that you only buy and wear one pair of bluejeans at a time, never own any dresses or suits, share whatever you have with anyone who wants something, and learn to live with just what you can carry on your back.

There is nothing new about parents teaching moral values to their children, but there seem to have been few times in history when children took such precepts so literally, and seemed to be equipped to do a good deal more than give them lip service.

This fact brings us to the second fundamentally distinctive quality in our childraising methods—the way in which I think we really changed "human nature" by the new psychological insights we brought to bear in our children's lives.

As a student of the newly emerging psychological theories, I believed that insight into human motivation and helping a child develop a sense of his personal worth would make him less likely to choose random targets for the expression of hostility.

Let me present two examples, acknowledging that these are an oversimplification of what was involved. Before we were given the newly emerging information that all human beings had all kinds of feelings, children were raised to believe that one could be either *good* or *bad*, actually a bald-faced lie that did great damage to the human psyche. An example: Johnny is jealous of the attention his baby sister is getting; he smacks her. He gets beaten for what he has done, and his parents tell him that only evil, bad children hate their sisters, and that God will punish him if he is a bad person. Johnny is scared to death of his hostile feelings. He blocks them out of his consciousness completely, but they are still there, deep-down. A number of things can happen to him as he grows up if this is the overall pattern of his experiences in the family. He may feel so guilty, so unworthy, so angry at himself for being a bad person that he develops a psychosomatic disease; he thus turns his unconscious feelings against himself. Or he may become a sweet, quiet, good, little surprise-killer if the deprivations of his life are strong enough and the buried hates bad enough—the kind of person who speaks in a whisper and says "please" and "thank you," and then suddenly runs amok and goes into a book depository and kills a president or climbs into the tower of a college building and shoots ten or fifteen students walking peacefully below. Or Johnny may find an outlet for his unresolved inner feelings by directing them toward some group whom he rationalizes are a *real* enemy, and therefore his hatred is not evil.

In most cases the Johnnies who are frightened by their "bad" feelings, grow up with less dramatic but certainly handicapping problems; too many headaches, serious marital conflicts, trouble in dealing with authority figures—and maybe more capacity for hating people and being ready to fight individuals and wars—than could be explained on any basis of social realities. They have been, throughout human history, very susceptible to suspicions of others, have disliked strangers and been jealous of others' achievements and property.

But we felt we could change that pattern. We helped our children to become aware of all their different kinds of feelings. We said, "Of course you feel mad at your little sister, Johnny, all children feel jealous sometimes. You can't hit her, because people must not hurt each other, but all people have angry thoughts and feelings, and there's nothing wrong with that. If you're feeling real mad, how about punching this doll instead?"

We also said such things as, "I know you are afraid of the dark. There is nothing to be ashamed of," and "The reason Frank and Jimmie ganged up against you, and made you feel bad was that they are little and not so sure of themselves, and ganging up on someone else makes them feel strong." Our children were the first generation ever raised with explanations for the meaning of behavior. We taught them to look for hidden causes. This has had two major effects: they grew up without undue guilt about their own human limitations, and they are very slow to make angry judgments about other people. Instead of saying, "He's stupid," they say, "Something is blocking his ability to think." Or instead of saying, "She's a malicious gossip," they say, "She's too insecure to trust her own ability to relate, without telling stories about other people." They are psychologically "hep"—but even more than that, there are no deep reservoirs of unresolved anger that need to be expressed in hating individuals or groups.

As I watch and listen to young people, I have the impression that no matter how rough and imperfect our new insights, no matter how much stumbling and uncertainty there may have been during this first half-century of experimenting with new psychological theories, those who truly tried them out on their children should be very pleased about these beginnings. The attempt to help children to understand the deeper meanings of their feelings and behavior, and to accept all that it means to be human, without condemnation of oneself or others, seems to have a great deal to do with the pacifism of our kids. *What they hate is social injustice—not themselves, not each other, not strangers.*

Few things have made me angrier in recent years than the pronouncements of Dr. Bruno Bettelheim about this generation of young people. His description of "the Hippies" is that they are all children who were raised too permissively and are just having a temper tantrum about the problems of the world. It seems to me that if he is right, and if our children are just spoiled brats, they would not be bothering about these problems, but would be doing everything they could to "get a piece of the action"—the spoils of affluence. It is much easier to be a submissive student, to pass your courses, to prepare for a profession, than it is to risk getting beaten over the head by the police in front of the Pentagon, or spend a summer in a Mississippi jail or lose a half-year's college credit, which happened to some of the college students on the Selma March. It is probably easier (and even less dangerous) to go into the army and serve two years in Vietnam than to spend three to five years in a federal prison for draft resistance. It is a nuisance to buy detergents without phosphates, to collect newspapers and bottles, to stop buying paper napkins and towels, and to live on organic vegetables —but these are the sorts of things these "spoiled brats" are doing. I can't see how overpermissive discipline could make them see, before most adults did, the obscenity of the war in Vietnam.

A friend who thinks I am slightly batty in my admiration

for the youth of today—a starry-eyed idiot, is what he thinks I am—gave me a copy of an article in *The Reader's Digest* (June, 1970) titled "I'm Tired of the Tyranny of Spoiled Brats," by K. Ross Toole, a professor of history at the University of Montana. Professor Toole believes that life is no better or worse than it has been for any other generation of young people; that steady progress has been made in this country, with each new generation, and that the middle-aged worked very hard for what they have, while the young are simply behaving very badly because they have not been properly disciplined. The article is not hateful or foolish, but well reasoned—the honest and loving assessment of someone who obviously cares about children and believes deeply in the idea that parents have abdicated from a kind of authority that is essential. But what bothered me is that his criticisms make no mention of the context in which this generation is rebelling. He writes in part: "I assert that we are in trouble with this younger generation not because we have failed our country, not because of materialism or stupidity, but simply because we failed to keep this generation in its place. . . ."

My husband, after reading the article, commented, "What puzzles me is that the article was written by a historian; how can he speak in the tones of normality at such a moment? Didn't he ever study the decline of the Roman empire and read about the orgies, the circuses, the increasingly selfish power-groups, the refusal to deal with moral issues?" The fault in Professor Toole's article was that it had nothing whatever to do with living during the fall of Western civilization! From my point of view, the spoiled brats are the middle-aged, trying to drown their perceptions of what is happening by a business-as-usual, don't-bother-me, attitude.

The radicalization of young people can be understood only in the context of *their* life experiences at a vulnerable and idealistic age. A friend tells me about her nephew: "Nobody in the family can figure out how Eric ever became a Maoist; he was a model student in high school, he had short hair and wore ties—he was a real stuffed shirt, just like his father. Out of the clear blue sky, he seemed to change—over-night—in his third year at Harvard. *I* know *exactly* when it happened, and it was one terrible moment. Eric was stand-ing on the sidelines during the riot at Harvard. He saw a policeman beating a student who was in a wheel chair, and Eric ran over and tried to cover him with his own body. The policeman cracked his skull instead and hauled him off to jail. He had a concussion, but was not hospitalized for more than twenty-four hours. He became a Maoist in the setting of his personal nightmare. Only someone utterly devoted to the ideals of this country could have been so *completely* disillu-sioned."

For those of us who feel we have raised a most civilized and idealistic generation, there is still, of course, the necessity to face the realities of drugs and copping out on life and one-self. I do not believe these are much related to affectionate discipline and the teaching of mental health concepts! They seem to me to be related to some of the things we could not possibly have imagined when our children were young, or to factors over which we had no control. It never occurred to us that if we raised a generation of kind, peaceful people, the world might be in such a state that it would have no use for them. Never, did it occur to me, for example, that my child would ever have anything to fear from the police. We came from a long line of law-abiding people, in which our only negative confrontation with the law might be a traffic ticket. The police, in our comfortable middle-class life, were always on our side. I admit with shame that I led such a protected life, I never had any idea of the quite different experiences with the police among the poor and the black. I never could have dreamed that a time would come when my daughter would be beaten on the neck with a night stick and have her coat ripped in half for demonstrating peacefully with a few hundred others in front of the Plaza Hotel, at a moment when she was simply trying to obey the policeman's order to move, but could not because the group had been surrounded on all sides by stanchions. I could not have believed that someone as peaceful and law-abiding as she is could constantly be harassed with car inspections because her boyfriend has long hair, or would live in terror in a lower-middle-class neighborhood, in which she is the suspect "Hippie," because she expects a midnight police raid in which they will plant pot in the apartment, as they have done to many of her friends. I am in a state of shock—the police have always *helped* me—but as her boyfriend explains ruefully, "What you don't understand, Eda, is that we are the niggers of our time."

There were aspects of our children's education that greatly influenced their attitudes. They are the products of the Sputnik hysteria, of the decade in which we lost our minds in a frantic worship of academic achievement, in which we decided that being well educated meant having your head stuffed with thousands of disconnected and irrelevant facts, and not with the challenge of learning to think or to reason. Our children were enslaved by hundreds of exams every year, three or four hours of homework every night, and the constant warning that their lives would be worthless if they didn't make it into an Ivy League college. All of a sudden all our social problems were going to be solved by computerizing the minds of our children. As a result, the large majority of schools made it clear to our children that nobody cared about their interests, their individual readinesses, their feelings, their social relations—all that mattered was getting high marks. It was a sick and incredibly stupid time in the history of American education, and we are now reaping the harvest of it all.

It is inhuman to have the school concerned only with your

mental gymnastics and not with your feelings as a human being. It may well have been that the imbalance—the emphasis on the activities of the cortex only—have had a great deal to do not only with the attraction of mind-expanding drugs, but also with the interest of young people in Yoga, mysticism, the occult, astrology, and the rest. All of these have to do with sensations, feelings, looking within one's soul; they are all the antithesis of memorizing and accumulating facts. We are both intellect and emotion, thought and feeling. We have many needs above and beyond merely knowing; we need each other, we need to be in contact with our feelings and our bodies. It is also no accident that there is so much interest right now in sensory awareness, in breathing exercises, in the therapies that stress touching each other. It seems to me that all of these are an adjustment of the unbalanced educational experience our children were victimized by. The catch is, of course, that we tend to go to extremes. In the search for balance, we may end up denying the appropriate and very real need for explorations of the intellect, for the development of mental skills. One can only hope that we can learn from these past few years, and allow children to have the kind of school experiences that truly encompass all of their varied needs and interests. In the meantime, we are stuck with the residue created by a time in which our children were treated like mental robots in school, and have therefore been turned-off by the academic life and instead are turned-on to their own mind-expanding (noncortical) experiences.

Another thing which we did not anticipate is that the prolongation of education and the relative affluence we enjoyed, would infantilize our children. If you are eighteen and your father is out of work and there are five hungry brothers and sisters at home, you go to work—and you grow up fast; there are no alternatives. If you are eighteen and your parents go to Europe every year and own a sailboat, and if you know that any profession you may choose will keep you in school in a passive and dependent role until you are almost thirty, you may not see very much sense in becoming independent. Nobody really *needs* your earning power, and it's no real sacrifice for your parents to supplement your livelihood, so you decide to spend the next few years thinking things over, figuring out what you really want to do. Or you earn as little as you need, just to get by, and try to do things that give you immediate pleasure, because there doesn't seem to be much advantage in planning for an unknown and maybe even nonexistent future.

We also could not anticipate that we would not use our new technology or the know-how in the social sciences for the betterment of mankind. One of the things that has distressed our children most about the quality of life today is that we know how to change the world and make it better, but we don't have the will to do it. Imagine if you can that the world had just discovered a cure for smallpox—knew how to make the vaccine, how to administer it, etc., but just refused to set up any kind of preventive program, because no nation would spend the money. Nobody gave a damn. It would be a monstrous kind of immorality and really quite unthinkable. From our children's point of view, this is precisely what is going on today. Rough and imperfect as our skills may be, for the past half-century at least, we have learned how to make life far better for the large majority of people but we have made minimal use of this knowledge. We have good understanding of the etiology of crime and its prevention, we have known how many people can grow up to be twisted, dangerous to themselves and society. We know how to plan intelligently for cities and towns, we know ways of educating children that can help almost every one of them to become caring, decent people; we know the social and emotional causes of the vast majority of those affected by drug addiction. We know it's a disease but we treat it as a crime. We know that if a child does not feel revered and cherished as a miracle of possibilities from the day he is born, he is doomed in many ways. We know how to demolish all slums, but we are only willing to create a climate for living on the moon. We know that race prejudice is a sickness— and we know how to cure most of it, by changing the quality of life.

We know the medical, the social, the psychological needs that are basic to the fullest fruition of human life—and we have thus far been unwilling to put our knowledge into practice to a degree that could really make a difference. We will not spend the money to develop the resources that could do the job. At this very moment there are, for example, enough expert criminologists to set up a system of prison reforms which would depopulate our prisons as much as 50 percent within the next two generations. But it costs too much. As soon as we acknowledge the possibility of prevention, we know we will be stuck with a great investment; it seems cheaper to hire more police and prison guards. Right now we know enough to halt pollution of our water and our air; but it would mean that a lot of people would have to give up the selfish motives by which they live—and it isn't about to happen.

There is, at this moment, a body of information available that could free most of the world's children of most serious diseases, could end malnutrition, but we won't use this knowledge. We have the technological means to end starvation everywhere in the world, but we won't do it. Our children have lived in this climate of life, and it has demoralized them. That is the obscenity that undercuts all else, and accounts in no small measure for the pain, the despair, the passive immobility, the copping-out of young people that distresses us so much.

We are, as a culture, insane. Many years ago a sociologist by the name of Luther Woodward told of a primitive society that had a very interesting and provocative way of measuring insanity. In the town square there would be a water spigot and the water would be pouring out into a wooden bucket. Next to the bucket would be a ladle. If you wanted to know if someone was sane or insane, you would ask them what could be done about the water spilling over the side of the bucket. If they tried to ladle the water out of the bucket, they were insane; if they turned off the spigot, they were sane. What contributes to the despair of our children is that we are a nation of ladlers; instead of treating the causes of poverty and crime and mental disease and prejudice and international hate and suspicion, we build more prisons, hire more firemen to keep slum fires from spreading, send more policemen into the ghettoes so the people won't riot, and build more and better missiles to scare all the people who are already scared of us. We need to concern ourselves with the reasons for our children's anguish.

In June of 1971 the *New York Times* reported on the "Voices of Despair" at the Dartmouth graduation. The highest-ranking student of that year's graduating class had said, "I have made no plans because I have found no plans worth making." These were the words of a mathematics major and computer expert who "did not feel any sense of accomplishment" after four years of college in which he had excelled over all his classmates. He continued:

> Take pity on me, those of you who can justify the air you breathe. Send me letters and tell me why life is worth living. Rich parents, write and tell me how money makes your life worthwhile. . . . Members of the class of 1971, take pity on a student who did not think, but only studied . . . tell me how you came to appreciate the absurdity of your life.

In *Slaughterhouse Five*, Kurt Vonnegut recalls the well-known prayer used by Alcoholics Anonymous: "God grant me the serenity to accept the things I cannot change, courage to change the things I can, and wisdom always to tell the difference." He says of his young hero, "Among the things Billy . . . could not change were the past, the present and the future." Our children easily identified with this point of view.

In spite of this generalized sense of hopelessness and helplessness, young people have made an incredible difference, whether they think so or not. There can be no doubt in any rational person's mind that it was primarily the youth of this land who finally made us take a good hard look at the war in Vietnam and American foreign policy in general. They also played an enormous role in sensitizing all of us to the ecological problems we must face up to. They have surely played a meaningful part in beginning the absolutely essential restructuring of our educational system, through their participation in Free Universities, storefront schools, street academies, noncampus high schools and colleges, and in general, their universal responsiveness to such over-thirty voices as Paul Goodman, John Holt, George Dennison, Nat Hentoff, Edgar Friedenberg, Jonathan Kozol, and Charles Silberman, who have raised serious critical questions about our schools.

They have also helped to clarify some muddy civil rights issues affecting students by bringing legal attention to such matters as the right of a male student not to cut his hair, or the freedom to express one's views in an underground newspaper. Until quite recently, few people were really thinking about some of the constitutional issues involved in school authority over children and their families, and it seems to me quite healthy that we now see an increasing awareness of the legal implications involved in suspension or expulsion of a student, for example.

The young have had a good influence on us! I think they have helped us to dress more casually, to live less competitively, and to be less hypocritical in our relations with others. I feel that my daughter and her friends have forced me to take a good hard look at many of my rigid and often phony assumptions about life, and if I feel that I am more relaxed, that I feel freer to be myself than I ever have before, that I have little patience with superficial and dishonest relationships, I owe this in no small part to her challenging me (as well as to my good will and flexibility!).

I have come to have a good deal of admiration for young people's unwillingness to choose a career before they have any sense of who they are or what matters to them. I share their cynicism and disregard for the formal requirements for most professions; they are saying what none of us ever dared to say, but knew perfectly well—that about 90 percent of the required courses we had to take for various professional degrees were so much horse manure and had nothing whatever to do with whether or not we learned what we needed to learn or became the kind of people who could do the job well. Certification in most professions has little or nothing to do with genuine talent or skill, but is, rather, a sophisticated extension of the "closed shop." The disenchantment with degrees is very real, and not only related to the fact that after all the yelling and screaming of high school guidance counselors, half the newly Ph.d'ed are unable to get jobs, especially in teaching and engineering, which were considered absolutely safe from any Depression. But what is even more important, our children have forced us to look with some candor at the misery of so many people who choose too quickly and settle too weakly for work they despise.

I find myself, after many years of self-examination (and all the anguish that that implies) truly on the side of young people who are taking a good look at marriage and are not so sure they see much meaning in its current forms. I do not find that they are any more inclined toward promiscuity and irresponsibility in their love relationships than any other generation. They are surely more open and honest than we were. I find their experimentation with new life-styles—trial marriages, communal living—a refreshing alternative to the current divorce rate among my contemporaries, and the quiet despair of so many who remain married. They are quite right in assessing this as a time for discovering new and perhaps more relevant ways for adults to love each other and raise children. They are also reexamining parenthood itself, in ways that make good sense to me. They see no reason why everybody should have children, and they are also deeply concerned with the limitation of family size for those who want children. Most of us, because of the brainwashing of our growing years, are horrified by what seems to us to be a sort of self-indulgence, a hedonism, when our children refuse to make long-range plans, but insist on enjoying the moment. In some cases of course this can be a symptom of a childlike need for immediate gratification of all one's wishes, but for many young people I think it is to "redress a balance"— and one that is much needed. It seems to me that if any of us are bitter or angry or discontented with our lot, it may well be because we have spent all our lives planning for the future and never daring just to enjoy the present. And having tried that lately, I must say there is a great deal to be said for *letting life tell you where you are going,* for living this instant for all it is worth. Again, it is a question of balance—but our generation needs to learn about just *being alive,* right now—and perhaps some day, as they get their fill of this intense pleasure, our children will also see the usefulness for some planning, some of the time.

What probably infuriates us more than anything else in this connection is when a young person seems to be "throwing away" something he has almost obtained—such as quitting graduate school six months before getting a degree, or giving up a fabulous scholarship to some Ivy League college in order to go cut sugar cane in Cuba for three months. "It's such a *waste!*" we say—but is it really? You may have discovered at the last moment that you don't really want to do anything connected with the Ph.D. and you may be making a gesture to acknowledge your own bitter disappointment with how little you have learned or earned it. Young people may be just as prone as we are to make mistakes in judgment and to make impulsive gestures that are foolish—maybe much more inclined—but I find myself impressed anyway, with a kind of purity that shines through these gestures; they are trying, at least, to be true to themselves and to their own system of values.

I have been talking about those of our children who are now somewhere between eighteen and twenty-five. They were an advance guard—the first young people to show how shaken they were by the state of the world. Middle-aged parents on the somewhat younger side serve to remind me of how quickly human beings get used to things and adapt to change. Younger parents have children who are turned-off by the same things that bother their older brothers and sisters, but there is a kind of security and stability about them. They have the same values, they look the same, but a lot of the groundwork of the revolution has already been done for them, and they do not seem so shook-up. The advance guard tends to suffer most during a time of change, and it is my impression that among the thirteen-to-seventeen-year-olds today, there may be fewer school dropouts, more attempts to work within the system and beat it into shape, a cooler and more self-confident approach to trying to survive and become part of a period of tremendous social upheaval. However, there are signs that we find disturbing, as well, among this younger group. They are bright, well informed, intellectually sophisticated, but emotionally immature. They bloomed too early and too fast. They tend to be too easily influenced by their peers, as a substitute dependency for leaning on us. A psychiatrist who has a residential treatment center for teenage drug addicts told me, "I don't know why parents blame themselves—*they* have no influence at all!"

I have the feeling that if I had a young adolescent today, I would want very much to try to counteract too much freedom too early—and if parents cannot manage this on their own, they might do well to consider the advisability of school and community controls, when children are too immature to withstand peer pressures.

Whether one's children are thirteen or twenty, one of our problems has to do with an inevitable feeling of jealousy and rivalry. I would like to hope that as parents rethink the meaning of their middle-age years, there could be less conflict with their adolescent children. What bothers parents most about their children as they emerge from childhood is that they are bursting with life, that they become sexual beings, and that they are struggling so hard against the authority (wishes, desires, dreams, expectations, anxieties) of their parents. Many adults feel threatened and angry, but I suspect that if we understood ourselves better, we would realize that a lot of the feelings we associate with the behavior of our children really have to do with our feelings about ourselves.

We can't and shouldn't try to compete with our children —we have lots of good things going for us, too! There is no denying that they are on the threshold of adventure, that they are beautiful and full of the juices of life, that their bodies are young and strong, that they feel themselves to be invulnerable and immortal. But we have a few things going for us, too! I remember how puzzled I was by the difference in the energy levels between myself and my daughter when she was fifteen or sixteen. She could outlast me in some sports and she could stay up talking to her friends half or all the night, and be bright and peppy at four in the morning. On the other hand, she also could sleep through half of the next day—and when it came to cleaning the house, or painting the porch, or even sitting at a typewriter for eight hours, I had her beat. We had different kinds of energy, based partly on where we were in age—but far more because of our interests and motivations.

It seems to me that middle-age/teenage relations have improved vastly since people like Kinsey, and Johnson and Masters have assured the world at large that we middle-aged are far from ready for the pasture. Human beings have a tendency to live up to what is expected of them. When you tell the middle-aged that they have had it in the boudoir, they are likely to accept this—and when you tell them they have another twenty or thirty years of sexuality left in them, and to make the most of it, the enthusiastic response is a pleasure to behold! I suspect that competition and envy have played a very real part in earlier generations, where parents saw the newly emerging young adult in their home as a kind of open sore, a constant reminder of their own decaying!

It seems to me it should also make a difference in our relations with younger adolescents if we see ourselves as going through very much the same kinds of things they are going through. They want to shed the cocoon of childhood; they know they must discover new selves and separate from the safety and dependency of the childhood environment. We are going to have to do something of the same sort, separate ourselves from the intense and necessary preoccupation with family and parenthood. It is a time for new beginnings for all the family.

Parents grow frightened and angry when their teenagers begin really to rebel; it seems so unfair, when you have tried so hard to be patient and understanding and loving. If, at such a moment, you go off by yourself and cogitate on what *you* want to rebel against yourself, what adventures *you* think you are ready for, what ways *you* want to develop a new identity, you may well discover that instead of being anxious about the children, you might try to learn a thing or two from them about the techniques of moving on to a new level of growing!

Much of the conflict between parents and children at this stage of life has to do with the fact that parents often cannot face the implications of adolescence; what it really means is that full-time parenthood is on the wane, and it is time to begin to think of being other things. For those who have been totally absorbed in parenthood, and have found the deepest satsifactions in a houseful of kids, this can be a frightening time. For full-time mothers and homemakers it is most frightening of all, for there may not be other avenues of fulfillment readily available. This happens less and less frequently as more women find all sorts of activities away from home, but it is still a common phenomenon to see both men and women go into a depression when the nest begins to empty, or try to infantilize the children who are still there. One example: a mother who simply could not face examining her own life and moving on to a new level of experiences, insisted on driving her nineteen-year-old son to college every day. She also spent sleepless nights waiting to hear if he got up, and if he did, she would cook for him at 2 or 3 o'clock in the morning. When it was pointed out to her by her son's therapist that perhaps his indifference to his work, his passive resistance in general might have something to do with her preoccupation with him and unwillingness to look at her own life, she insisted that her son leave therapy.

I have written elsewhere * about how hard it is to free our children to do their necessary growing away from us; but it occurs to me now, with the focus on ourselves, that when we begin to deal with the crisis of our "middlescence," and try to discover our own new adventures in growing, this will become less of a problem for us.

Sometimes an adolescent has trouble separating from his parents because of an unconscious feeling that he hasn't been a satisfactory child. You really need to feel good about yourself before you can assert your independence. It may be that

* *How to Survive Parenthood* (New York: Random House, 1965), *The Conspiracy Against Childhood* (New York: Atheneum, 1967), *Sex and Your Teen-Ager* (New York: David McKay, 1970), *Natural Parenthood* (New York: Signet Books, 1971), and *How Do Your Children Grow?* (New York: David McKay, 1972).

some of us have had a rough time letting go of our children because of a residue of guilt, a feeling we have somehow failed as parents. I hope I have been convincing in saying that quite the opposite is the case, and on those grounds we certainly ought to feel free to move ahead into our own lives. It should encourage and sustain us that, in fact, we have been a remarkable generation of parents! Our aspirations were worthy, we made a profound emotional investment in our children; when we were called upon to show great flexibility— to love our kids even if they seemed to be creatures from Mars—a lot of us have come through with flying colors. We tolerate with considerable grace a great many things we once thought of as unendurable: our children openly living together, a wedding on the banks of a river in bluejeans instead of that gorgeous affair we planned at the Plaza when that daughter was three weeks old, expressing our misgivings but still adoring the Harvard senior who quits to study the sitar, or being able to say, "My son the fruit-picker" instead of "My son the doctor." Many of us have done very well in adapting to the new life-styles, and I think our children would agree that we have been tested and not found wanting in the unconditional love department.

We should also be reassured (and therefore freed to move on in our own lives) by the fact that while the forms may change, loving and caring are as real and important to our children as they ever were to us, and that is the true basis of all morality. A friend tells me, "My daughter was moving into an apartment with her boyfriend. Nobody had ever done that in our family before, and I was ashamed. Then my daughter asked me to go shopping with her on the day they were moving in. I saw her shopping list—this child who never hung her clothes in the closet, left her dirty dishes in the sink for me to wash and to my knowledge had never even *watched* me wash a floor, had this list of necessary items to buy: garbage can, shower curtain, bathmat, extension cords, hammer, hooks, liquid floor wax, scouring powder, mop and broom, dustpan, Lysol. It's crazy, I know, but that list reassured me more than anything else!"

Moving forward into our own lives can take many forms, but we need to give serious consideration to the ways in which we can be very much in touch with our children, and an integral part of their "army" of concerned citizens. Vista has an apt slogan: "If you're not part of the solution, then you're part of the problem."

We need to have more courage than perhaps we have ever had before, for we must try to free our children of the burden of our fears for them. A student at San Francisco State, in the midst of the demonstrations and police brutality, said, "I have to be part of all this, I can't back down from the issues, if I did I feel my life would become meaningless; but I carry with me, all the time, an awful load of guilt because I know my mother is hysterical. She wants me to mind my own business and play it safe—and I can't. I wish she could encourage me—I'm scared myself, and it's hard enough sticking with your principles, but if your parents add to your anxiety, it's a bad load to carry."

In *Report to Greco*, Kazantzakis tells of a monk who dreamt that he met a young boy in terrible trouble; he was in agony over the state of the world, he could not endure the pain he saw all around him. He was dressed in rags and had no shoes, and no way to earn his living. The monk gave him some clothes and shoes and taught him a trade, and told him not to worry about the world, and so, "Jesus became a happy carpenter." What a terrible story! If ever the world needed anxious, sensitive, saintly people willing to take responsibility for trying to change the world, it needs them now; we have no shortage of happy carpenters; I would hate to be responsible for turning a saint into one of them. We must learn to live with our anxieties and to encourage and support our children in their demonstrations, their strikes, their struggle to change the climate of life. The only thing that has really worried me in recent years is that they would be too discouraged, too wounded by their defeats to keep on trying—and the current silence on the campus may well be an indication that their hopelessness has immobilized them. That is the worst thing that could happen, for if there is anything at all we can teach them, it must be that the only way for life to have any meaning at all is to continue to struggle, even if defeat seems all but inevitable.

Our children need our optimism and our support, and as part of a reassessment of our lives we need to think about our own activism and commitment. Is the struggle just for the young? I think not. There is the old joke about the definition of a liberal: he's a radical with a wife and two children to support. That isn't a good enough rationalization anymore. If the house is burning down, it's time to participate in the firefighting, whatever the dangers. One way that is guaranteed to take the poison out of parent-child conflicts is for parents to join the children on the barricades!

For years now, the young have carried too heavy a burden of agony. They have been screaming alone in the wilderness, struggling against adult hostility and blindness. It is time to share that agony: to take part of the load off their young shoulders; to weep with them over the war dead on both sides, for no reasonable cause, in Vietnam; to scream with them against the plundering of our planet; to fight the necessary fight for redress of grievances among our poor and our disfranchised minorities.

If we want to be close to our children, it behooves us to get involved—to commit ourselves to whatever kinds of social action seem called for. Most of us are scared to death to confront the law; we never have before in our whole lives, and having grown up in a time when we really believed that the police and the law were protecting us, it is terribly painful to face the possibility of arrest; in our day, only criminals got arrested—or so we liked to tell ourselves, since our contacts with the poor and the black were nonexistent. A friend of mine was one of the people picked up in the insane arrests of about seven thousand people in Washington in April, 1971, when all were herded into one amphitheater without food, water, or bathroom facilities for many hours. The cases were almost all thrown out of court, the arrests were illegal, and there was little violence on the part of police or peace demonstrators. But my friend described her sensations: "I wanted to run—God, how I wanted to run. But I was ashamed—the kids were so beautiful, and they weren't doing anything that warranted arrests on such a mass scale. Only a handful were really disruptive. But I was too ashamed to back down. When a policeman grabbed me, I wanted to tell him that I was a grandmother and that I lived in a wealthy suburb of Boston and that my husband was the vice president of a bank. In other words, I wanted to use all kinds of irrelevant status symbols when the only reason he should have respected me was because I was a citizen expressing my dissent. I was scared and plenty unhappy about the physical discomforts of that day—but I lived through it, and God, did I feel *proud* of myself for not quitting! Once you have been through the civil disobedience thing, it doesn't hold such terrors for you."

If there is one thing I am really certain of about our teenage and young adult children, it is that they are not really turned off—they want to hear what we think, they want to test their own thinking in a confrontation with us. In the last few years, when I've been doing a good deal of writing about them and have sought them out in a genuine search for their ideas, I have found myself surrounded by *sponges*, eager to soak up whatever communication I was willing to take the time for. Many of them were turned off because none of us really could listen; we were too busy making sure that our position was well stated. We forgot two important factors:

(1) we are out of our heads if we think our children don't know what we think; that's all they've been absorbing for fifteen or twenty years; (2) we have to realize that while *we* need not lose any status when we listen, the young person feels, inevitably, that he is putting himself in jeopardy—for when you listen, you play a more passive role, and if you are still very young, and your relationship is that of a child to a parent, you are bound to feel endangered in whatever degree of hard-won independence you may have got. It isn't necessarily that parents infantilize you—although that can be a big part of it—it is that you, yourself, still seeing yourself as someone's child, become threatened. As one boy of sixteen put it, "As soon as my father starts talking—I can't help it —I feel he's lecturing me, and I begin to feel like a little child again. I guess that I'm still too close to being a child or it wouldn't bother me as much as it does, but it takes a lot of courage for us to be the listeners because it makes us feel so young and dependent again." They need us to do a lot of the listening as a sounding board for them to do their own changing and growing.

There is a very touching song, written and sung by Melanie, that seems to me to be a very clear message to us from our children. It is called *The Good Book* (Buddah Records, 1650 Broadway, N.Y.C. 10019), and she sings of the fears and loneliness of young people:

> Tell us you love us so we don't feel alone.

If we tell them we love them, *we* won't feel alone, either.

July 1972: *Addendum*

It is impossible to write about young people and not have one's observations become obsolete in less than five years. That has happened to me with every book I've written, and it has happened here.

I am now in the process of making final revisions on this book; I have been working on it for almost two years, and foolishly, this chapter was one of the first I wrote. It seems quite incredible that so much can change so quickly, but it does—and because adolescence is a time of turmoil and great sensitivity, the reaction to change is always sharper.

We seem to be seeing a serious malaise among many of the young people who were so vocal and committed just a few years ago. At first glance it might seem that our children are ungrateful and lazy; they've got the chance to make a difference, and they don't have the guts to take it. My own impression is quite different. I think that in spite of my own earlier awareness of the unhappiness of our children and the hostility of the adult community against them, even I underestimated the amount of psychic damage that was being done.

A great many of us whose children are now in their early and middle twenties find ourselves greatly alarmed. The rebels of four years ago often seem completely indifferent to what they accomplished. Many of us find our children wandering, aimless, unable to direct their lives or find meaningful goals. Some are doing what may be irreparable damage to themselves with drugs, with destructive relationships, with denial of their gifts, their potentials for accomplishment. Much to our shock and dismay, most of us find that we or our friends or relatives are having the experience of older children coming home to live—a pattern of regression and dependency that we cannot understand at all. A thirty-year-old son, brilliant student, Phi Beta Kappa at Yale, on the way to becoming a lawyer, lives at home and drives a taxi when he needs spending money. A twenty-three-year-old daughter, after several love affairs and an assortment of jobs, announces she and her boyfriend are unemployed, she's going to have a baby, and they have decided to come and live at home. The young man with six months to go for his doctoral degree in biology drops out, becomes a junky, disappears for months at a time. The Harvard senior, headed for medical school, goes off to an Indian Ashram to search for meaning, and not having found it, settles for giving sitar lessons. A bereaved mother tells of being called to her son's college: he had cut his wrists, after a bad LSD trip. She says, "And *he* was the *easy* child to raise!"

Some of our children "found themselves" as they discovered it was possible to play an effective role in social change. Some of our now-grown children are beautiful—as partners to a love relationship and as parents; as a new kind of citizen who lives by individual, self-styled moral laws that are awe-inspiring.

But some of those "McCarthy kids" who had so much vitality and courage seem to have had some kind of breakdown. They seem paralyzed, unable to focus energy and attention on making something of their own lives. I think it *is* a kind of breakdown, but a variety I have never seen or heard of before, that has more to do with social anguish than neurotic conflicts.

It would seem that we are to pay a terrible price for the revolution we are living through. The upheaval is too much for some young people; they seem profoundly damaged by what they have lived through. They are probably the kind of people who needed a certain solidity in life; perhaps less freedom, fewer open options for choice. Just as some kinds of young people were throttled by the rigidities of earlier days, it seems quite possible that today's open uncertainties can shake up young people who are overwhelmed by chaos. What it comes down to is that there are some people growing up—from ten to twenty and over—who are too sensitive, too delicately balanced, too vulnerable to be able to make it in a world where we are planning new rockets although we can already blow the whole world up, and Vietnamese children run through the streets with their clothes on fire.

Most of my contemporaries, despite acknowledging that this country is going through a frightful period in its history, still blame themselves for the unhappy, wasting lives of their children. Nothing could immobilize us more in trying to find ways to help those of our children who are in trouble.

Instead of wasting our energies on self-condemnation we need to try to think of ways in which we can be helpful to our children, without adding further to the pattern of regression and dependency. How do you let a child know you will always love him, that you are not rejecting him, but still feel that it is inappropriate for him to be living at home with no plans for the future, at the age of twenty-four? How can a parent be compassionate without fostering further infantilization? And what about our right to greater autonomy and freedom in our own lives, now? As one mother put it, "What drives me wild is the assumption that I have to adjust to *their* life-style—that they can change my home, my way of living. I can't and I won't!" For our sakes, as well as for our children's, we must refuse to start the childraising years all over again. It is no help at all if we passively accept our grown children's inability to function as adults. We are not showing genuine affection and concern if we accept indications of psychic breakdown and make no demands at all.

If our children are in trouble, we need to try as hard as we can to encourage them to get help. Unfortunately, many of these young people have been burned by misguided psychotherapy that was totally irrelevant to this new disease of social breakdown, and it is hard to convince them of the truth, that there are still some people who can help. It is legitimate to offer financial assistance for therapeutic help, but it is an encouragement to further immobility not to insist on some realistic expectations. There is no reason why, at this time in our lives, we should be supporting our grown children unless they are so ill they need hospitalization. Sometimes, hard as it is, the kindest thing we can do is to force just that question to be settled. It is all but impossible to get loving parents to do it—but when they do, it is often the first step to recovery, when they can finally say, "If you are too sick to work or go to school, then you had better go to a hospital."

One of the ways we can help is to be flexible about the fact that new life-styles are open to our children that may make a great deal of sense, despite our resistances. It goes against our grain to believe, for example, that it is possible to make a good living without being trained for a profession, but that idea was a foolish one and our children keep proving it all the time.

David quit college after three semesters. It was perfectly clear to him that there was nothing he wanted to know that he couldn't learn far better on his own than in a classroom. He read constantly, took all sorts of odd jobs, discovered a natural ability for carpentry and architectural design—but could not stand the thought of going back to school. (People were building houses for thousands of years before you needed a college degree to do it.) He was moping around, doing just enough to earn some pocket money, bumming around the country, when his father offered to advance him the money to build a house. David was delirious with joy; he brought together all the young artisans he knew, they accepted the fact that some of the building had to be done by licensed people, and they built a hand-crafted house of great beauty and sold it for twice what it had cost to make, and now plan to continue to build other houses.

There are all sorts of perfectly decent and realistic ways for young people to work and live that have been discarded for several generations. We can help them to see that they have some choices if we are flexible about the options open to them.

One mother told me, "My husband's grandfather was once an itinerant peddler in New England. He was smart and ambitious, and eventually he had his own general store, and I'm sure that during all his struggles, his main goal was that his children and grandchildren would not have to work at such jobs, but could sit at desks and wear white shirts and ties. At the moment, his great-granddaughter—our daughter—has got herself a peddler's license to sell leather bags as a way to earn money. Grandpa would have a fit—all his hard work for this? Well, why not?"

If there are signs of a social breakdown among some of our young people, it is only accentuated by stereotyped ideas about work. There has been a ridiculous overconcern in the past half-century with academic achievement and professional degrees, leaving no room at all for craftsmen. If we can help some of our young people have a sense of personal pride and accomplishment—so necessary to a meaningful life—they may be able to recover their strength and courage. The fact that they are taking their time about accepting the obligations of maturity need not frighten us quite so much; after all, *we* were all responsible and studious and goal-oriented before we were twenty—and how many of us are happy with what we are doing? It is healthier to say when you're hurting and let it all happen, in your twenties, than to carry the burdens of unhappiness into your forties, as we did. We can take great comfort from that very important difference. And who can tell how obsolete these observations may be in another year and a half!

ERICH SEGAL
WAS A
COWARD

Chapter 6

went to see the movie *Love Story* with a middle-aged friend whom I had not seen in some time. She was visiting New York and we had spent a couple of days catching up on each other's lives. At that particular time we were both feeling a lot of pain and had been comforting each other by topping each other's traumas! That afternoon, deciding we were in the mood for a sentimental, slushy movie that would provide a further excuse for a good cry, we stocked up on lots of Kleenex and went to Radio City Music Hall. But we didn't cry, and we both felt disappointed and cheated. My friend muttered, as we walked out, "Erich Segal is a coward; it's a real cop-out to kill off the young wife while they are still in the first blush of romance—it would have taken a lot more courage to let them live through marriage-in-middle-age!"

There is no doubt whatever in my mind that the toughest challenge of the middle years has to do with love and marriage. We are a generation of men and women who were taught at our parents' knees that marriage was an exclusive contract for life, and that with the proper attitude, sensitivity, and imagination, one could stay happily married all of one's life. We were unprepared for the fact that marriage is a social institution of great complexity that is now in the middle of a major revolution as to its purposes and its future—and if ever a generation was caught in the middle, we sure are *it!* We were too late for the arranged marriages of our forebears, and too early to have been able to foresee the problems of romance-oriented monogamy. We were also almost, but not quite, the first generation to believe in love marriages, to be placing the enormous burden of love onto the relationship designed primarily and originally for the survival of the human race.

Many of us believed in Snow White, awakened by the handsome prince and living happily ever after. As an adolescent I accepted the notion that I ought to be "pure and innocent" until I married, and then immediately become a sexpot for the rest of my life, offering such an assortment of mysterious delights that my husband would never get bored with me. Of course this cultivated sensuality was to be entirely focused on that marriage bed. Emotionally, and in spite of twenty-odd years of psychotherapy, I still feel at home with these attitudes. I am psychologically monogamous to the core! Intellectually, I think those attitudes are cockeyed and obsolete. Human beings do not, after all, seem to be monogamous creatures; left to their own devices, and without stern social pressures, this is not the way people behave.

What we were *not* taught as children was the idea stated so well by an obviously married person: "All marriages are happy; it's the living together afterward that causes all the trouble."

One of the sharpest commentaries I've seen on marriage is that of Robert Tyler, professor of history at Southern Connecticut State College, writing in *The Humanist* (December 1970):

> . . . marriage is impossible. It has *always* been an impossible institution. . . . it has clamped some kind of social control on sex [to] . . . serve such stuffy values as child-raising, the inheritance of wealth, or the transmission of social status or tradition. . . . Yet every society . . . has come up with the institution of

marriage in one form or another. . . . American marriage has been especially impossible. From the beginning, Americans frowned on all those extramarital sports discovered by older and wiser cultures to make the institution livable. They were probably no more successful than other people in keeping frisky sex within the marriage corral, but their hypocrisy was certainly very serious. Also, America rejected the old-world practice of arranging marriages.

. . . They set out to mix in one stew what older societies had discovered to be unmixable: romantic attachment, sexual adventure, love, domesticity. . . . The strain on American marriage, of course, has been terrific. Before the escape hatch of divorce began to open up in the early 1900's, . . . probably millions of persons had been chained to each other, hating each other's guts more . . . each year. . . . In the early phases of our sexual revolution, after World War I, the cracks in the old, crumbling edifice were papered over by the well-meaning romantics who wrote marriage manuals, trying to show old bedfellows how to be exciting to each other after five, 10, or 20 years. . . . By now attempts to save the institution have become pretty desperate. The suburban wife-swapping and the weekend gang bangs of the upper middle class, for example, seem to be only more adventurous extensions of the old marriage manuals' advice. . . . Already one can see the future taking shape in the experiments of the present college-age generation, which has apparently decided to deal with the institution by ignoring it as anachronism and hypocrisy.*

This view of marriage is expressed by one wife who put it: "What do you do about the inevitable boredom that has to be part of living with one person for forty or fifty years? No matter how you love each other, no matter how congenial, no matter how good the companionship and sense of security, people have almost never been expected to live together and love each other so long, when it wasn't a matter of survival to stay together."

* Reprinted with permission of *The Humanist.*

One husband observed, "You know, I'd never really thought about the heavy burdens we put on marriage today until I spent some time visiting some old graveyards in New England. You realize then how many husbands and wives died at an early age, and how many remarriages took place. Just looking back into my own family, a few generations ago, there were so many step-parents, and families with children who came from two or three earlier marriages because a spouse had died. In earlier times people changed partners through death; now they do it through divorce; maybe there's really not much difference in the staying power."

A particular complication in middle-aged marriage is that it is bound to reflect our emotional reactions to signs of aging. A wife says, "I was so upset about the onset of menopause that I accused my husband of not finding me attractive anymore; but it was really how I was feeling about myself, not at all his feelings." Or a doctor says, "When a man begins to notice a decrease in his sexual drive, this is often so painful that he blames it on his wife; nothing's happening to *him*, you see, it's just that she's boring or indifferent."

Another burden that must be borne by the middle-aged marriage is that we were taught to believe that if you were unhappy before being married, marriage would change you. It has been painful to discover that nothing could be further from the truth. All the evidence clearly points to the fact that no man or woman can expect to feel happier as a partner in marriage than he did when he was single. The same kind of false hope occurs when a couple think having a child can save their relationship. Marriage can be only as satisfying as the sum of its parts, and we are each responsible for our own happiness; to place this burden on the relationship is to place the marriage in serious jeopardy.

One of the most destructive burdens we place on marriage is when we make the assumption that we have to do something for the partner that we really don't want to do. We say for example, "Oh, I can't do that—my husband would kill me!" or "I'd like to change things around here, but my wife would never forgive me." If I choose to do or not do something I need to understand that I have made that choice—no one has made it for me. If I make a decision I don't like, then I am the one who did not want to face possible conflict about it. Very often we misjudge and underestimate the capacity of a spouse to respond very well to our challenges, if we would only give them the opportunity. We are responsible for our own lives and we cannot displace our choices and decisions on anyone else. This doctrine may well lead to more honest confrontations, and they may be painful, but they are really essential to a meaningful relationship.

If I seem to have started off on a negative tone about marriage, it does not mean that I do not value it greatly. I do—and I hope I will make that quite clear. But I care enough to feel that it is absolutely essential that we view it with candor and face the realistic problems, frustrations, and limitations.

I suppose I ought to admit at the outset that there *are* some calm and collected marriages that seem to keep on a very even keel much of the time. When they occur, it seems to be when the partners are very similar in temperaments and needs. They share a common relatively low threshold of excitability. This is not a value judgment at all—there are many advantages to such a way of life—but I am struck by the fact that the marriages which seem to be most steady are those where both partners have the same somewhat limited aspiration level. Both want and are contented with a relatively low emotional level; they like being where they are, in their own growth and development. They do not hunger for great excitement, they do not have any great ambition or drive. They tend to be terribly good, decent, kindly people, who want to live simply and without a great deal of turmoil.

These often tend to be the marriages where husband and wife call each other "Mother" and "Father"! This may be significant in the sense that such couples seem to find their deepest marital gratification in their roles as parents, and see themselves in this role all of their lives, long after their own children may have grown and gone.

Some of the most difficult marriages seem to turn out to be the very best, in the sense that although the partners may live through an awful lot of hell with each other, in the process of striving for the fullest use of their own potentials, they eventually find a deep and solid foundation for their relationship. The problem often is that one partner does more growing than the other. A wife says, "I am not very ambitious; I like the way I've lived my life, I feel I've done most of the things I wanted to do. I could very happily settle for more of the same; but my husband isn't like that. He has a kind of divine discontent; no matter what he's accomplished, he always wants more; he's an adventurer, and his attitude is that life is such a tiny spark of time that he's hellbent on not missing any experiences which might enrich him. He is restless and discontented—not in a negative sense, just wanting the search and the challenge and the growing to go on and on and on. If I want him to go on loving me, I have to be willing to become more, myself; I have to try to use my own possibilities more fully; I have to be willing to share his adventures, and I find this exhausting. Sometimes I think I can't go on; I'll just have to find myself some place where I can be simple and live quietly. But on the other hand, I also feel how exciting it is to be pulled along by someone so passionately alive—it's hard, but I know it's good for me to have someone nudging me along."

Having found ourselves caught in the midst of a sexual revolution which has affected us as much or more than the young, many of the middle-aged married suffer from a kind of free-floating anxiety because there is such a feeling of uncertainty. We were unprepared for how our own marriages would change, and we also did not anticipate the degree to which a new sexual morality and the difficulties associated with the nuclear family would place marriage as an institution in such jeopardy.

We were not emotionally prepared for the inevitable fact that marriage relationships change, that it is exceedingly unlikely, with all the things that happen to us, to go on with the lovely romance of the beginnings of being in love. Constant proximity, diapers, throwing up with the flu, getting along with the in-laws, the rotten teacher who scares your child, fatigue, disappointments at work, financial worries, the stuck plumbing, the garbage—how could the most romantic young lovers survive all this and still be dewy-eyed? What is so remarkable is not that so few do, but that so many do some of the time!

We are also unprepared for the ways in which our roles change. Husbands and wives have to adjust not only to newly emerging selves but also to partners with a New Look about them. All these years you've thought you were married to a lady who wanted to have babies and keep house; now you discover she's considered the best choice possible for the State Democratic Committee-woman from your district. Or all along, you thought of yourself as "the Principal's wife" —and here he is retiring, and wondering what to do with his life. You both feel uneasy in the transition—you wonder to what degree changing roles and images also change the person you once felt you knew so well.

For many, the fear of divorce becomes greatly accentuated in middle age. While the children were at home, dissatisfactions and discontents were often put aside. Realistic responsibilities were too heavy, and both partners were more likely to feel that their lives would become unbearably complex if they were to separate. Those who *do* divorce before middle age tend to have experienced very intense and dramatic kinds of incompatibility, but many marriages that manage to sustain themselves during the parenting years do so on shaky grounds.

It is hard for our generation ever to see divorce as anything but tragic. This is another part of our childhood roots. We are the generation in which divorce has become commonplace, but when we were children it was still a rarity. It is hard to see it in the context of the changing nature of marriage rather than as our failure as human beings. Divorce was uncommon when marriages were made for other reasons than love alone. It is not easy for us to begin to accept the idea that divorce can often be a testament to courage, to human integrity, to idealism; that it can mean a refusal to settle for half a life, or less. Most of us, including those who do divorce, cannot shake that sense of failure and shame which may have nothing to do with the merits of the situation at all but is simply a residue of what we learned when we were most impressionable as children.

In the course of living together for twenty or thirty years, if both partners continue to grow, it is possible that they may become strangers. Life changes us whether we want it to or not, and when one considers that most of us chose a life partner when we hardly knew anything about ourselves or what we would become, one begins to marvel at the fact that so many people stay together.

We are one of the first and few generations to try the experiment of "the nuclear family." As children, most of us had far more experience with an extended family, in which we either lived with, or close to, some of our relatives, where we saw them far more often, and where grandparents, maiden aunts, and others cared for us many times. We are a generation suddenly and dramatically cut off from this pattern. The sharp increase in mobility after the Second World War meant that most of us experienced for the first time living far away from our closest relatives, and the heavy burdens of responsibility and our sense of isolation have added to our current anxieties about divorce.

A typical example of what so many of us fear is the story of Estelle and Frank who fell in love in high school, married in college, couldn't have been "better suited" in terms of interests and temperament, had two children, lived through all sorts of agonies and frustrations before they were in their forties: the prolonged illness and death of her parents, involving years of care and self-sacrifice; a child's bout with rheumatic fever; a one-year mysterious illness with Frank in the hospital continually, and Estelle the sole support; the rebellious and sometimes self-destructive adolescence of a daughter, including great concern over a period of experimenting with drugs. And through it all, their friends and relatives would have sworn there couldn't have been a more devoted and congenial and mutually supportive pair. Frank changed jobs at forty-two—a really exciting and rewarding new world for him, involving a great deal of travel, a lot of attention from the press and public. In Geneva, at the age of forty-eight, he met a young journalist of twenty-four, fell in love, got a divorce, and married her. If there were hidden problems in the marriage, they were no worse than must have occurred in the marriages of their parents, grandparents, and more distant progenitors; there had never been a divorce in the family before. Estelle is full of self-doubts and self-condemnation; did she take Frank too much for granted? Was she unaware of signs of early difficulty? Was she too preoccupied with the kids? Maybe, maybe not; surely one cannot ignore the fact that living in the midst of a cult of youth, many men worry about aging. The opportunities for adventure have never been greater. The revolution in birth control affects the middle-aged as much as the young; and the fact that marriage is no longer essential for physical survival is not to be ignored as an element in such surprise divorces.

What seems to be happening even more frequently is the

divorce that surprises one's relatives and friends, but which the central figures in the drama have known was coming. However, each of them has needed a long time to face it directly. Ann and Bill began to be bored with each other after seven or eight years. Neither could accept divorce as a viable alternative and, without ever facing their growing indifference toward each other, tried to push it away by taking trips, joining clubs together, taking dancing lessons, having children. By the time they were in their forties, Ann especially had a sense of having missed out on something important, and almost unconsciously began her own search for something more exciting. She went back to college to get a degree, majored in art education, and after two years of almost full-time study, seeing less and less of her husband and no longer needed by young children, fell in love with one of her teachers, who was divorced. Bill, unable to handle his sense of isolation and loneliness, had fallen into a halfhearted affair with a woman in his office, and his wife's request for a divorce came when he was already numb with a lost marriage.

Their friends and relatives could not believe it; what a wonderful couple! So good to their children, seemingly so compatible. Nobody had ever heard them argue, much less fight. Ann was so good to Bill's mother and Bill was so loved by Ann's parents. They'd always shared so many things—trips and social groups, they even took dancing lessons—what is the world coming to, when such a solid marriage as this can be set aside!

Many men and women have a great fear of being rejected, discarded. When we were growing up the possibility of living alone was considered quite dreadful. "Old maids" were scorned as second-class citizens, and old bachelors were greatly pitied. As a result of this kind of brainwashing, many women and some men are terrified of desertion—and some who might otherwise initiate a separation or a divorce themselves, because they are living a life of quiet despair, cling to their marriages because being married is less frightening than being alone, no matter what.

We need to gain a new perspective on the issue of divorce. It is not always a symptom of terrible failure but may represent a courageous attempt at living more meaningfully. To fail at marriage in a time of such complexity and change is no disgrace; the challenges have never been more overwhelming. It seems quite clear that many middle-aged divorces represent an affirmation of one's ideals, not a copping-out.

In addition, second marriages in middle age tend to be quite successful. Of course there are many cases where neither partner has much insight into why the first marriage failed and each tends to repeat the same mistakes a second time, but that seems to be becoming less common. These days a great many people who are in crisis recognize that it is extremely difficult to have the perspective or the insight into their own unconscious motivations and that it makes sense to get professional help at such times. When those involved in the death of a marriage can really have the courage and honesty to examine the dynamics of the relationship, they tend to bring greater self-understanding to a second relationship.

When a couple have stayed married for twenty to twenty-five years and one or both have been discontented and unhappy for a long time, it may well be that unconsciously they are simply waiting for the children to leave home; they are already well aware of the problems in this marriage, and know what will have to be different in a second relationship.

Another aspect of a divorce is that, when we were young, it was assumed that we all had to get married; only neurotic or thoroughly unattractive people remained single, in the eyes of our parents. I recall very well that I was getting pretty nervous and fearful that I would be doomed to a half-life of misery because I wasn't yet married at twenty-one! These days, in a far freer atmosphere with fewer institutionalized demands, young people are giving very serious consideration to whether or not to marry—and many are deciding that marriage is not for them. There is a far wider variety of options open to them than there were for us—and among our middle-aged numbers are many men and women, natural loners, who probably should never have married in the first place, or might have been most fulfilled by some other style of living. As one comes to the existential crisis of middle age and realizes that time is running out and if ever there will be a time to be most oneself this is it, some men and women are likely to begin to face the fact that they need to be alone or in relationships of less emotional commitment than marriage.

There are many who see serious flaws in their marriages, but decide carefully and consciously not to separate. There can be sound reasons for the compromises we make in life; change is not a cure-all, and some couples feel that the known difficulties may well be more comfortable than the unknown possibilities.

The fact that there are no general answers suitable for all to the crises we may face is expressed in the viewpoints of many middle-aged married people, that while their marriages were surely not made in heaven, the sense of mutual responsibility and caring is not to be lightly dismissed as the specter of old age becomes more real. This feeling was articulated by a woman who said, "I think Joe and I have made peace with our marriage. We each have our own interests and activities, but just living together for thirty years, and the knowledge you accumulate about another person, makes you care a lot; you know each other's strengths and weaknesses, you feel each other's pain, and you have shared your joys. No matter how much you try to go on learning and growing and becoming more of a human being, you have to face the fact that as you get older, you may need someone to take care of you, and someone else may need your care. If either of us were to

become sick or develop some chronic handicap, we care
enough about each other to want to help, to take responsibility for each other. I feel that having the companionship and
concern of someone I have shared all my adult life with is not
something to be taken lightly. I would rather accept the fact
that there are some things I will never do, some parts of myself that may never be fulfilled, in exchange for knowing that
I will have someone to share old age with; from what I see of
older people, old age can be frightening and I don't want to
be alone."

Some kinds of change are inevitable. No matter how well
prepared we may think we are, there is a very real adjustment to the time when children leave us. I would have
thought that no one could have been more prepared than I
was. I had been a career woman all along, I had many interests and activities, I was well launched and successful in my
work; my husband and I shared the same fields of work and
had always been interested in what the other was doing—
what better preparation for the departure of our daughter?

It wasn't that easy. Most of my friends are also career
women, articulate, insightful, aware of the need for planning
ahead for their changing roles; almost all of us have been
shocked to discover that no matter how well prepared we
thought we were, there have been major adjustments and
unexpected upheavals.

The most common pattern seems to be a period of unacknowledged mourning for what has passed, which the couple
do not share with each other. Perhaps this is even more characteristic of couples who *do* have many interests, for what
seems to happen is a period of growing apart, during which
neither partner is fully aware of what is happening.

Men who have felt that the children were slowing them
down in achieving all that they might in their careers see
being alone again as an opportunity for full steam ahead professionally. There doesn't seem to be as much reason for com-

ing home for dinner when one isn't motivated by the wish to be a good and attentive father. There seem to be fewer opportunities or motivation for sitting down and discussing unshared experiences; each begins, inexorably, to move apart. There is no longer any reason for either husband or wife not to accept speaking engagements in other cities, or go to interesting professional conferences, or maybe take a refresher course in one's field. You are not deserting a spouse who will be in sole charge of the children.

Where is the renewed togetherness you thought would happen—those candelit dinners alone, those wicked-seeming "matinees" in the empty house on a Saturday or Sunday afternoon? Instead you may have both become much lighter sleepers and find yourselves sleeping separately now that there are empty rooms, engrossed in work, spending less, not more, time together.

When the children leave, marriage faces a moment of truth; is there strength enough to sustain it without the excuse of parenthood?

We frequently find ourselves having to face unfinished business of earlier years. During the time when a couple are raising a family, a lot of issues may be postponed temporarily. It's not a good idea, but it happens—even to people who really think they are dealing with their problems all the way along. For example, vague but chronic sexual disappointments tend to come into clearer focus once the children have grown and gone. While they were calling for a glass of water eight times a night, while they were having croup, while summer vacations usually involved the whole family sleeping in a tent—the fact that one partner seemed to want more sexual activity than the other could be masked by parental emergencies and duties. Once the children are gone and there is no child sleeping in the next room, and no kids underfoot of a lazy Sunday afternoon, the lack of mutual pleasure and gratification becomes a clear and present problem, hanging in the air, palpably, and can no longer be avoided.

It may very well be that middle age doesn't bring with it new marital problems; it only tends to accentuate those that have been there all along, but have been successfully avoided by such ingenious devices as a struggle for economic solvency and having children! Sometimes, when people really love each other and care about each other's feelings, this kind of postponement of issues is the way in which a husband or wife "protects" his or her partner. I recall one woman who told me it was only after discovering that her husband was having an affair, after twenty-five years of marriage, that he was finally forced into admitting some of the negative feelings he had had about their relationship all along; the times he felt he was being manipulated; the times he became utterly weary of her histrionics; the times he had felt imprisoned by her dependency and proprietary attitude. She said, "He kept telling me that he hadn't wanted to hurt my feelings—so instead he took the chance of destroying our marriage!"

We need to learn from those unrealistic "kindnesses" we did for each other that the repression of genuine feelings and escaping from the confrontation that will hurt so much only leads to alienation, loss of trust, and may end a relationship that might have been viable if both partners had been more honest with each other about their dissatisfactions. There is no more time to waste now that we are middle-aged. If our remaining years are to be satisfying and fulfilling, we cannot be polite to each other.

"I think I underestimated my husband's courage and flexibility," one wife told me. "I never shared with him my unhappiness that he was so undemonstrative, nor did I ever express the resentment I felt at his attitude toward my work as a dress designer. I always had the feeling he saw this as 'busy work,' to keep me out of trouble! I met a man in this field, and he not only admired my work, but fell in love with me and made me feel I was the most attractive woman in the world. I thought that if my husband ever found out he'd kill himself. Well, of course he did find out—I suppose I was deliberately careless because I couldn't endure the cheating. Afterward I had to talk openly about some of the things in our marriage that bothered me, and he didn't fall apart. I was full of compassion and sympathy for his misery, but I confronted him openly and honestly, as I never had done before. I expected him, at long last, to be able to grow and change and understand—and he did. He was no weakling, and I insulted him when I didn't do this many years before. People *can* change; those few that can't, well, then the marriage may end. But if there is a lot of genuine affection and caring, it can happen."

For some, the years after the children grow up become a disaster. It is not merely that the couple cannot adjust to change, but they simply do not seem to have the inner resources or the necessary courage to develop new roles in relation to each other. A friend of mine had just returned from a two-week trip to visit her sister and brother-in-law. She said, "You know, I don't think I'll ever feel sorry for myself again, not being married. I had quite a lesson in how some marriages can be so much worse than living alone. Marge and Richard were high school sweethearts. She was valedictorian, he was captain of the football team, the perfect couple, the perfect marriage. I guess they were happy for a while; they both loved the children and I think they did a pretty good job as parents. But now the kids are gone and they're alone. They never talk to each other. All the time that I was there, each spoke to me and I spoke to each of them, but I don't think they directed five words to each other. Richard comes home, eats, watches TV; they never go out. They have no sex life anymore. Marge wants to go to work, but he gets furious. She suggested that they get some marriage counseling and he hit the ceiling; he won't even let her go alone. You know what she told me? That she really wished he'd go out and have an affair; maybe it would make him more human, kinder to her. They have lost touch with each other completely—

they just go through the motions of living, but they are caught up in despair, hatred, and misery. I just could not understand why they stayed together, but now as I think about it, they are both so miserable, so disappointed in life, that it wouldn't matter if they stayed married or not. They don't seem to have any of the resources you need to change and grow. All they were equipped for was being high school sweethearts, and you just can't keep that up for a lifetime."

Where a basically good relationship exists, the adjustment may mostly be a matter of consciousness on the part of each person that a period of adjustment is necessary and inevitable. Sometimes one or the other partner needs to offer special help at this crossroads in life. It may be that a husband may need to make a special effort to reestablish a closer relationship with his wife, who will be the one who is hardest hit at first. A woman told me, "About a year before Michael, our youngest, left for college, Ben began to call me up every once in a while and ask me if I'd like to meet him for lunch. Or he'd call and say he needed to stretch his legs for a few minutes—would I like to meet him for a quick walk in the park. At one point, he bought tickets for a Wednesday matinee and took the day off. We felt very wicked and it was fun. I will always be grateful to Ben for his thoughtfulness and sensitivity. I think he did this to help me over the period of adjustment to the empty nest, and to bring us closer again."

A husband said, "I have four daughters, and I can really say that I enjoyed being a father more than anything else I ever did! My job is okay, but primarily it was just a way to make a living—my real fun was with my family. When the youngest daughter got married, my wife did a very smart thing; she talked me into taking a cruise, and when we got back she nagged the hell out of me to start doing some kind of volunteer work with children. She was a very smart lady; the cruise reminded us both that we still had each other, and now I'm tutoring two children in a ghetto school, and they remind me that children are the greatest joy and hope we've got. I think I avoided a lot of heartache by having a smart and bossy wife!"

Middle-aged marriage starts, of course, while the children are still home. In fact, emotional and financial responsibility may be at an all-time high. It is hard to find time alone together to work out differences or worries. It is not easy to deal with all the problems and challenges of middle age at the very same time that your children like you the least, and are, in fact, inclined to be devastating in their cruel judgments of your shortcomings. Because parents tend to worry more and to feel more helpless about their children during adolescence than any other time, it becomes increasingly difficult to reassure oneself or each other about the future.

Another factor which inevitably occurs is that parents become more self-conscious and uneasy about the privacy of their relationship. As one father put it, "If a two- or three-year-old hears some giggles or moans through the wall when he's in bed at night, he may be curious or even upset, but you sure as hell don't feel like having a sixteen-year-old hear anything like that!" Another father said, "It's not just the kids 'making out' at a drive-in movie; sometimes it's the parents trying to get a little privacy!"

An additional burden on marriage at middle age is that the normal range of defects in the relationship are likely to show up, to appear in sharper focus. For example, if a wife has been totally dependent on her husband and both have allowed him to "manage everything," things may run fairly smoothly for many years. He takes care of the checking account, the insurance premiums, the mortgage payments, and taxes; she takes care of the house and children and asks for money as she needs it. Both are healthy and competent in the areas in which they function and it seems to be a perfect arrangement, well suited to their temperaments. But in middle age the husband becomes seriously ill. He has a coronary and is hospitalized for many weeks; for some time his life is hanging in the balance. His wife's complete helplessness and panic, the fact that she barely knows how to write a check, has no idea what their assets are, and has never made, or even participated in, the major financial decisions suddenly shows the marriage up as having very severe flaws. Unless she can begin to measure up to the necessity for changing her role, the marriage may never recover.

During the first few years of marriage, it is not too difficult to "rekindle the flame"; in point of fact, it *is* the romance, the passion, that helps couples make the necessary adjustments to such realities as who leaves the cap off the toothpaste, whose mother visits too often, and who leaves dirty underwear on the bedroom floor.

While we are preoccupied with childraising, we have little enough time alone together, and we savor it; we still feel young. But in middle age, we find ourselves alone again, faced with one terrible challenge to most people—and marriages; we know we are getting older, and we are therefore more frightened by any signs of waning ardor.

As one woman put it, "My husband had been out of town for several days, and some great and important victories had occurred in some business deals, so he came home feeling very affectionate, glad to see me, very expansive and self-confident. We spent the weekend like a couple of honeymooners—a real sex orgy, with the steak and wine and the walk in the park and sleeping late. I felt young and attractive and our marriage seemed the most wonderful ever. By the following Wednesday, everything had deteriorated. We got a notice that our rent was going to be increased, a very important project that had seemed to be settled, collapsed, and my husband was worried and defeated. We heard his mother was sick and that meant finding time for a trip to Minnesota. I sprained my ankle, and needed to be waited on.

I looked at my husband as he was watching TV on Wednesday night. His face sagged; it was getting a craggy look, he'd gained a lot of weight recently, which I hadn't noticed before. His hair was all gray; because we were both out of sorts and tired and mad at the world, both our perceptions changed—suddenly I felt old and ugly and it frightened me. When marriage is wonderful, you expect it to stay that way—but it can't and doesn't."

Being married to a middle-aged person is a constant reminder that *you* are middle-aged too! Another woman told me, "You know, the fact that we live in a milieu that places so much importance on youthfulness is far from the whole story. Getting old *is awful*, under any circumstances; life is too goddamned short—and unless you're really miserable, who wants it to end? And who wants to get old and sick and feeble? I think it's perfectly natural to be repelled by constant reminders that you are getting older every minute, that there are fewer of the good years left. It's hard to see yourself aging, but you can see the signs in a husband or wife; every once in a while you become aware of some change, and it shocks you into realizing that you're both getting older. I can understand very well why a middle-aged man might want to spend his time with a younger woman—and a woman might find herself very much attracted to younger men; you aren't constantly reminded by the aging of your partner that you are getting older too. And the worst part of this is that you remember each other as you once looked! As my husband gets balder, I find myself feeling sadder and sadder. I have an awful nostalgia for the way he looked when we first met—that marvelous shock of wavy hair, that slim waist and exciting vitality; I long to go back in time."

The subject that seems to be the source of greatest anxiety and pain for many middle-aged couples is the matter of infidelity. It was my impression that the rapidity of social change is nowhere more evident than in this aspect of marriage. As one woman said, "Even ten years ago I would have been shocked at the idea that *really happy* marriages would have to face this question. I felt then, and still feel now, that there is nothing like faithlessness to break down self-assurance and play on one's deepest insecurities. But I don't personally know any marriage—I swear, *any marriage*—that hasn't either battled that experience through or broken over it."

A psychiatrist, born in France, told me, "Americans are simply *ridiculous!* Human beings are *not* monogamous creatures—and with the increasing longevity and general good health until people are quite old, it is insane to expect them to be faithful to one love relationship. And because that is such an impossible goal, it almost never works out that way; when it does, I really worry about how neurotic the people must be!"

On the other hand, several marriage counselors told me that they feel there is far less actual infidelity than we think, just lots more talking about it. In either case, whether it be conjecture or fact, one thing is clear; it is a matter of great concern.

A crucial dimension of this issue is the fact that we were taught as children that it was possible to be truly intimate with only one person at a time. We find ourselves wrestling with the question of the true nature of intimacy; does it necessarily imply exclusivity? I don't know of any middle-aged person who has found an entirely satisfactory answer to this question. We are so much a part of our training and environment that it is impossible to look at this issue objectively. The typical feeling of many people is, "Intellectually and rationally I believe that it is possible to share a genuine intimacy with more than one person; I've seen it happen, I know it exists. And yet, emotionally, I still feel there is some very serious violation of the intimacy that exists between marriage partners if either or both are sharing a profound and meaningful experience with someone else."

There are situations—apparently there are lots of them —where a husband or wife is deeply in love with his or her marriage partner, does not want to end the marriage, feels a deep loyalty and affection, and still does not want to give up the second relationship. And apparently this kind of thing can happen to people who describe themselves as "monogamous to the core." Typical of such situations, one woman said, "My husband, Jack, and I have never been closer. He found out about my affair with Larry two years ago, and we have lived through such pain and suffering and have reached each other in ways we never imagined possible before. We love each other less possessively and more really and we're not afraid of each other anymore. But I still love Larry; it was real, it was a shock to me, but it happened, and in spite of feeling terrible guilt at hurting someone I truly love, that simply does not make me love Larry less. If anyone had told me five years ago that it was possible to love two people simultaneously I would have said they were out of their minds; and even crazier, if I were to find out that Jack was having an affair, I think I'd kill him! I'm really a very monogamous person—but this *did* happen to me. What I feel for Larry is private and internal and it simply does not preclude my being committed to my marriage—and even as I try to explain this, I think I sound crazy!"

A woman in great conflict about her continuing need for a variety of relationships said, "I seem to need the drama, the romance—some sort of new declaration of my value in someone else's eyes—but the truth of the matter is that only my marriage is really important to me. Bill and I and our life together is the still point of the turning world."

In some cases, the decision about whether or not to have an affair seems to rest on the question of whether or not one's spouse is capable of changing and of fulfilling one's changing needs. One woman told me that there had been no real warmth in her and her husband's relationship for the past fif-

teen years. Four children were now grown. She and her husband had grown very far apart as they were raising their
children—in fact, after the first ten years of marriage, she
began to suspect that she had made a serious mistake. She
said, "I knew I had married beneath my emotional level. Ted
is a cold, withdrawn kind of person; he can't show his
feelings—except he did to some degree with his children,
whom he adored, but none of them really ever got close to
him. He was a very authoritarian father—couldn't seem to
be anything else—but I always knew he loved us to the degree he could, and heaven knows he worked terribly hard to
make us all comfortable. I know he needs me, in his own
way, and I decided against a confrontation while the children
were still home, because—well, there was no alternative
that seemed better, or would make the upheaval in our children's lives worth it. I'm sorry for him. He loves his home, he
wants to go on just as things are—his golf club, his church
activities, his garden. One of our children was a stutterer, and
some years ago I insisted that we had to get psychological
help for him. My husband absolutely refused to see the therapist, but in the course of getting help for my child, I began to
see the effect of my husband's rigidity and impossible expectations on myself as well as on the children. I began to grow
as a woman. I realized I had to become more of a person, use
my abilities more fully, or I would wither and die. I began
selling bread and cakes and preserves—I was a great cook
—and now many stores buy from me and I have a thriving
business, which I love. I have an active, useful life: I make my
own clothes, I work in a children's museum, I go to classes in
business management to learn how to run my business. I have
a lot of affection for Ted. He's a sad, limited person who just
can't give of himself. I would feel very guilty if I left him,
and he's absolutely opposed to divorce, on religious grounds.
There is a man I've met through my business who is very attractive to me and vice versa. He wants me to meet him in a

city between our two homes. I feel that I have been deprived of the kind of warmth and spontaneity he could give me. Do you think I could do it—be for myself, and yet also continue my marriage? Could I tolerate how guilty I would feel?" Based on the experiences of most married people, she will feel discomfort whichever decision she makes. Perhaps all anyone can do is to try to choose one's ambivalences!

There are many middle-aged people in similar circumstances who feel that their marriage partners cannot change. The more she talked about her husband the more I was inclined to agree with her that any attempt to try to help him to grow and change and to meet some of her legitimate needs was really most unlikely to succeed.

A husband says, "On the whole I feel I have had a good marriage; I care very much about my wife, and we have the accumulated memories of half a lifetime to share. But I was very young when I married, and there are many areas of growing that have occurred since then which my wife has not shared with me. Her interests are more limited than mine, she has remained quite inhibited sexually, and does not want to change. I need something more vital, more volatile, more adventurous in my life, and I suppose that's how the affair started. When my wife found out, she gave me an ultimatum: she would leave me if I did not give up the affair. It was a terrible choice to make. I tried to imagine us getting a divorce—of not sharing the experience of seeing our kids get married, of becoming grandparents together. I really look forward to us taking our grandchildren off on vacations. I miss that part of our relationship—with children—very much. We have shared so many joys and sorrows—I love her! But I need some things that she can't give me, and I feel that life is too short to deny bringing as much of oneself as possible into being. If only it were possible for both partners to understand that you can have a central marriage relationship which is relatively indestructible, and still need other relationships which have nothing to do with that."

There are some situations where there may be so much affection and understanding that it may be worthwhile to allow a marriage to continue, recognizing its limitations and seeking for growth and fulfillment in other places. Whether or not this can succeed depends very much on the integrity and maturity of the partner who is having the affair; his or her ability to carry the burden of guilt without ever having to confess. There are times when a marriage relationship may actually be improved under such circumstances. The greater psychological fulfillment of the partner having the affair brings a new dimension to the limited marriage. There is more gentleness and compassion, more acceptance, a general climate of elation, of hope, of good will—all of which can have a positive effect on the marriage. The deception may, of course, be a most insidious danger to the relationship, but what seems to happen in such cases is that the marriage remains pretty much as it was before—or if it improves greatly the affair is eventually relinquished, having served its purpose. That there is hurt and heartache goes without question—but all growing seems to involve these ingredients, and the quest for living more fully seems to me to be healthier than settling for despair and hopelessness.

The hurt to the partner almost always takes the form of confirming his or her own worst fears, of being hit in the area of greatest vulnerability, and this accentuates the sense of disaster for both people. The flat-chested wife is confirmed in her feelings of not looking sexy, as is the short or bald or overweight husband. One husband said, "It is uncanny how Marilyn sensed what it was all about. She never doubted her sexual attractiveness, because she knows she's a beautiful and desirable woman. But her immediate reaction on discovering I was having an affair was that it must have happened because she didn't go to college and isn't smart enough to challenge me intellectually. It was uncanny how the fact of my affair immediately brought to the surface her own sense of where *she* had failed."

Another kind of anguish has to do with our perceptions —often our illusions—of how many roles we can play effectively in our marriages. One wife commented: "My first reaction when I found out my husband had had an affair was a sense of great loss and deprivation; I could never play that role in his life again—never be a mistress to him—even on vacations! That game was over; but later, as I had time to think it over, I realized I was living in a dream world. No wife is ever her husband's mistress, no matter what games they play!"

Where an affair is in progress this question of deeply wounding a marriage partner and seriously threatening the marriage is a matter of stormy controversy—internally as well as in current public discussion. A typical feeling about telling a spouse was expressed by one woman who said, "I know in my deepest self that I cannot share my truth with my husband. It would destroy his love and self-respect. I deceive him to keep him, and I feel very guilty. But he is jealous, possessive, insecure—a lot of things that simply won't accommodate themselves to my reality—but I need him and love him, and because I've had to do so much thinking about it, I find my marriage more precious than ever. If I could tell him, if he could understand why it has happened to me, he might be able to grow and change; but he can't since I don't tell him. The only good part is that I know my marriage is better and more solid than ever before."

Some psychiatrists take the point of view that affairs may be valuable in some cases, but that they must be kept secret. One psychiatrist, Dr. O. Spurgeon English, believes that an extramarital affair is necessary and desirable for some men and women and should not be condemned. He does not recommend affairs as a part of treatment, but he does not try to dissuade anyone who has decided to have one. He feels that some people need to seek a type of person with whom they can have different and significant kinds of sex relations that they cannot achieve in marriage. Rather than being branded as neurotic behavior, having an affair may be a way of moving toward greater maturity and emotional well-being. He feels, however, it should be kept a secret from the spouse and all others who might be hurt by it.

There are, of course, times when a marriage partner finds out about an affair when the partner has really not wanted this fact to be revealed, but most experts and couples seem to agree that in the majority of cases where the spouse is "found out," unconsciously it is because he or she was ready to relinquish the relationship or was so flooded by guilt that one or both wanted to be punished. Husbands and wives who "never suspected anything—it was a complete shock" are frequently not consciously aware of what is happening because they are not ready to face it, but unconsciously they may have felt anxious for some time. Typical are such comments as, "I saw my husband walking on the street with a woman who works in his office. There was something about their manner which made me very suspicious—a sense that *I* was the intruder. That night I told my husband that I had been suspicious for the first time in our marriage. I also added that if he ever was unfaithful, I didn't want to know about it. He took me at my word! A year later, when I found her letters in his desk when he was out of town and I needed an old checkbook, I thought at first that it was a complete shock —but it wasn't; I must have known, unconsciously, from the very beginning."

Anyone who makes the decision to have an affair and to keep it a secret needs to examine the hazards carefully, in terms of both inevitable accidents of fate and unconscious sabotage due to feelings of guilt. One psychologist told me, "One does not come to the point of telling a life-partner that there has been a liaison with someone else until one has reached the readiness to be without it—it has fulfilled its purpose because all along there was an underlying awareness that it was never the enduring thing, the deeply necessary thing. It was only a means to uncover things within the marriage that had to be revealed. Then, despite the awful pain, one becomes willing to go through whatever is necessary to keep the marriage alive and both partners growing."

Sometimes there is a conscious determination to end the relationship before being found out, as in this case where the wife said, "It was one of those crazy things—a wedding we had to go to, and that my lover and his wife also attended. My husband's obvious anguish and almost-asking-me caused me to let go in some massive way inside. I suddenly came up against the fact that the way I have come to love my husband encompasses his needs as much as mine. I wanted it to be true if he ever asked me directly, it would really be over. It's a real death but not a denial—the other love was a living thing—it will always be part of me."

There was general agreement with what one person said: "When you fall in love with someone, and you love the person you are married to, there are no formulas, no absolutes. You have to follow your feelings as honestly as you can, and endure the contradictions and ambivalences. You have to *live* it out, not *think* it out."

When the decision "to tell" is made, either consciously or unconsciously, there is almost always a period of great suffering for both partners.

Johnson and Masters (*Redbook* magazine, September 1971) offer advice on what to do after an affair has been discovered: "Once the fact of adultery is out in the open, the only constructive course of action is to have a confrontation—a quiet and, if humanly possible, an unemotional face-to-face inquiry." Even if it were "humanly possible," it would seem to me to be very poor advice, because it would be an unnatural and over-controlled reaction for most people. It is entirely human to react to terrible pain with screaming and kicking, and it would seem to me that a better prelude to eventually discussing all the serious implications of the affair in relation to the marriage, would be an honest and spontaneous expression of genuine feelings on both sides.

One of the most disastrous after-effects of finding out about an infidelity, is the husband or wife who is hurt so profoundly that he or she takes immediate and devastating action, out of deeply wounded pride, before stopping to think about whether this is really the desired solution. Where there are still strong ties of caring, and where the couple have the courage to face the implications of an affair, marriages almost invariably are improved by the crisis. In fact, I cannot recall one instance among those I talked with where this was not admitted.

The same phenomenon is true in parent-child relationships. In every case where an adolescent, for example, had acted out—through experimenting with drugs, through an unwanted pregnancy, through playing hooky from school— the degree to which there now could be an open confrontation and real communication, was the degree to which the relationship improved. The typical reaction of parents who had lived through a major crisis with a child was, "We have never been closer; terrible as it seemed at the time, it was the best thing that could have happened—we learned so much about each other, and our love for each other measured up to the test." Exactly the same pattern seems to be true in marital upheavals, where there is still a basically sound relationship that neither partner really wants to give up.

Today, many couples are not only able to tolerate individual affairs, but are exploring and engaging in other alternative activities which they consider to be "marriage-savers," such as switching partners, group sex, communal marriages, etc. It seems to me that it is too early to assess such arrangements as either (1) manipulative, exploitative, and mechanistic, or (2) genuine, sensitive, imaginative responses to the challenge of marriage in today's world. We will have to wait and see, but for the majority of the currently middle-aged, these options will probably remain interesting but academic; most of us are too deeply embedded in the value system of our childhood to find such alternatives possible.

There are still many people who consider infidelity to be an indication of serious individual neurosis, a very sick marriage, or just plain immoral. It cannot be tolerated at all. For those who feel that way, it may be helpful to try to prevent its occurrence long before it might happen.

A woman who had had several affairs told me, "The ultimate deception is of oneself, feeling that answers to *anything* can come only through personal liaisons outside of the marriage. I've learned that this is usually a rationalization for being afraid of openly facing one's needs and feelings and working it out in the marriage relationship."

The advent of an affair is so often related to differences in rates of growing that it seems the better part of wisdom for couples who are not yet ready for the "brave new world of sexual freedom" to be sensitive to the changes that are taking place in the partner, and to try to see to it that one partner doesn't outdistance the other to such a degree that a real chasm develops between them.

Most people seem to underestimate the fact that a great many cases of infidelity have little or nothing to do with sex. Marital sex may be very satisfactory and the affair may occur because a spouse feels lonely and wants someone to talk to! Anxieties about finances, feelings of hopelessness about getting a better job, wanting to be with someone who isn't constantly making so many demands, being able to talk to someone who is interested in one's work are some of the other factors that frequently enter the picture.

But it is also true that sex can be a major factor, especially because we live in a period when so much fuss is being made about it. It is very difficult to be caught up in the sweep of the current preoccupation with the techniques of lovemaking; it makes us feel so deficient and defensive. One woman told me, "Much as you try to say you don't believe in all this new stuff about experimenting with new positions and being adventurous, you still get caught up in it. My husband and I finally bought a book with all the different sexual positions, and it was really crazy. What difference does it make which position you use, if you're having fun, enjoying yourself, and expressing your feelings toward each other? This obsession with techniques can drive you crazy. It isn't *how* you do it, but what doing it *means* to you."

More helpful, to the middle-aged marriage, than a preoccupation with becoming more technically varied and skillful is giving more attention to such things as how to be more open and honest about feelings, how to become more sensitized to each other's wishes. We are constantly bombarded by such expressions of the mood of our time as "the sensuous woman," with the idea that newness, variation, is the goal, and yet so many middle-aged marrieds know from their own experience that in many ways familiarity, a long-term awareness of another person's needs and pleasures, the warmth of an extended affection, the comradeship of having lived through so much together can be a basis for sexual fulfillment and pleasure. One wife explained, "My God, we've had *thirty years* of practice! We know so much about each other—maybe we 'do it' in the same old way, but I *like* it! Practice *does* enhance what you can do for each other— when you really know all the shortcomings, all the weaknesses, all the fears of another—when you still love another human being anyway, then lovemaking is a kind of testament of unconditional love, a surrender, an openness, a vulnerability that is so deeply rewarding."

It is a source of surprise, wonder, and delight for many couples that no matter what they've been through, no matter how different they may be at fifty from what they were at twenty—the added weight and lines and arthritic fingers and gray hair—so many still feel a hunger, a delight, in each other. And for those who have truly grown and are ten times the people they were at twenty, there can be a kind of communion, both spiritual and sensual, at fifty that beats the wedding night by a mile.

Because we have high expectations and inevitable feelings of boredom sometimes—and a pervasive fear that maybe we're really missing something—we tend to overemphasize the importance of variety in sexual relationships. In talking to a number of therapists who are working with middle-aged people, I found that most of their patients who still loved a spouse, but had wandered into greener pastures, admitted that their extramarital sexual adventures were often far less satisfying than their marital relationship, that the adventure had often been quite a frustrating experience. One patient had expressed this as, "I seem to be afraid that I might miss something, or that I have to prove I'm still attractive to men, and I put on a good performance, but the truth is, I haven't reached an orgasm in any of these relationships, and much prefer sex relations with my husband." There is a good deal to be said for familiarity! And practice *does* bring improvement if not perfection! The growing knowledge of another person's body; the continued experimentation with what gives pleasure and what doesn't; the comfortable and secure feeling of making love with someone you have known very well and for a long time can make sex infinitely satisfying in its own particular way. Sex at fifty is not the relief of pent-up drives, characteristic of an adolescent or young adult; what it can be and often is, is a great tenderness, a long-time union of old friends who care deeply about each other and who have a deep sense of togetherness.

This is not to suggest that doing the "same old things in the same old way" is the only alternative to the experimentation of new relationships. Imagination, creativity, a spirit of adventure are entirely appropriate within a long-term marriage relationship. A conscious effort to rekindle the flame some of the time is surely a desirable thing, if the couple are willing to accept the fact that there will be ups and downs in any such relationship. But sometimes an overselfconscious attempt at finding new roads to passion can be quite ludicrous. A group of us were talking one day; we had all just read a new book on sexual techniques and we had a hilarious discussion about the recommended ways for keeping the marriage lively. One of the women said, "Remember the part where the writer was advising women that one way to get a husband sexually interested again was to get all undressed and hide in the coat closet when he came home from work? When he came in and hung his coat up, there you'd be, stark naked in the closet! I tried to think what would happen if Len came home and found me in the closet. I know exactly what would happen; he'd call an ambulance and have me taken to Bellevue Hospital and locked up in a closed ward with the other mental patients!"

In making a satisfying and meaningful adjustment to marriage-at-midstream, there is growing evidence that many middle-aged couples are trying very hard to develop a new system of values for themselves. A psychologist, Dr. James Bugenthal, writing in *The Journal of Humanistic Psychology*,* seems to me to have summarized the elements of a new humanistic ethic when he wrote:

> Probably the epitome of intimate encounter is sexual intercourse between a man and a woman who deeply love each other, who are mutually self-and-other respecting, and who are free to invest themselves fully in their coming together—free, that is, of fear, guilt (etc.). . . . It can mean a transcending of the separateness which is usually part of being human, a transcending of the difference between giving and receiving . . . of the boundaries of time and daily concerns. . . . The wise lover knows, however, that there is a Gresham's law governing such

* Vol. XI, No. 1, Spring 1971.

experiences. One may select the discipline of being selective in his relationships and thus preserving their transcendent potentials, or he may yield to the invitations of opportunity and content himself with pale simulations of the fullness that is potential. . . . It is not possible to be both an indiscriminate playboy and a fully authentic lover. . . . The humanistic ethic does not include the idea of exclusivity in relationships, for that would amount to a kind of ownership. . . . Rather it counsels a selectivity or discrimination such as one would exercise in the care of any precious talent. This means that promiscuity will be seen as sad wastefulness, but that the same can be said of blind fidelity.

There are a growing number of marriages in which there is a serious attempt to deal with the reality that fidelity for thirty or forty or fifty years may be stultifying and almost impossible for people living in the current climate of individual freedom. Many couples have been experimenting with an honesty and openness in which they both recognize that the marriage is the central relationship but each may have temporary affairs with others. They feel that deception is a more serious danger to their marriage than infidelity. In some cases there is an honest idealism involved and a very serious and healthy attempt to adapt to changing times and circumstances, and do as little damage to each other as possible. Where both can make this adjustment, it can work. The danger lies in two areas: first, in few marriages do both partners choose this with equal enthusiasm, and second, how does a couple evaluate the degree to which this solution may disguise other kinds of needs—where, for example, such arrangements may represent a kind of titillation, a voyeurism or exhibitionism, or where they are really trying to shore up a marriage that has serious flaws and limitations?

In one successful arrangement of this kind, the wife said, "When you feel most married, you can tolerate the pain of your spouse having another relationship. But it takes tremendous security and an almost absolute clarity on the part of both that the marriage is central, permanent, a deeply necessary relationship. If you feel that secure, then you don't want to deny your partner the right to experience himself in other ways." A minister told me, "Fidelity in marriage is essential —but to me that means loving, caring, taking responsibility, not necessarily being faithful sexually."

Sylvia had had several love relationships before she met Glen, but he had had only the most superficial sexual encounters. When they married Sylvia said (possibly because it seemed to be an academic question) she would not feel threatened if at some time during their marriage, he needed to have some other relationships. The only thing she felt she could not tolerate would be deception between them. About six years later, Glen did have an extracurricular relationship— a most intense love affair—and he could not bring himself to acknowledge it openly, for he simply could not believe Sylvia really had meant what she said or could live up to such a level of understanding and acceptance. Sylvia did not find out until several years afterward, and for a time it seemed the marriage could not be healed. It was the deception which was to her intolerable in a relationship where trust seemed so important.

Sylvia and Glen have now been married for over thirty years. From time to time, each of them has had a relationship with someone else; both feel that it is perfectly possible (based on their experience) to love two people in different and unthreatening ways. They have not hidden what was happening from each other. Sylvia says, "We could do this because we both came to feel that our marriage was indestructible—that what we had together was so deep, so absolutely necessary to us, that nothing could threaten our relationship. There are times, in a long life together, when a man or a woman may need to fulfill some needs that cannot be met with each other—some striving for growth, some different way of relating; all in all, we feel that all the things that have happened to us separately enhance what we feel for each other."

But this is no easy goal. The conflict between one's deepest prejudices against sexual freedom and a growing acceptance, at least intellectually, that today's marriage is doomed unless each partner to it is free to fulfill himself and to grow—and therefore to do whatever he or she needs to do for this quest —is expressed by the woman who said, "My husband wants me to be able to love with an open hand. He wants me to let him 'fly free'—he says that a butterfly is only alive and beautiful when you hold it in an open hand; if you clutch it it will die. The trouble is that he's the butterfly, and while he says I have the same rights, it isn't the same thing at all. I'm not a butterfly; I have no wish to roam, I am madly in love with my husband, and in twenty-six years of marriage, have never met anybody as attractive or interesting."

It is possible that in this changing society with its greater flexibility and wider opportunities, it may become a kind of social ideal to accept the words of Kahlil Gibran. He writes of marriage, in *The Prophet:*

But let there be spaces in your togetherness,
And let the winds of the heavens dance between you.

Love one another, but make not a bond of love:
Let it rather be a moving sea between the shores of your souls.

The goal of self-actualization for each human being would suggest that it might become possible for us to make the necessary adaptation so that love between marriage partners could, indeed, be of such maturity, wisdom, tenderness, security, and selflessness that we could tolerate affairs on both sides in which neither felt hurt or threatened, and did not have to deceive. At first glance it might appear that this is true in some European countries, such as France and Italy, where it is an accepted idea that each will have a romantic liaison outside of the marriage; but these are predominantly Catholic countries, and it may be that the capacity to accept this kind of marriage structure rests largely on the fact that the marriage remains intact—that there is the structure of the church which defines the marriage as permanent, so neither partner ever feels threatened by the other's extracurricular activities. Whether or not this is possible without that institutional control is hard to say. This position implies that in a stable and mature marriage anything that is good for the partner is good for oneself. One woman told me, "I'm glad when other women are attracted to my husband; I want him to feel that good about himself; and I'm glad because I know that in spite of other relationships, he still wants me the most and forever. If he is fulfilled and happy, then he makes me feel that way too."

It seems clear to me that if we want our marriages to last and if we also want to go on growing, we have to begin the long hard struggle to free each other from the kinds of bonds we learned as children were proper to marriage. The challenge we face is to cultivate our separate identities and to acknowledge a conception of marriage that we were not taught, but which may be more viable for the times in which we now live. I know this has been terribly difficult for me to learn, and it is my impression that in almost every marriage one partner wants this more than the other, and takes to it more naturally. I had an experience recently, which pointed this up so clearly. I was visiting a friend in another city, and called to speak to my husband. We talked for a few minutes and when I hung up, my friend said, "You know, you sounded like an inquisitor; I could feel my own hackles rising as you kept asking what he was doing, where he was going, what his plans were. It's exactly what Ed does to me, and I can't bear it." I hadn't been aware of what I was doing at all; I like it when my husband is interested in my whereabouts and concerned about my feelings and experiences. I am constitutionally *dis*inclined to feel a need for privacy or separateness, but as my friend explained, "It's not that people like us necessarily have anything to hide; it has something to do with our sense of the integrity of self—there just has to be a part of us that we don't share."

Despite living in a time when people are discussing how obsolete marriage has become, and are either talking about or experimenting with new life-styles, I find that I must accept who I am and what my life experiences have been. It will do me no good to force myself to change or to hate myself because I can't change. I do the best I can to understand change and to keep an open heart and mind and assume that I have no idea how my feelings might change six months from now or six years. I have learned, at least, to live without a program! The best we can do is to let life unfold, to happen, and to be as consciously aware of how we feel as we can as we go along. I am still a sentimentalist; I still get weepy when I see families meeting or separating at airports. *There is something there*—of that I am sure—the joy in the greetings, the controlled but brimming eyes when a son or husband or father is leaving. Whatever may be wrong with us and with marriage, I have sensed too often myself that exultation in loving and being loved which is above and beyond any other experience I ever had. In spite of all the anguish that is an inevitable part of two individuals struggling to make a life together, there is something quite miraculous and beyond my powers to describe, which can only be shared wordlessly by those who have experienced it. If marriage is either impossible or ridiculous, as some now feel, why is it that there are so many couples who seem to prefer this arrangement to all others and frequently manage to stay in love—really in love —all their lives?

I suppose the explanation (which doesn't really help very much!) is that we are ambivalent, and have strong drives in both directions; exclusivity appeals to us as well as variety, and there are emotional values in a wide range of adventures as well as in the intense intimacy of a long-term marriage. We are, again, a generation caught in the middle of changing values and behavior, and we really have no choice but to roll with the punches, meeting each individual human experience as it comes, and using it as best we can for further growing. Boredom, at least, seems to me to be almost entirely avoidable. If two people constantly pursue their own growing, then each is constantly encountering an exciting stranger in the other!

Most of us must sooner or later accept the fact that change in one's marriage is inevitable. We were immature and far from being most ourselves when we married, and in the period in which we married, we were surrounded by romantic illusions. With that background, it becomes inevitable that marriage must change, that it can't stay where it was. It is a dynamic, not static, relationship, made up of both pleasure and pain.

One of the most valuable attributes of marriage is that one's partner can truly be one's best friend, and friendship was never more important. If one defines a friend as someone who loves you in spite of knowing your faults and weaknesses, and has even better dreams for your fulfillment than you have for yourself, it can surely be the foundation for what each of us needs most in middle age—permission to continue to quest for one's own identity.

During the period when my husband and I were courting, I became more and more impatient for some declaration of intent on his part. It had been love at second sight for me; it was in the midst of the Second World War, and I was impatient for the commitment I wanted so much. Unable to endure the suspense any longer, I finally asked him if he would tell me how he felt about our relationship; what did it mean to him, and where was it going, if anywhere? I asked this provocative question at a railroad station in a town where he was stationed in the army, and where I was about to board a train crowded with soldiers, to return home after a brief visit. As I was swept along the platform, he shouted his answer: *"It's a friendship with possibilities!"*

I was crushed, both figuratively and literally, and spent a miserable six hours sitting on my suitcase in a jammed aisle, misreading his meaning quite completely, for we were married less than six months later. What I have learned in the intervening years is that he was talking about marriage, and that he was quite right; it is most surely a friendship with possibilities. That's a lot—and enough.

THE

HEAVY BURDEN

OF OUR

MASKS

*
*
*
*
*
*
*

Chapter 7

My husband and I spent a day with some friends who own a farm in Pennsylvania. We happened to be in their neighborhood, and called to see if we could stop in. We hadn't seen each other in several years. The day was lovely; we were given vegetables from their plentiful garden, we had a delicious dinner, we hiked to the top of the hill to see their beautiful view, we talked about our work and the increasing horrors of city living and their adjustment to the rural life. What none of us spoke about was their main reason for moving to the country: so that they could better care for their brain-damaged child—too normal for institutionalization, yet too difficult to handle in a city apartment, as she got older and more restless and destructive.

A few years ago we went to the theater with some friends one evening, laughed through an early dinner, made small talk during the intermissions, and parted saying it was a shame we didn't see each other more often. It was more than a year later that they felt able to tell us what they had been going through on that evening; their son had been arrested for possession of marijuana, had spent a day and a night in jail, and they were waiting for his trial date to be set.

In the case of our farm visit, we had grown apart in the

years we had not seen each other, and I suppose neither couple wanted to cloud the day's pleasures with old agonies. In the second instance, even the closest of friendship relationships may not help until one has had time to deal privately with one's anxiety and suffering.

As I began writing this book and asked people to talk to me frankly about their experiencing of middle age, I began to realize more fully than ever before the degree of pain and tragedy there is in every person's life. How little we really know about each other! How easy it is to envy those who seem better off, free of anguish.

The greatest burden we carry into middle age is the burden of our masks. To some degree each of us is an island; we devote enormous amounts of time and energy to keeping up appearances, maintaining a good front; "everything is just fine"—while each of us weeps in the privacy of our own souls. One woman told me, "At eight o'clock on Christmas morning, John and I were discussing getting a divorce after twenty-two years of marriage. At eight-thirty, I was standing at an open window, wishing I had the courage to jump. But at noon we were at my parents' place in the country, with all the children and aunts and uncles, making merry—nothing showing."

When we were children, people kept their troubles (and their pleasures!) to themselves; "nice people" didn't wash their dirty linen in public. And certainly no one confided the more sordid facts of life to children. We feel a deep reticence, an unwillingness to sacrifice our privacy for the comfort of sharing our griefs. But even more burdensome is the fact that despite our awareness of our own pain, and the problems of those who are closest to us, there is still some place, deepdown, where we really don't believe in the tragic nature of life; where we still believe in magic and fairy tales, in good winning over evil, in an orderly and just universe—for we were told that such things were possible when we were very young and impressionable. The fact that it was untrue and that we know it now, doesn't take away that childish inner wish not to know.

Our children are just the opposite. And we played as much a part in their tendency toward cynicism as our parents played in our romantic illusions. As I look back I realize that honesty seemed terribly important to me in raising my child. At the time I was not so much aware of the effects overprotection had had on me, as I was concerned with honesty as part of a psychologically therapeutic milieu in which a child could understand his own complicated feelings because the feelings of others were being openly discussed. If my child were told "the truth" about the human condition, I thought, she would be able to accept her own fallibility without self-condemnation and paralyzing guilt.

When we knew that close friends were having serious marital difficulties, we discussed it quite openly in front of our daughter, even when she was only seven or eight years old. She heard many discussions in which we analyzed how people "really felt" underneath their superficially polite or happy-looking behavior. Although we tried to protect her from our major personal fights and crises, we never pretended that we were happy all the time. The one thing we tried to do, if she saw me crying or her father depressed and aloof, was to make it clear she had nothing to do with it—that these were grownup troubles.

A lot of other parents must have been doing the same thing, for our children are not burdened with the illusions of our growing years; sometimes I think we went too far and they know too much!

For my television series *How Do Your Children Grow?* we asked a great many teenagers to express their opinions on many subjects, and the one almost universal response that startled and unsettled us was that they did not want their lives to be like their parents' at all. While this loss of illusions has its dangers in some ways, our children have few of our hang-ups about how hard it is to be a human being; they *take for granted* that all human beings are sometimes weak and scared and jealous and angry and selfish. They live with both sides of the human experience in far greater comfort than we.

No matter how I fight it, no matter how much I know from my own experience, I still find myself looking at a couple kissing goodbye at an air terminal, or an old man and woman holding hands at the Central Park Zoo—or the beautiful people, so rich, so self-assured, so gorgeously dressed at the opera—and find myself thinking, "Those are the lucky ones." Part of lifting some of the weight of our own masks, is finally facing how foolish it is to think that anyone escapes all that it means to be human. The only ones who do are those who are already dead inside and feel nothing, neither pain nor joy. When we were growing up it almost seemed as if expressing one's real feelings was a kind of unfortunate defect in our makeup. There was something wrong and shameful about shouting in anger or crying or shaking with terror; such feelings were to be suppressed, got rid of. Strong feelings of hostility and pain, especially, seemed to us to be unwanted parts of life. In truth they are essential to the full human experience.

When I was supervising young nursery school teachers, the hardest thing for them to accept was my insistence on their allowing a child to experience his own grief. During the first weeks of school, when the children were having their normal separation problems, I would go up to a child and say, "I know how sad you feel, Suzy, because Mommy left you here for a little while. Maybe you need to cry for a few minutes—come sit on my lap." The teachers were horrified; I was putting ideas into the child's head. Instead of helping her to feel happy, I was making her feel worse. Their tendency was to say, "You feel fine, Suzy—look at all the toys you can play with, and how about sitting next to Kathy and drawing a picture?" Evasion and denial of the most natural kind of grief at a first major parting. This is the way it has always been, and it turns out people like us, who don't know what to do with our pain. After a while, most of the teachers would begin to see that the children who were allowed to experience their real feelings most fully were able to move on more easily to enjoying themselves.

Hiding one's feelings from others is the first and more obvious burden; but the deeper issue is how we hide our feelings from ourselves. Both are issues we need to take a look at, for they greatly influence what we do or don't do with our middle years.

One rarely sees a genuine sharing of feelings among large groups of people. Even at most funerals, the goal seems to be to show as little of one's feelings as possible. One of those unusual public sharings of feeling occurred when President Kennedy was assassinated. For a few days the shock was so great that people cried quite openly; strangers talked to each other on the streets and subways. I remember it as being a time when one felt safe on the streets of New York, when out of the sharing of genuine feelings, something happened and people reached out to each other; it felt good.

The night of the "Great Blackout" was another such time. People were afraid together, they joked together, they shared their panic. There was a great camaraderie of shared feelings in a city where people ordinarily barely acknowledge each other's existence. It would change the quality of life in the most profound ways if nothing else were to happen but our ability to share our human feelings with each other.

Each of us finds his own ways to lighten the burden of our masks. The least successful in the long run is denial. We may try that for a while, and when that doesn't work too well, we may turn to a special friend or relative for comfort and support. The opposite technique from denial—spilling one's guts all over the place—is just as ineffective and may do one serious damage, but there are times when we can't help ourselves because we just don't know what to do with our feelings. Later we suffer great misgivings and discomfort.

I find that I change and grow—and regress and then grow again—so rapidly and so disorganizedly that if I pour my heart out on one day, I may regret it terribly a day or two later when I have better perspective on the problem and really don't want five other people figuring out what I'm doing with my life. There are times of such stress that we cannot help ourselves—we all spill at the wrong time and to the wrong person sometimes—but I find that I do this less if I try to be consciously selective. A question that seems to be helpful is: Which of my friends seems to have had parallel growth experiences? For example, you don't see someone you have known a long time, and you wonder whether you will bore each other to death. Sometimes that is exactly what happens—you discover that you have both changed so much and gone off in such different directions that you have become complete strangers, even if you've known each other for thirty or more years.

But then there are those other times. I remember going to Washington a few years ago and wondering if I should look up a friend I hadn't seen for four or five years. Enormous changes had taken place in my life: I felt I was almost a totally different person from the last time we had met, but we had been very good friends and I decided to chance it. I stayed with her for two days, and the only frustration was that we got tired and needed to sleep at night, which seemed terribly unfair when we had so much to say to each other! Our growth during those intervening years had been unbelievably similar, and we could again use our friendship for emotional support and comfort and complete understanding.

Everyone has some experiences with feeling betrayed. But it seems to me, on the basis of my own experience, that the responsibility for what happens rests with oneself; if I talk too much, my lack of caution is expressing my own needs and feelings at the moment; I may be saying, "Please don't tell anyone," but at some deep level I want the information to get around if I talk indiscriminately. When we choose a confidante, we ought to try to get in touch with what we are really feeling; do we want to be gossiped about? People often do! Do we want to be babied and made to feel that we are the poor victims of someone else's perfidy? Do we feel like running home to Mommy and having her kiss our wounds? If we really want advice and counsel as well as the comfort of unburdening, then we have to be selective and cautious in deciding to whom to tell our troubles.

When my daughter was young I had a friend who was a social worker and a wise and perceptive human being. When I would be at the end of my rope, after my daughter had been home from school for several weeks with the mumps or the measles, and there had been many sleepless nights, and I was feeling very sorry for myself, I would call her up or we'd have lunch, and I would pour out all my complaints, wallowing in self-pity. She'd listen, and she'd be very sympathetic—and then the ax would fall! I would get a blistering lecture about myself, or she would point up how my daughter or husband might interpret some of the things *I* was saying or doing. She was loving, but tough, and I tried to do the same thing for her. We were each able to reveal our feelings, without fear—but the most important part of the relationship was the fact that we were able to give each other some sound and important new perspectives through which we could work at our problems.

This matter of whom we select to tell our troubles to is in itself often an important revelation of what we want to do about our problems. One woman told me, "I realized that I wasn't going to solve my problem, when I began to see that the only people I turned to for comfort were people who would just feel sorry for me, and would agree with my wounded feelings. One day, on impulse, I began discussing my problem with a young niece. She was sympathetic, but also critical of what I was doing, and she gave me a completely different perspective, from the vantage point of her generation. I realized later that it wasn't until I took my miseries to someone who I knew would not just be sympathetic that I was ready to try to solve my problems."

We reveal a good deal about ourselves in our selection of intimates. One person tells her sisters and her brothers, her neighbors and thirty "close friends" the details of her husband's sexual inadequacies; another person complains to Mother about his wife's bad cooking and sloppy housekeeping. Or another person tells no one that her husband is becoming an alcoholic. We can learn a good deal about ourselves, and what we want to do about our difficulties from where we take them—or don't take them.

It takes a great deal of courage, but sometimes one needs to ask oneself: "Am I looking for someone to encourage self-pity? Am I trying to get back at someone who has hurt me, by telling other people things he or she would not want them to know? And perhaps most important of all, am I trying to avoid facing my own responsibility for my difficulties by blaming others? Or, when I keep really serious problems to myself, am I unconsciously unwilling to give them up?"

One of our special problems in deciding what to share and what to withhold has to do with the difference between the way we were brought up and the current climate in which total revelation seems to be what's "in." Privacy still seems to me to be a very precious commodity, and what I have to try to figure out is how to protect the integrity of my right *not* to share everything with everybody, and my awareness of how foolish and costly it is to build a high wall of defenses by which I lose touch with others as well as myself.

It's a tough problem for those of us who find ourselves appalled by the total self-revelation of a book like *Portnoy's*

Complaint, for example. One can do such awful things to other people, when one tells everything. I find myself equally turned-off by the kinds of groups in which total strangers make what seems to me to be a pretense of intimacy, in which they reveal their deepest feelings to each other over a weekend. After focusing a great deal of attention during most of my adult life on who I am and what I can be, I am sure I cannot discover my "authentic self" among a group of people I've never met before during a weekend marathon. I *like* being a private person. I like choosing very carefully whom I tell what. I don't believe in instant insight, instant truth, instant "real feelings"; life is far more complex than that.

I do not believe in giving up one's masks completely. I am extremely uncomfortable with people who feel that in order to be real to themselves and others, they must tell the whole world every detail of their feelings and experiences.

Just recently I read an autobiographical book by a man I know. He was describing how he had changed under the influence of a therapeutic experience. Among the many things I found out about him that I did not feel I needed to know in order to sense his authenticity as a human being was the number of girls he'd laid, and how one of them gave him syphilis. I suppose every writer and playwright reveals much of himself in everything he writes, but it seems to me that fiction offers ambiguity; it can make use of all human experiencing, without having to identify just where the understanding came from. Self-revelation is inevitable—and necessary to the creative experience—but is it improved by such specificity that what finally comes through is not a human story but the "true confessions" of one person?

It seems to me that what many people are searching for these days is some kind of better balance between the hypocrisy and illusions of the past, where people kept their masks in place all the time, and the current trend toward total self-revelation. Privacy is to me an integral part of being at home inside oneself, of having a special and unique identity. Never privacy *from* oneself—that's really the key. The sense of burden falls away to a large degree when one can begin to tolerate revealing oneself to oneself. It is *not* the business of the rest of the world to know every detail of one's problems and wounds; when we allow this we lose a sense of selfhood, I think, and become only half of what we really are. One is revealed in all the naked pain of one's experience—but then all the positive things are left out or dimmed. The bitter pain of life is no more a true picture than the hypocrisy of the past in which we lived a kind of fairy tale: "All parents love their children. People marry and live happily ever after."

Recently there was a newspaper interview with a well-known couple who happen to be our friends. What a perfect life the author described! Such a sharing, such richness of living: the model marriage, the beautiful people living only a gorgeous life. I knew their pain, their suffering, their wonderful, courageous struggle to grow, to change, to become more real with each other, to find their own selves in a deeper way. The truth about them is far more beautiful than that perfect story. The truth is full of such poignant humanity. And yet I would be the last to tell them to reveal the truth, anymore than I would go into explicit detail about my own life. I just felt sorry for the readers; the thousands of people who read such stories and really believe that it *is* possible to be "perfectly happy." By now we know that movies and books we grew up on didn't tell the truth about life. But one does tend to believe what one reads in newspapers and magazines. We should not! We need to keep our perspective and not allow ourselves to become depressed by the thought: *They* made it, they conquered the tragic part—why can't we? Nobody gets off that easily! It's an impossible goal, for the two halves are equally necessary and real.

I am equally turned-off by anyone telling me about those wonderful families where everybody loves everybody all the time, as I am by the psychotherapist who feels he is making progress with his patients only when he's got them in a screaming rage and therefore expressing their "real" feelings. In both cases, one-half of being human is being ignored.

At the same time that there is a great deal to be said for the dignity of privacy, it seems to me that we can overcome some of the more nonsensical defenses we maintain, which exhaust us and lead to a kind of basic fraudulence in our relationships with others. When we "keep up a good front" all or even most of the time, we often end up lying to ourselves as well as to everyone else.

Special days are a good example of this kind of thing. I was shocked some years ago when a psychiatrist told me that she had more trouble with serious depressive states in her patients on Thanksgiving, Christmas, and Mother's Day than any other times during the year. She explained that on such occasions people build up fantasies of the way life *ought* to be, and when reality refuses to cooperate with these dreams, people become very angry and depressed. "These holidays intensify the 'shoulds' in our lives," she told me. People *should* be kind and loving; parents *should* enjoy playing with their children; and children *should* be in an ecstatic trance over the presents they receive. Apparently Mother's Day evokes the worst "shoulds" of all! Its very existence in our lives suggests that mothers *should* be better than other people, and that their children and their husbands *should* treat them as some kind of super-heroic beings, larger than life.

There is such an awful letdown because we lose sight of our humanness, our limitations; we are seduced into a fantasy that life is all sugar and spice and everything nice. We would have a much better time at family reunions and holiday celebrations if we were to take stock ahead of time and throw out all those "shoulds." It is fun to get together with people you love, but that doesn't mean you won't get testy and snappish with all the noise and confusion. It's great for the kids to visit their grandparents, but they will begin to drive everyone crazy if the visit is too long. It's good to have a chance to have fun together, but that doesn't mean that all the normal and natural tensions that exist whenever people are genuinely close to each other will just evaporate into thin air. Plain Jane will be jealous of gorgeous cousin Jill; no mother worth her salt really ever believes that her son's wife takes proper care of him; siblings who once competed for the high school football letter compete more subtly now, with who is in the higher tax bracket. Old slights, old wounds, the unfinished business of childhood, misunderstandings, poor communication, old jealousies—they are all there when we sit down together for Yuletide Merriment. Such feelings can be set aside; sometimes just the effort at good fellowship neutralizes old wounds, but it does no good at all to deny the existence of human imperfection and normal human problems. We can have a marvelous time if we let reality in, if we know it may well turn out to be an Excedrin Headache day in spite of the fact that it is also good to be together. There will be more genuine gaiety and robust good humor, more real affection and love if we acknowledge the fact that there is no such thing as a fairy-tale family—no place on earth where peace and love and goodness exist in pristine purity.

Instead we are human: we love and we care, but we also get cranky and tired; we want to be close to people we love, but we also need to be by ourselves; the past memories of a cozy Christmas may be warm and filled with delight, but at the time there was that flat tire that made us late, and Richie's disappointment over the sand truck that didn't live up to expectations, and Liz wetting her pants right in front of the Christmas tree, and Grandma's hurt feelings because the awkward misery of adolescence keeps her grandson from kissing her with his previous enthusiasm.

We are less likely to suffer an aftermath of disappointment or depression if we don't let ourselves expect too much in the first place. Often it's just when we demand the least that we get the most. A mother told me recently, "I expected Thanksgiving to be a disaster—too many hidden tensions to be absorbed in the turkey stuffing this year—but the nicest thing happened; some of the kids began to sing around the piano, and then everybody joined in and we had a marvelous musical afternoon." It's the unexpected pleasures that are the best—not the ones we grab for, or demand from life.

A large dose of wry humor helps a lot. The following is an excerpt from a letter I received from a friend after a recent Christmas:

> The kids have come and gone for the so-called holidays. We managed to stagger through with an impressive patina of poise and pleasure, despite Jerry's announcement that he's leaving school and Helen's disclosure that she's in love with a married Japanese exchange professor with two kids! I poured eggnog and turkey gravy over the whole. All I have left of the holidays is a staggering number of bills that I failed to recognize, a bunch of useless red and green candle stubs, a turkey leg that isn't quite rotten enough to throw away yet, and letters from the girls with cheery bits such as, "I'm terribly sorry but I forgot my left iceskate," or "Could you send my allowance ahead of time?" I find it a source of comfort that there is only one Messiah's birthday to be celebrated.

This is a mother who loves her family and has raised three quite marvelous human beings. A little perspective and a good sense of humor have left her with no serious postholiday depression.

I know a sweet and gentle Grandma who twinkles with good cheer and love as she faces the holidays—baking and shopping and wrapping packages, looking for all the world like a Madison Avenue version of American Grandmother of the Year. One pre-Christmas week she greeted me with, "Isn't it wonderful, looking forward to the Christmas holidays again, with all the family coming to visit?" And then she whispered in my ear, "It's almost as wonderful as the day they all go home!"

There is no clearer place where our masks show up than in those Christmas letters some people send! I have to admit I find them appalling (there goes one of my masks). I can just see all the lists on which I'm being crossed off! A typical example: "The big event of the year is: Diane and Robert had a darling baby girl last February. Mimi is now almost a year old, and a delight to all with her sunny personality, sparkling beauty and bright mind. Robert is finishing up law school this year and Diane is still a struggling young painter."

I saw this Grandma not long ago. Behind this cheery news are these facts: Diane and Robert were living together for several years, Diane dying to get married, Robert swearing marriage wasn't for him. They broke up, Diane had such a serious depression she had to be hospitalized, Robert found he missed her too much and they reconciled, during which period Diane became pregnant and they finally married when she was in her fifth month. Mimi was a colicky baby, and Diane was beside herself with anxiety, fatigue, and frustration. Grandma went to visit and was really worried for a while. She thought there might be something seriously wrong with the baby, she seemed to have so much pain after each meal, threw up so much, etc. Grandma was also worried because Diane was leaving the baby with a sitter too much of the time, and escaping by becoming a model for a painter she knew. Grandma was worried about the emotional investment in this relationship, and was afraid Diane would leave Robert and the baby. She talked to Diane at some length, finally persuading both Diane and Robert to go into therapy, and she would pay the bill. Things seemed to be better, especially because Mimi had overcome her gastro-intestinal problems.

This doesn't mean that the letter is lying; all those good and happy things are also true. But they are half the truth, and rather than spreading good cheer, I think they depress the reader, who again dares to hope it is the *whole* truth. I think these letters represent the worst in us, not the best, for they seem to me to be symbolic of a kind of denial that is misleading and hurtful to both sender and recipient. Real friends can share both the tragedies and the joys of life; acquaintances don't really gain anything from these euphoric declarations. They are depressing, for they deny one's genuine humanity.

Sometimes the masks fall away even when people are trying to assure us that everything is just wonderful. There was, for example, the Christmas letter that had two pages telling about an older son's accomplishments: the newly acquired Ph.D., the paper presented at a professional convention, the adorable fiancée, the plans for a European honeymoon. Then another full page about mother's activities: the problems of the city government she worked for, her trips with the mayor, his plans for getting into national politics, her contributions to developing a "White Paper" on welfare program revisions. On the last page there was a paragraph about a husband and a younger son: "Fred is still busy working for the telephone company, and increasing the variety and number of his tropical fish—the hobby that fascinates him. Patrick decided to leave college for a year and has been traveling around the country in a camper. He's been picking fruit in Florida, lately. He's having a chance to try to find himself, and we are hoping he will return to school in the fall." Five lines for them, three pages for number one son and mother. It doesn't take a psychiatrist to read between the lines!

The main thing is for each of us not to have to wear our masks all the time, and not to make the masks so impenetrable that even we ourselves think everything is always just great. I've noticed, for example, that sometimes it is when I am trying hardest to believe I have no problems that I get pains in my shoulder, or a cold that lingers for weeks, or find myself unable to write. The mask has been so good that even I have been taken in by it. Our bodies, our minds, our total selves have a way of sending out warning signals when we are least alive to ourselves, when we are closing up and living on the surface of life.

There are many ways of getting in touch with yourself. Some do it through meditation, others through religious communion; some come to it in group therapy, some find that their daily work offers them the avenue: the poet, the teacher, the actor, for example, who in developing his craft has moments of discovering inner realities that foster great spurts of growing.

My personal choice for the best way to do this has been through psychotherapy. I have been in psychotherapy off and on for over twenty years. I have worked with four therapists. I was never psychotic. I was never even terribly neurotic. I could have had a reasonably happy and constructive life without one day of therapy, but when I think of the young woman I was before I started, and where I am now, I shudder to think how much more limited my life would have been without it.

In recent years I have become increasingly critical of many aspects of orthodox psychoanalysis, sometimes called "Endless Analysis," and too frequently deserving that name for its intensity and prolongation. It has seemed more and more unnecessary—and even harmful—for the patient to see his therapist five times a week, and to persist for five or ten years. It has seemed to me that this kind of dependency— the cocoonlike quality of life—was not truly therapeutic. This attitude may appear at first to be quite inconsistent with the facts I've just given about myself, but they are not. It isn't the length of time involved, but rather, the basic philosophy underlying one's approach to psychotherapy. In its earlier years (less and less today, one hopes) psychoanalysis took the point of view that life should be suspended during the therapy; the patient was not supposed to make any important decisions, there was to be no or very little focus on the present, the whole technique was designed to lead the patient toward a concentration on his childhood experiences. The insight one gained was supposed to free you to make new and better decisions in your life—but only after therapy was "completed."

The therapy that I sought—and still seek—is quite different in orientation. While it is perfectly true that one's childhood experiences are an inextricable part of one's present feelings, and one must again and again examine one's behavior and attitudes in the light of the past, the therapy that I have experienced has always used the past only to throw light on the present. Therapy was also never isolated from the rest of my life. I went right on making decisions, enjoying the helpful ones and learning from the mistaken ones. Therapy was simply one avenue for becoming more aware, more sensitive, more in charge of my own destiny.

There are people who need to be in therapy all their lives because they really are too sick to make it outside a mental hospital otherwise, or who are so frightened that they need constant reassurance, or who have problems which are so overwhelming (a handicapped spouse or child, a chronic illness themselves, etc.) that they need guidance and comfort all along the way. But then there are also some people like me, who come to feel that therapy is searching, it is one of many possible ways to go on growing, continually, and if it is used simply as an avenue—a tool—for self-exploration, then it becomes part of your life. You don't turn to it constantly, but it is there, available to you, when you feel you have reached a new level and can't go any further on your own, or you are faced with a new crisis in your life, or feel blocked in your work or relationships.

I find that for me, having a skilled professional person, who is also a cherished friend, helps me the most to go on in the never-ending search for whatever possibilities I still have, un-realized, in my being. And when the painful crises of life ar-rive at regular intervals, this is the place where I try to get my head together and search out the ways in which I can bring whatever resources I have to bear on my problems. There are no rewards, there is no expectation of a symptom-free unneurotic life—just the promise of growing, if I can bring whatever courage and creativity I may have to the task. In this sense I see therapy not as a crutch but as a prodding to keep growing. I think this attitude is exemplified beautifully by the patient who called his therapist for an appointment after almost a year's absence, and said, "I need to give myself some advice, but I have a poor connection!"

In spite of my personal commitment to psychotherapy, as a profound and meaningful avenue to greater self-realization, I understand very well why so many people feel disillusioned with this procedure. Especially those of us who are middle-aged and who have been, in a sense, victimized by the fact that this field has been in its infancy during our lifetime. There have been very good reasons, indeed, for being turned off by many of the theories and practices we have been wit-ness to either directly or indirectly. Any new art-science has to go through all kinds of birthpangs and growing pains, and in a very real sense those who are willing to try something new may often feel like guinea pigs. But in making a decision in middle age about what to do with the burdens we carry, it seems to me we have to take a new look and examine the ways in which psychotherapy has struggled to improve its philosophy and methods.

I can feel a deep compassion for those who feel that psy-chotherapy is destructive at worst and useless at best. Part of the reason for such feelings is that so many of us expected too much, too soon. When I began reading the works of Freud and his followers, it seemed to me that *the* answer to all human suffering had been discovered! There were such magnificent new insights in this psychological revolution that, for a while, we lost our sense of perspective. Instead of realizing that we were learning just the first faint, stumbling beginnings of a whole new world of fascinating new understandings, we tended to make a new orthodoxy, a new religion out of psychoanalysis.

Freud was certainly one of the greatest geniuses of all time; his insights into man's nature have forever changed the face of the earth. But he would be the first to insist that the greatest testament to his pioneering will be the changes and modifications, the refinement and broadening of our understanding as we go along. But both laymen and professionals were too drunk with new power to understand or acknowledge how very primitive and experimental the early gropings toward new insights had to be. Our naïveté thirty years ago is only matched by those who now think encounter groups are *the* answer! There is no such thing, only marvelous new ideas, new leads, new worlds to explore continually. But any new field tends in its infancy to fall in love with its earliest observations and take them too seriously. That is why we all know so many people who were badly burned by their experiences with psychoanalysis and all the splinter forms it took in the years of our feeling our way toward new insights. We were dealing with a tool that would become more and more remarkable and beneficial, but the beginnings were full of traps.

The first and foremost trap was really inevitable. The concept of the unconscious as a force which moved us was so dramatic and overwhelming that at first it seemed that patients had no control over their own destiny, but were just the passive victims of unconscious drives. Freud and his followers were working with a population that none of us can really even imagine, because their work put an end to such kinds of problems! These were rigid, repressed Victorians, who believed that some people were good and some were bad, and if there were bad thoughts or feelings in *their* unconsciouses, they sure didn't know about it! Most of the early research dealt with people who were emotionally and often physically paralyzed because of repressed sexual wishes, or had phobias because they couldn't recognize their hostile feelings, or were enslaved by compulsions as a way of keeping their normal human terrors at bay. The large majority of the earliest patients studied came under this category of "conversion hysterias." However, if a psychiatrist comes across a conversion hysteric today, he calls up all his colleagues to tell them about this great find, for the revolution which discovered them also cured them!

The result of seeing this kind of population was that in the early days psychiatrists treated patients as if they had no free will, but were merely passive victims. A typical response on the part of a patient caught in this web was, "When *I* do something, it always has some deep meaning—but what about when my analyst does something? How come he's not under the same rules?" A very good question, and one that has led to a great deal of investigation.

It is easy to see how resentment against the therapist would build up when he or she was free to choose, to take action, to have opinions, but the patient was not. Typical of this feeling of being trapped was the secretary who quit working for an analyst, saying, "Whatever I did, I was sick. If I came early I was overanxious, if I came late, I was hostile—and if I came on time I was compulsive."

We have since learned that while everyone is sometimes influenced by forces he does not consciously understand, we all are basically responsible for our actions and can take control of our lives. For those who feel that therapy is "just lying there," being told why you did what you did, without there being any expectation of your taking action or behaving in terms of some meaningful values—let me assure you, good therapy isn't like that anymore.

In the early years, the patient was instructed to leave reality outside the office door; whatever was happening to him right now was irrelevant, the problem was to clear away the debris of childhood misunderstandings, fears, and confusions. Typical of this attitude was the patient who called a social worker at a referral service to ask where she could get advice; her husband was seeing an analyst, but had just received a salary cut and could not continue to pay his regular fee. The social worker said, "But he's *seeing* his therapist, why doesn't he discuss it with *him?*" The wife answered, "He says he can't because that's a reality problem." This approach is also disappearing. One therapist, who many years ago was in the advance guard of change, shocked many of his patients who had been in psychoanalytic therapy before coming to him, by saying, "Now before we get started, let's face the reality problem of where you are going to park your car!" It is certainly no longer necessary to think of therapy as some kind of isolated island, far from the mainstream of life. Quite the contrary, there tends to be so *much* concentration on the here-and-now that sometimes one wonders if there is enough attention being given to how we got where we are!

A major source of disenchantment with analysis was the fact that creative, artistic people began to be afraid of it— with good reason. In the early years, all kinds of deviations from the norm were viewed with a jaundiced eye and seen as "sick." I think it is a fair judgment to say that a lot of marvelous, talented people, who ought to have been helped to have the courage to beat out their own special music, were seriously harmed by a therapy that was preoccupied with early childhood trauma and some mythical "healthy norm" of behavior. But there are therapists available today who are excited by deviation, by specialness, when it represents a unique creative energy and intelligence, and see their role as enhancing what needs to come to life most fully. As one therapist put it, "There is nothing wrong—only something wonderful about being a little crazy. But it depends what kind of craziness; if it sits in your throat and chokes you to death, it's not good, but if it hits you in the back of the neck and drives you like an outboard motor to fulfill all you have in you, then it's good!"

A basic difference in the orientation of psychotherapy now was expressed by the patient who went to a new therapist after three years of orthodox psychoanalysis. She said, "I guess we have to start out all over again to find out what's wrong with me." The therapist replied, "I'm even more interested in what is right with you."

The relationship with the therapist has been the source of the deepest disappointment and dismay for many people. In the early years of research it seemed to make sense for the therapist to remain hidden, neutral, distant. The first patients were so repressed, so ashamed of the feelings that began to emerge, that they probably needed to be lying down, not facing anyone. It was also easier for the therapist, who was not at all sure of what he ought to do, since no one had ever before done what he was doing. With so much focus on early childhood, it also seemed useful for the therapist to remain relatively unknown as a person, so that the patient could transfer old feelings onto him—reflect feelings that were associated with parents, siblings, etc. To a large degree, this has changed; it is certainly possible to find a therapist who faces you as another human being, who expresses opinions, who expects you to decide for yourself how you feel about working with him.

One of the worst features of the earlier years was that patients felt that if they couldn't stand the analyst or the treatment, it was their "resistance," not anything in the situation. Many of us know people who stayed with an analyst for years, not liking him, feeling they were getting nothing from it, but absolutely convinced that these feelings were an indication of just how sick they were! This has changed almost completely. The mystique of therapy is disappearing as it becomes a familiar and relatively ordinary aspect of life. A characteristic comment of a patient seeing the light was the one who went to a new therapist after seven years of analysis and said, "One day, on the way to my analyst's office, I suddenly had an impulse to stop at a newsstand and pick up a magazine to read during my fifty minutes on the couch. It finally dawned on me that I was crazier for staying than I'd been for starting!"

A frequent complaint from patients has been the fact that they never felt they really knew what kind of person the therapist was: his philosophy of life, his politics, his personal feelings even about the patient. This again was something that seemed appropriate in the early years, as researchers tried to assess the effect of the therapist on the patient; but we have come a long way from there, and it is now possible to find a therapist who is spontaneous, open about his feelings, and not at all hesitant to share his ideas with his patients.

During the early years there was a kind of aura of black magic about psychoanalysis: it was mysterious, it was the promise of happiness, it could cure you of any psychic discomfort. When of course it turned out to be a remarkable but clumsy new tool, people who had been too enthusiastic turned violently against it. There were enough bad experiences going around to confirm the suspicions, the hostility of many. One of the factors which has led to a rejection of therapy, in whatever form, has been the reports by researchers that in "careful scientific studies" it has been "proven" that therapy doesn't really do any good at all; that people with the same problems who don't have therapy get better just as frequently, in the course of four or five years.

This kind of research is meaningless. Scientific methodology that may be appropriate to physics or chemistry is simply not applicable to the complex factors which influence human behavior. Psychotherapy is at least as much art as it is science, and it seems to me quite impossible to design objective standards for evaluating how a person feels about himself. But there is certainly clear subjective evidence that people have found therapy a helpful way *to learn to face the problems of life more effectively*. If one makes that the goal, there is no question it "works." The problem has been that we often started out with unrealistic goals, because of our expectations that this new field was going to make everything perfect. Psychotherapy is a drama, a struggle to be more alive —and to me that is a creative, a religious experience in the deepest sense, and only the individual can make a meaningful judgment of its value. Of course it will be a subjective reaction. How could it be otherwise? I find ludicrous the comment of one scientist who said, "A lot of people *think* they get better, but it's just self-delusion." What nonsense! Who is to decide how one is growing—except oneself?

I brought unrealistic expectations to my early experiences with therapy; I came to it with very specific problems, symptoms, that I wanted removed. But I learned over the years that while it was true that therapy could help to relieve, even "cure" some kinds of problems, that wasn't really what it was all about. What could happen was that you became more sensitive, more compassionate, more insightful, so that you could bring greater strength and courage to all the new problems that kept cropping up!

It was a great shock to me one day when someone asked me what I'd got out of the first seven years of therapy, and without thinking, I heard myself answering, "I got to like the opera and I developed a green thumb!" I can assure you the problems I'd started out with were far more clinical and serious than *that!* But when I began to think about it, I realized that sometimes what we blurt out in humor touches a deeper wisdom. For me, learning to enjoy the opera was getting decerebrated; learning to allow myself to respond to sensations of color and sound and movement, without having to intellectualize every experience. And the green thumb had to do with the fact that I began to love growing things, to want to spend time, quietly, just appreciating the wonders, the miracles of nature. Both represented something of a profound change in my very being.

I mentioned earlier that, for me, growing is like a lobster, regularly risking awful dangers to shed its shell and move into a bigger life-space. The risk and dangers seem very great, and since all of us are weak as well as strong, terrified as well as courageous, neurotically trapped as well as healthfully hungry for growing, I find it easier to live with these ambivalences if I have someone to help me during the times when I am relinquishing a shell that has become too small and cramped for me. But I don't underestimate for one moment how important it is to have the right partner to help me on my way. I was very choosy about the therapists I selected, and it seems to me that if one thinks this might be an avenue of help, one must be just as discriminating and careful about the choice as one is about choosing a pediatrician or a lawyer. In the early years of psychoanalysis, the idea of the patient as sick and passive often interfered with feeling that one's personal feelings and judgments were valid and important. This was a very serious error.

Looking back, I think I was looking for a therapist who was familiar with all the various schools of psychiatric thought, had experienced an eclectic psychotherapy himself, and was therefore in touch with himself and able to respond to others, and had selected what he felt were the most sound and helpful practices and philosophy. It seems to me that anyone who is going to practice such an inexact art ought to have a very considerable background in information and experience, ought to know with comfortable familiarity all the different schools of thought, the history and development of the field, have a background knowledge of what has been tried, what has been accomplished, what has failed. Then beyond that, a practitioner must have developed a philosophy of life that he can be articulate about, so that the would-be patient can see how this relates to his own ideas. And beyond having a good educational and therapeutic background, some years of experience, and a reasonably well-formed philosophy, what I would look for most of all, if I were searching for a therapist right now, would be someone who can say, "I don't know," someone who makes no promises, offers no panaceas, but rather, says in effect, "All I can offer you is my companionship in an adventure. Neither of us knows where it will take us—but I think I can help you find your way." I liked, for example, the comment of one psychologist, who responded to my question about her background by saying, "I have studied Freud and Jung and Adler and just about everyone who has followed since, and then I made up my mind which pieces made sense to me, and now I am a person who does it her own way!" Or the comment of a psychiatric social worker who, when asked what philosophy she believed in, said, "How can I give you an answer to that, until I see the *patient?*" I chose therapists who took the attitude that there were rich treasures to be mined in the ideas of all the masters who have emerged, and that one can take those parts of each philosophy that seem to make the most sense to oneself, and about which one feels comfortable and which one can use with ease. I would not be very trustful of a therapist who wasn't well grounded in the whole development of this field of mental health, but after that, one has to begin to select what fits in with one's own life-style and emerging philosophy.

When I began to look for a therapist, the first criteria was, "Do I like this person? Does he make me feel comfortable, hopeful, at ease?" I could never have chosen anyone who didn't have a good sense of humor. And I don't think that's too bad a criterion for anyone to use, for humor is almost always a sign of warmth, humility, and humanity and an awareness of human fallibility.

It takes time, effort, and expense to find the right person. I hated the first three therapists I went to see; one was a haughty, distant man who behaved as if I were boring him beyond endurance. He had written a book I greatly admired, and my disappointment at finding his humanity more literary than actual was very great. He referred me to a woman therapist who looked like the "Wicked Witch of the North." I wasn't sick enough to suit her, and she said she would "have to get a Rorschach" on me before she could tell what was really the matter with me, since I wasn't telling her the truth. The third therapist I tried wanted me to lie down on the couch the first time I came to see him, with my back to him. I figured we ought to at least face each other for the preliminaries; talking to the wall in a stranger's office didn't exactly thrill me.

The fourth therapist was a friend of a friend. I knew nothing about her except that my friend said, "She's just an adorable woman." She was. She spoke with a French accent, she was soft and round and very feminine, she clicked and clucked over me like a mother hen. Her office was full of books and paintings—she was a "Sunday artist" herself, and one of the most cultured and well-educated women I had ever met. My "homework assignment" during the first weeks was to reread Dante's *Inferno* and some Edna St. Vincent Millay! I remember that after our first session, I ran to a corner telephone in exhilaration and joy, to call my husband, and said, "I think she really *likes* me!"

That is the heart of the matter: you have to find a therapist who makes you feel you are a wonderful person, worthy of love. Sooner or later you are likely to go through a variety of periods of personal hell, in this process of self-exploration, and you need a companion who really cares.

In any discussion with lay people who are seeking some form of psychotherapy, one question almost always arises: How do you decide if you should go to a social worker, psychologist, psychiatrist, lay analyst, or one of the various other kinds of specialized counselors? Only the psychiatrist and psychoanalyst need be medical doctors; beyond that, any or all categories (including medical doctors!) may or may not have had a good grounding in all that is known to date about mental health issues and treatment procedures. Schools of social work tend to emphasize social concerns to some extent; psychological training tends to involve more emphasis on testing and statistical research; each of these professions can be prepared for within the framework of a particular school of thinking. My own experience over the past twenty-five or thirty years is that there simply are no rules. There are great artists in all categories, and about the same ratio of dullards and idiots in all of the categories. The crucial factor seems to be what the individual brings, within himself, to the experience, the training, the insights he acquires. I have never seen any useful correlation whatsoever between successful therapy and the particular background training and present professional category of a therapist; there is *every* correlation between successful psychotherapy and the quality of the human being, the wisdom, sensitivity, compassion, and honesty of the therapist.

Money is sometimes an accurate key to a therapist's philosophy. I know one psychiatrist who charges his rich patients $75 a session, so that he can take some patients whom he charges nothing at all. I like that philosophy. I think that a sliding scale of fees is, in general, a fairly good barometer of a man's point of view. It seems to me that if you spend ten years of your life getting the training to help people with their problems, you really ought to be the kind of person who cares so much about human suffering that making a lot of money cannot be the central goal of your life. If it is, become a stockbroker, I say. If a therapist says, "I have a flat fee of $35 an hour, no exceptions," I would run, not walk, to the nearest door (paying the $35 as I depart!). Or a therapist may say, "I have to charge a minimum of $25 a session, in order to just cover my expenses and support my family, reasonably well. However, if you can only afford to pay $20 right now, maybe we can work out a system of delayed payments, so that you can manage over the long haul." I know of one therapist who tells his patients that he charges a lot, but they shouldn't worry about that—his patients all "get so healthy" that they will end up making a lot of money! He has a very full practice in this materialistic society. I just hope I never meet him.

Clinics have become so expensive that it seems almost foolish to suggest this resource as an alternative to a private therapist. However, there is usually some difference in cost, and in some communities a clinic or hospital outpatient facility may offer the best professional resources. Here too, choice is important. Although one is given a specific counselor, and it is usually assumed by both patient and agency that this is an irrevocable arrangement, it is nothing of the sort. Any good agency recognizes the importance of "mutual chemistry" in the therapeutic relationship, and the client has every right to object if he feels he cannot work with the person he is assigned to.

Each therapist has his own way of relating the past to the present, of dream interpretation, of the degree to which he gives his own opinions, how direct or indirect he is in responding. I suppose it's like choosing a marriage partner; if it starts with the right chemistry then these individual differences don't matter too much. Having had four therapists up to now, I find that my dreams adapted themselves to each of their ways of interpreting them, and in each case, it was helpful. The particular school of thought was far less important than the human being who was using specific procedures or interpretations.

"Why four therapists?" I can hear readers asking. Well, in the first place, as I have already said, I see therapy as a way of life, a way of growing and changing—and if you change a lot, you may outgrow a therapist. Sometimes you feel you have moved beyond their ability to help you further; or you realize they are beginning to stereotype their view of you, and you feel cramped; or, as in my case, you may give a good therapist over to a spouse and need a new one for yourself! We have had a somewhat incestuous experience in our family, with all three of us seeing and/or knowing very well each other's therapists, and that seems quite appropriate to me in the sense in which we all use therapy, from time to time. *It is talking with someone who can help you take a better look at where you are and where you are going.*

How do I decide when to stop and when to start again? By now it is almost second nature to try to keep in touch with myself so that I know if I am ready for a plateau—if I have reached a place I want to be for the time being. For awhile I seem to be functioning pretty well, working hard, feeling no special pain or problems with those around me; then gradually I begin to realize that I'm getting depressed; I eat too much; I find myself getting angry at my husband about old wounds I thought had healed. I usually develop a writing block—and then I'm really in trouble, then I'm scared. I know it is a symptom of becoming less alive and at home in myself. Maybe within a day or week, I have some dreams, or something occurs to me while I'm walking across the park or washing the dishes—a sudden flash of awareness that gives me a good clue to what it's all about. In a day or two I feel good again and I'm back at work, feeling creative and optimistic. I have grown enough to have worked that out by myself.

But sometimes it doesn't work. I find myself feeling depressed and anxious. I begin despising myself. Then it's time for a refresher with my therapist, and it may last three weeks, or it may mean that I am back in regular therapy for three years, if what I'm ready to wrestle with is something important.

The decision to return to therapy can also come for causes external to myself: difficulties with or about the people I am close to, relationships in working, or problems in my writing.

Another factor in my decision often has to do with physical well-being. One of the serious mistakes made by many of the middle-aged and elderly is that physical disabilities are always or even most often a reflection of aging. While no one in his right mind could deny the good sense of regular medical checkups, preventive programs for good health, the necessary care and attention given to illnesses, it still remains true that most of our difficulties are, at least to some degree, psychosomatic—and that "psycho" part often gets lost in the shuffle.

If you get a pain in your stomach at twenty, it seems so inappropriate—you are so young and healthy—that the possibility of its being an ulcer derived largely from tension seems plausible. How could there be any other reason, when you're so young? If you get the same pain at forty-five— well, you're just getting old, what's the use? There are more middle-aged being treated in internists' offices than there should be; a great many of those with "diseases of aging" really belong in some psychologically therapeutic milieu instead, whether it be group therapy, individual psychotherapy, or growth-center seminars and workshops. Most internists would agree. All medical symptoms ought to be investigated medically, of course, but what we need to remember is that even in middle age most of our somatic complaints come just as frequently from the problems of our psyche. It is too easy for the middle-aged to assume they must simply endure their new infirmities. What is likely is that as the body becomes less resilient, the psychological tensions of our lives affect us more dramatically; but the source is still the same—the feelings and frustrations that generate in the brain. The number of middle-aged physical disabilities that have been cured by some good psychotherapy, a 'round-the-world tour or a remarriage of the widowed, are legion! Having observed this more closely than most (because of my husband's research in the field of psychosomatic medicine), I have made myself a firm pledge: as I get older, and as there may be increasing symptoms of organic deterioration, I am never going to assume that the only recourse open to me is my friendly neighborhood internist. I am always going to assume that there is no meaningful or useful separation of psyche and soma, and that the cure or the improvement must always be approached as one totality. The interplay and interdependency between feelings and physical symptoms seems to me to be so valid and so important that I cannot imagine trying to understand or treat one without the other, including the common cold!

A final reason for my own pursuit of psychotherapy is that all of my professional life has involved trying to help other people with their problems, and I have learned more about the human condition from this experience than I could have learned from attaining ten Ph.D.s.

All kinds of crises come into all our lives: the illness or death of a parent, the unemployment of a spouse, the school problems of a child. Sometimes we can get in touch with our inner resources in such a way that we can work toward some resolution of our difficulties without a therapist. Often there are other people who come to our aid. A favorite aunt, a childhood friend, a minister or rabbi. There are so many therapeutic relationships in our lives. I recall, especially, two or three of those wonderfully gifted teachers who were able to help us see our child through their eyes and, because of that, set off a real spurt in our growth and sensitivity. Part of growing, in or out of a therapist's office, seems to be one's ability to listen to others without feeling threatened. What they say may be wrong—and we don't have to take the advice—but they may have a different way of looking at something that can give us just the clue we need, just the perspective we have not been able to attain.

Of course not all fears of therapy come from the outside

(what one has heard or seen). Far more important are the inside fears. A characteristic response was that of the man who said (when someone told him he needed psychotherapy), "Not on your life—I couldn't look at all that ugliness!" The very nature of a neurosis is often its tenacious hold on us *not* to change. The unconscious is primitive and powerful, and there is always a struggle, a battle between the forces of being most alive and most unalive. The strength of the wish not to examine one's feelings and fantasies and childlike perceptions was brought home to me clearly when I watched a friend in the throes of a truly agonizing anxiety attack. When I later suggested it was time to get help, she said, "I'm used to the way I am."

Too often our inner terrors keep us from taking care of our lives; we don't love ourselves enough to insist on fighting for greater fulfillment. We need to try to nurture our lives and assert our right to be the most we can be. It *will* be painful, there *will* be times of great anxiety and anger and suffering, but none of it comes anywhere near the horrors of unliving.

It is hard to explain what a therapist can mean in one's life; all the intellectual and academic words still miss the background music. A therapist once showed me the following letter which says, I think, all that one can say about what the experience ought to be:

> Why My Therapist Deserves a Vacation, or
> Why I Love Her, Even Though She's Leaving Me
> Alone and Stranded for Four Weeks
>
> Because she usually has her feet off the ground, allowing herself to progress to that higher intuitive level, enabling her to understand me nine-tenths of the time—sometimes even before I finish a sentence.
> Because she has a marvelously expressive face enticing me to continue relating to it.
> Because she has a rare spontaneous humor, enabling her to

laugh with me and cheer me up even when I'd rather feel depressed.

Because she understands my poems and cries when they touch her.

Because she seems to have no conception of what is normal.

Because she has never failed to answer any of my questions except directly, honestly and after careful consideration.

Because she's smarter than I am and doesn't allow me to trap her into illogical and untenable positions.

Because she occasionally comes up with an insight so brilliant and intuitive that I want to fly out of the office (and incidentally wonder why I hadn't thought of it myself).

Because she releases inspiration and at times even lets me see and share her suffering.

Because she gives me extra hours when I ask for them.

Because she never fails to enter her own experiential self when she feels it might help.

Because she waits for my Blue Shield check to come.

Because she's always real (sometimes even nervous and confused).

Because she has a rare capacity for empathy.

Because she works damn hard!

Because she has made a successful appeal to the freedom of this patient.

Because I want her to have a great time, and I wish she were back already.*

I can speak with more authority about individual therapy because that is what I am most familiar with. Today the choices are greater than they have ever been before for a wide variety of individual and group experiences. Family therapy is one of the newer approaches which seems to hold promise of being very useful, in which a whole family sits down together, as "the group," with a therapist, and begins to confront the ways in which they relate to each other. The most widespread of the newer approaches is the encounter

* By Diane Levenberg, and printed with her permission.

group, and I confess that my knowledge is limited to hearsay and observation, not to direct participation. I have heard reports that have horrified me, and I have also heard wonderful things about this approach from people I admire and respect greatly.

The range of possible experiences is as great in group therapy as in individual therapy, and one must be just as cautious and selective about the group leader and the philosophy he represents. In evaluating encounter groups one is handicapped by the very same problem that existed in the early days of psychoanalysis: the encounter group movement is in *its* infancy and has just as many "bugs" to work out, has the same orthodoxy and religiosity of its advocates that made progress difficult and disillusion frequent in those earlier times. An additional problem with the encounter group movement is that in general there has been far less care, far fewer precautions, about who can call himself a trained leader. The range is from someone who has been an excellent therapist, both individual and group, for thirty years, to someone who can call himself a group leader after going through one or two encounter group experiences himself. There are growth centers in many parts of the country where teachers, lawyers, students, salesmen, and housewives are leading groups after a personal "transformation" that may have involved participation in only one kind of group, who have no additional educational or professional background in psychiatry, psychology, or psychotherapy.

There is little question in my mind that many of the requirements for calling oneself a professional therapist have had little or nothing to do with the human skills and artistry that are really essential to the task. On the other hand, it seems to me that unless one has a broad background in understanding the possibilities and problems that may arise in a therapeutic relationship, one is likely to do far more damage than good. One group leader, for example, tells the group when they first meet that he is not responsible for anything that happens; if someone in the group "wants to go crazy," that's his responsibility! This is the exact antithesis of the early psychoanalytic notion that the patient was not able to decide anything for himself. This new extreme, in which a therapist does not take responsibility for knowing more than the patient and using his special skills for guidance, is just as dangerous and destructive.

Just as in individual therapy, so too in group therapy, one has to shop around. The most important thing is to feel free to leave a group in which one feels uncomfortable, and sometimes that is more difficult in a group than when seeing an individual therapist for one session. Now it is the group, rather than the therapist, who may make one feel that one's resistances are a form of disease, not a healthy distaste for something that just isn't right for a particular individual. Instead of the learned doctor, looking wise and saying, "We must examine why you do not like me in the light of your defenses against facing your sexual fantasies," we have instead, far too often (because we should have learned better from the first experience), a whole group of people who pounce on the nonbeliever, the one who wants to leave, with, "Face it! Face it! Show us your anger, show us your self-contempt— don't be afraid!" In the first instance we found out that sexual hang-ups often had nothing whatever to do with disliking a man who always was sure he knew what was healthy and unhealthy, and in the second instance, it is equally possible that the only feeling one might want to express to a group before leaving is that they are silly, boring, overzealous bigots, who like only people who are angry!

But often a subtle coercion does exist, and makes some people very uncomfortable. You enter a ballroom at one of the professional conventions of encounter-type people, and you really don't think you want to start touching people you never laid eyes on before, or you don't feel like telling five hundred strangers what your fantasy was in being instructed to think about a magic forest. Too often you feel you are being looked on with pity, as a soul who can't be saved, as you make your trembling, barefooted way over a sea of bodies, and stagger to the hotel bar. There is no reason to assume that the things that bug you about some encounter groups are any indication that you are sick. Twenty years from now, looking back, we will undoubtedly see that a lot of the resistances to some of the excesses now indulged in, were very sound judgments indeed. "I was just in an encounter group," a colleague reports, "where they were all concerned about helping us become 'more truly human.' That is, a tape recorder was telling us how to be more human. I'm not about to take such instructions from a machine, and if that makes me resistant, well at least I don't run on batteries."

But just because one ought to be critical in evaluating encounter groups, this doesn't mean make snap judgments or decide ahead of time that it's going to be awful. It takes a little time to get an accurate impression. In a group, the first day or two may be awkward and uncomfortable for everyone; there needs to be a kind of shakedown period as the group finds its own special character and begins to gel. We need to give it a chance; some of the best group experiences people have ever had started off terribly.

Typical of this was the young black woman who was horrified by the instruction to close her eyes and move around a room, touching and hugging anyone she came in contact with. But she was too embarrassed to leave, so she started following the directions. Her immediate thought was, "If those people had their eyes open and saw I was black, they wouldn't be so loving." Then she found herself wondering if this were true—and suddenly she felt flooded by *her* defenses, *her* anger against white people. "For a few moments, in that common darkness, I faced my longing for unconditional acceptance, my hunger for human intimacy, with no barriers," she reported. "It didn't make me over or change my life, but I will never forget how good it was, and I will never quite settle for what is."

One of the serious drawbacks to psychoanalysis was the original idea that for therapy to have any real significance, it had to take at least five years of working at it five days a week. One of the serious drawbacks to some of the new encounter groups is the notion that major changes in one's nature and one's life can take place in a day or a week—or even in an hour. Both extremes are equally foolish. I recall coming home on a train from an educational conference with a colleague who was in a state of ecstasy, because in an encounter group she had run the evening before, one young woman, who had never had any therapy at all, had "faced the terrible feelings she had about her father's suicide." The implication in this report was clear; the young woman might be pretty shook-up for some time, she might even need further help, but "the worst was over." As a tired old veteran of the pioneering days of psychoanalysis, all I could think was, "Here we go again." In those days "insight" was the magic word; all you had to do was understand your unconscious feelings and you could leave your neuroses behind you. It has taken fifty years to see how simplistic and untrue this was; life just isn't that well ordered. Now here we go again: instant self-revelation to others is the new magic cure. It won't fare any better.

But just as there was much that was truly helpful, even in the stumbling, confusing early days of psychoanalysis, there is a great deal that is sound and extremely promising in the field of encounter psychotherapy. No one who has ever spent any time at all among its advocates and participants can doubt the decency and sincerity of most of the people who are involved in this new field. And it is not maudlin or inaccurate to say that one does experience a sense of great warmth and love in this environment. The best thing that has thus far emerged from this kind of therapeutic approach is the very real attempt to help people care deeply about each other, to feel compassion for others and for themselves. When a group becomes a loving focus on oneself, when the search for self-understanding and self-acceptance is real, wonderful things can begin to happen.

A widow, married for forty years, was unable to stop mourning. She felt that her life was over, that nothing could ever again have meaning for her. After a great amount of urging and encouragement, she went with a friend to a two-week encounter group. It happened to be an exceptionally fine group of people, with an experienced and sensitive leader, who were able to help her relinquish the past and begin to think about herself, her present and future. Her report was: "I was never so frightened in my life—but my depression, my despair was so great that I knew I could not go on as I was. In all my life I have never felt so loved by others, I never felt more *safe to feel*. It changed my life completely." It is surely possible to get new strength, new perspective, to gain the courage to move forward in an intense sharing with other people. But it is only the beginning of new growing, as in any other kind of experience. If one sees it in such terms, it can be an enormous thrust forward.

On the other hand, another widow in another group, a shy, reticent woman still in the throes of grief, who was catapulted into something she was not at all ready for: "At the very first session the leader made us do exercises in touching each other. I have never been so embarrassed in my life. I *loved* touching my husband and my children, but touching strangers made me terribly uncomfortable. And when I just could not do it, they made me feel that it was a sign of some deep defensiveness and fear of people. It was some time before I began to realize that they have a right to their attitudes and I have an equal right to mine—but at first they made me feel I was a sick, silly old woman. I went home after the second session, more miserable than ever."

Some of the new group techniques for self-examination and

self-strengthening are fascinating and productive. Many of them help to redress a balance; by focusing on feelings, on body awareness, on sensory experiences, they are attempting to help us get back to a healthy "wholeness of being" that many of us lost in childhood. Most of us were raised to think, not to feel, to become disconnected between our brain and our body. In some ways the earlier approaches in psychotherapy have encouraged a verbal, intellectual experiencing without concern for one's physical well-being, and it seems to me to be a promising and sound idea that we find so much new interest in reconnecting the body to the mind. But new excesses also occur as we search for a better balance. One of the strongest advocates, a pioneer in the encounter movement, the late Dr. Abraham Maslow, observed: "I think some of them [encounter groups] hover on the edge of antiscience and even antirational feelings in their enthusiasm for 'experiencing.' . . . I believe that experiencing is only the beginning of knowledge (necessary but not sufficient)."

In pursuing the possibility of having a meaningful experience with a group, it might be helpful to get a list of the Growth Centers now spreading all over the country, and this can be obtained from the Association for Humanistic Psychology, 416 Hoffman Street, San Francisco, California 94114. On the whole, this list represents responsible professional groups, but it is still absolutely essential to bring all of one's own critical judgments to evaluating a particular experience in a group. In addition, I heartily recommend reading a clear, precise, beautiful book, *Carl Rogers on Encounter Groups.**

Aside from the question of a specific type of therapy, it seems to me that there is a general philosophy, a point of view about the nature of man that can be very helpful and meaningful to us middle-aged. My own introduction to it came through the man to whom this book is dedicated, the

* New York: Harper & Row, 1970.

late Dr. Abraham Maslow, formerly head of the Psychology Department at Brandeis University.

In his research and writings, Dr. Maslow came to feel that two earlier views about the psychological nature of human beings left much to be desired. The first view, which appeared in the early 1900s when psychology was being born, was called Behaviorism, and was represented most generally by the writings of John B. Watson. In essence, this point of view suggests that one can use scientific methods previously only applied to chemistry, astronomy, and physics to study man; that man is basically nothing more than a very complex machine; that he can be conditioned to behave in predictable ways. For a while (especially during the heyday of psychoanalysis) Behaviorism went into disfavor among most psychologists, but our technological age, our tendency to worship "pure science" as the only path to salvation has given it new life. Today it is represented most by the work of Dr. B. F. Skinner at Harvard. Skinner contends that if man were a little less arrogant he might survive, might even become as well adapted to his environment as the rat or the pigeon. He believes that all our troubles stem from the notion of man being more than a bundle of responses to the environment. He denies the existence of ego, personality, spirit, character, or soul—of Autonomous Man, having free will and deriving inalienable rights therefrom. I find this approach to the human experience without merit; it leaves out too much, it dehumanizes, it oversimplifies. But most of all, I simply cannot personally endure a mechanistic view of human beings, and that is precisely what it is.

In the second view of man, psychoanalysis, which began to emerge over the same period of time, there was an attempt to look more deeply and to find the qualities of life more profound and mysterious. But there has been all along an intense preoccupation with pathology, with a view of man as a passive victim of his unconscious drives. I recall a time when,

while working in a child-guidance clinic, one was considered
a real jerk if one ever described someone as "courageous" or
"honest" or "compassionate." Psychiatry did not concern itself
with such foolish concepts; what was important was "fixa-
tions, regressions, compulsions, anxieties, fantasies, and repres-
sions." Slowly but surely a great many people, including Dr.
Maslow, began to have to reckon with something that had
been far too little discussed by psychoanalysis, and that was
the evidence all of us see, constantly, of bravery, kindness,
selflessness, and creativity among people.

Dr. Maslow found himself as fascinated by people who
seemed psychologically healthier than anyone else as Freud
had been by people who were sicker than anyone else! He
observed that people who seemed most fulfilled, who expressed the greatest capacity for creative and love-filled lives,
who seemed to be able to meet adversity with most courage
and ingenuity, were people whom he called "self-actualized,"
and by that he meant people who had been able to search out
what was unique and true about themselves and were using
their potentialities in ways that had great meaning for them.
They were also people who were involved in a cause outside
themselves, working at something that was very precious to
them and to which they were singularly devoted. They were
all people in vigorous search of ultimate values. They were
fully experiencing—vividly and consciously—their own
inner selves.

In his book *Toward a Psychology of Being*,* Maslow
writes:

> Every age but ours has had its model, its ideal. All these have
> been given up by our culture: the saint, the hero, the gentle-
> man, the knight, the mystic. About all we have left is the
> well-adjusted man without problems, a very pale and doubtful
> substitute. Perhaps we shall soon be able to use as our guide

* New York: Van Nostrand and Co., 1962.

and model the fully growing and self-fulfilling human being, the one in whom all his potentialities are coming to full development, the one whose inner nature expresses itself freely, rather than being warped, suppressed or denied.

Rather than focusing on what made people emotionally sick, Dr. Maslow wanted to discover what was involved in making a person most whole, most alive, most at home in himself and in the world. In a book published posthumously, *The Farther Reaches of Human Nature,** he says:

> All the evidence that we have . . . indicates that it is reasonable to assume in practically every human being, and certainly in almost every newborn baby, that there is an active will toward health, an impulse toward growth or toward the actualization of human potentialities. But at once we are confronted with the very saddening realization that so few people make it. Only a small proportion of the human population gets to the point of identity, or of selfhood, full humanness. . . . This is our great paradox. We have the impulse toward full development of humanness. Then why doesn't it happen more often? What blocks it?

I highly recommend that all middle-aged who want to be more in touch with their own "impulse toward full development" read both of these books. The Association for Humanistic Psychology can also provide a reading list for those who wish to pursue this question further—and having found this philosophy so meaningful in my own life, I urge others to do likewise! It is the basis for the point of view expressed in this book. In addition to lifting our human burdens by sharing one's life and thoughts with others, by growing through one's work and one's love relationships, by seeking help through some form of therapy, I also believe that one can grow and change by reading and studying. I know of no current thinking in the field of psychology that can be more rewarding as

* New York: Viking Press, 1972.

we try to examine the nature and possibilities of being middle-aged.

The psychologies of the past, with their focus on passivity and pathology, really had little to offer the middle-aged. But a psychology that is full of hope and wonder at our still-to-be-discovered possibilities is just the shot in the arm we need! So much of the burden of our masks has had to do with feeling hopeless and helpless, unable to gain mastery over ourselves and our lives, that we retreat into a sterile and lonely inner isolation.

The central problem we are dealing with in lifting our masks is in being "real," in trying to find some balance between an infantile, dependent, self-pitying wallowing in the tragic part of life, and the equally destructive and unreasonable denial that we are fallible, that we hurt, that we experience the pain of uncertainty, fear, anger, and anxiety. I find myself equally appalled by people who see nothing but misery in life, and tell everybody all their troubles, as I am by the popularity of "smile" buttons, posters, stationery, T-shirts, etc. There is something quite awful about wearing an idiotic smile on the surface of oneself at a time when the whole world is in agony and utmost danger; it is a kind of ultimate escapism.

It seems to me that we find our way toward some balance only to the degree that we stop lying to ourselves; that is surely the first step. Once we begin to experience ourselves fully, in all our complexity, we are able to drop our masks at appropriate times and places. We are less likely to try to impress and please other people, to be always happy and lovable, to try to win applause for our efforts. If we focus on trying to be honest with ourselves, there is no audience, and we stop being actors—and this inevitably carries over into our relationships with other people.

In looking within, we really taste the reality of the truth that pain and joy are two sides of the same experience, and that the intensity of the one is the beginning of the intensity of the other. What I have discovered is that if you can experience yourself as fully as possible as much of the time as possible, you lift the mask at least to yourself, and that helps enormously. The burden becomes insupportable when you can't even reveal yourself to yourself.

CAN THERE BE
A RENAISSANCE
IN OUR
MIDDLE AGES?

*
*
*
*
*
*

Chapter 8

An old school friend—we'd known each other since we were six—was visiting me at the seashore. My next-door neighbor had been complaining to us over the fence about her baby, and my friend and I began to talk about our own experiences as young mothers. She has lived in California since getting married; I live in New York. Suddenly we looked at each other in astonishment and dismay; as close as we had always been, neither of us had ever seen the other with a baby or a small child. We both felt a sense of shock and grief; one of the most important phases of our lives had passed without being shared at all. "That's what it's like to be young," she said, "to be so sure there is always time that you never stop in your tracks and realize what you have now will pass. We just never believed that part of our lives would end, so we felt no compulsion to try to see each other."

It is also true that we were too busy with mothering young children to travel three thousand miles, and we also could not have afforded it then. But that wasn't the point; the point was *it had never occurred to us that time was important.*

If there is one single thing we really have going for us in middle age, it is a more accurate and sensitive awareness of time. And if we don't get ourselves too caught up in nostalgia for what is past, we can use this more acute perception to excellent advantage.

The trouble is that nostalgia and grieving seem almost inevitably to accompany the new sensitivity to time passing, at least at first. I was sitting on the terrace of an apartment with another old childhood friend one summer day. The sun was shining, but despite having been sun-worshipers most of our lives, both of us were sitting in the shade. I can remember so clearly when this friend was fifteen or sixteen. She was one of those statuesque, golden girls—tennis player, swimmer, horseback rider—a wealthy girl with a gorgeous glow cultivated by spending at least four months of the year in the sunshine. She was remembering too, "Oh, Eda, remember how I could lie in the sun all day long, and what a gorgeous color I was? I don't think *anybody* ever loved sitting in the sun as much as I did." I had noticed some increased sensitivity to the sun myself in recent years, but for her it was really forbidden; she had had cancer of the skin. "God, *everything* is downhill from now on," she muttered miserably.

And then there was the letter from my cousin, a sane and sensible lady, mother of three, who had created a rich full working life for herself as her three children had got ready to leave the nest, who had carefully nurtured a happy marriage, and who expected there to be no wrench at all when the last one left for college—which said: "Just got back from taking Betsy to college. I'm afraid I'm going to miss her much more than I expected. Despite all the psychological preparation for the event, it is a wrench to be suddenly childless after twenty-five years. A '*wonderful* crisis'? You're nuts!"

No matter how cleverly or wisely we plan, such moments are inevitable. There's not much point in fighting them; it seems to me it makes more sense to ride them out—and then use them for creating "a Renaissance in our Middle Ages."

We have been so steeped in the idea that "the green years" are the best, that we tend to have accepted this without questioning it, even though the evidence of our senses often belies this notion. What do we have now that we didn't have then? Experience, which has given us more poise, more self-possession, and a broader perspective about ourselves than we have ever had before. We have learned not to take every momentary crisis too seriously. *We know about survival;* we have every reason to believe that heartaches never kill, and that wounds heal; we've been there too often to doubt it. We are smarter, as well as older, and strangely enough, even though we now understand that time passes, we are less in a hurry, less likely to be future-oriented. We respect *now* more than ever before, and we can savor the present without always planning for what happens next. Until I was about thirty-five, I think that probably more than half of my thinking had to do with the future; that has changed completely; now I feel today is all that I have and deserves far more of the focus of my attention.

Someone once said that middle age is like rereading a book that you haven't read since you were a callow youth. The first time around you were dazzled by impressions, emotions, and tended to miss the finer points. In middle age you have the equipment to see the subtleties you missed before and you savor it more slowly.

One of the best attributes of a more acute sense of time is how unimportant unimportant things become. I believe it was Clifton Fadiman who once said that at fifty a man realizes he only needs one suit! We spend the first half of our lives accumulating things: mates, children, houses, lawnmowers, cribs, chinaware, cars, washing machines, lamps, clothes, and all the things our children ever made in the school art department. A frequent fantasy of mine in the past few years has been that either we had a fire in our apartment, or I somehow found a way to talk my daughter into taking all our furniture, and we moved into a trailer, and just wandered! I find this strange and surprising, when I think of how acquisitive I was for so long.

The essence of whether one experiences "a Renaissance" or "the Dark Ages" in middle life seems to me to depend a great deal on the degree to which one can use change effectively, rather than denying its existence and trying to go on with business as usual.

The most unhappy of the middle-aged and older seem to be those who cannot change. One woman of sixty, who had devoted her life to her family, found herself suddenly widowed. Bitterly she observed, "Now I'll always be an extra person. I gave my life to my children—now they don't need me. I might as well crawl in a hole and die." When old friends made overtures, she sent them away. ("They think they're doing me a favor. They never really liked me, they only liked Jack.")

She objected to her children's suggestion that perhaps now she'd like to see something of the world. ("Do you expect me to go by myself?") A niece gave her a three-page single-spaced list of very much needed volunteer jobs and was rebuffed. ("Nobody respects you when you don't get paid.")

As I've talked with so many of the middle-aged, I've come to the personal conclusion that the only truly sad and depressing people I've encountered are the forty- and fifty- and sixty-year-olds who still think and act as if they were twenty or thirty. It seems to me we have some very important choices to make, and that continued years of fulfillment are almost entirely dependent on how well we choose.

Despite the responsibilities we still bear for caring for children and perhaps for aging parents, both emotionally and financially, middle age still remains a stage of life in which we can make conscious choices more clearly and strongly than ever before. We know much more about ourselves; we have now had enough years of living to know our reactions, our feelings, our needs, and we have a rich experience from which to draw conclusions about what makes us feel most imprisoned and immobilized and despairing, and what makes us feel most alive, most used by life, most hopeful and full of zest and enthusiasm.

Making choices is not easy; there are many times when we long nostalgically for the times in our lives when decisions were made for us, and we could blame others for what happened to us. If we sit back and just let things happen, if we take the course of least resistance during our middle years, it is much harder to find a scapegoat to blame our troubles on —but it is a testament to human ingenuity how we still manage to try to get away with this kind of copping-out: "I can't *possibly* become a travel agent, as I've always longed to be, because Jim would have to live alone sometimes." Or "How can I go back to school? We're sending two children to college and giving my father $125 a month—where are we going to get the money for me?" Or, "Yes, the children are grown, and we could retire and move to Oregon and live in a trailer, as we've dreamed of doing for thirty years, but how could I go so far away from my parents, when they are so sick and old?" We talk ourselves into believing that we don't have any choices at all and are merely victims.

But we *do* choose whatever we do, and we might as well own up to it. Doing nothing, sitting tight, not taking any chances is making a choice. Maybe it's the right one for now —if it is, let's own up to making it and live with it. If it's absolutely wrong, if cowardice is more to blame than any reality, then we need to look at that choice. "I complained all the time about our living in the city," a friend told me. "I was constantly saying I couldn't breathe, and it was a horrible, dangerous place to be, but after all, what could I do? Paul had to be near his work. Then one day, he shocked the hell out of me by saying he'd give up his job and start all over again in Maine or Florida or wherever I wanted to go. Suddenly I realized I didn't really want to leave at all. I like buses and nearby movies and no driving and the anonymity of life in the city. I'd been choosing all along, but I'd never admitted it before!"

We can, at last, choose to spend more time on ourselves, no matter how much others may demand from us. Our children are old enough to do many more things for themselves; it will be good for them if we give them some responsibility for supporting themselves and allowing us some leeway. We may have to learn to live with some feelings of guilt for not satisfying the endless needs of parents, relatives, friends, co-workers, but if ever there is a time to say "I am for *me*," it is middle age.

It is amazing how well other people can rally when we insist on having our own lives! To think that we are indispensable is the height of egotism. We are indispensable to our own lives, and we must begin to choose to live those lives or we will despair and die. To the degree that we make this choice, the next twenty or thirty years can be the most fulfilling of our lives. We need to take a chance on new beginnings. The challenge of the increased lifespan is that it creates the necessity for a kind of reassessment and renewal. A charming fifty-year-old mother of four, widowed and remarried, a woman of sensitivity, imagination, and courage who had created a rich and loving environment for her children, found herself confronted by her seventy-two-year-old mother on the day her youngest left for college. Mother, who had become a concert pianist at thirty-eight, looked at her expectantly and said, "Well, Connie, it's time for you to make something of yourself!"

The gradual departure of children is probably the first and most dramatic indication to us that our lives are changing. At first it may seem like a lark; we are alone with our mate— at last!

In one family, mother and father finally found themselves

alone in a quiet house. They walked from room to room, affectionately patting an old teddy bear, picking up an array of clothes on the floor, closing a closet door on old beer cans and hockey sticks—and finally, sitting down in the living room, they looked each other in the eye and said, "Alone at last. Isn't it *great?*"

Perhaps an even more persuasive and reassuring example of this is the story of another middle-aged couple who were discovered necking in a car on a college campus by a policeman. The embarrassed man in the car said, "Sorry, officer— we're parents of a freshman student we just brought here —he's our youngest, and this is the first time we've been alone in thirty years!"

It would be foolish to deny the profound impact of the process of letting go of one's children. But it would be equally foolish to deny the opportunities that are created by this gradual change in our lives. First of all, it does make a difference if we have tried to prepare ourselves to whatever degree is possible. The woman who has slowly moved toward finding other enrichments which can become a new focus of energy and talent is certainly likely to adjust to her new life better than the mother who clings to mothering too long and too well.

I invited a friend to spend a weekend with me in the country while her husband was out of town. She told me she couldn't possibly come because Walter would be home alone. Walter was almost eighteen, a senior in high school, who had traveled to many parts of the United States and Europe in the past few summers, who had dozens of neighborhood friends he'd known since early childhood whom he could call on for any problems, a great big strapping young man, more than capable of taking care of himself for a weekend. But what was most interesting to me was that Walter's two older brothers had been allowed to become more independent and were far less hovered over by their mother when they were

Walter's age. He was the last one at home, and quite unconsciously my friend was clinging to the role that was really
coming to a rapid end.

A period of adjustment is unavoidable, but planning ahead
can be helpful. To have talked about future plans, to know
where one is going to find some new areas of fulfillment—
travel, a move back to the city, or out to the country, courses
of study one may take—all help to get one over the early
months.

The empty nest actually is crowded with possibilities.
Whatever self-examination, whatever mutual explorations
may be necessary, I believe with all my heart that no matter
how much one has loved being a parent, just as rich or even
richer experiences can lie ahead. That is why it is so important to let whatever has to happen, happen; in the struggle to
understand what one's new life experiences can be, one has to
clean house first. What shadows lurk in what corners? What
inner voices echo through these now empty rooms? Are we
truer companions than ever before, or strangers wandering
through what seems to be an arid place in life? Are we ready
to take stock, to look at who we are and where we are, and
to take the first next steps toward a new life? It has seemed to
me that for those who are having a true "Renaissance," there
must be a period of "the Dark Ages" first. It seems necessary
in history and in human psychology! I don't believe that it is
really possible for almost anyone to move smoothly and easily through this change in one's life, no matter how solid
one's marriage, how sensible one's planning has been, how
bright and constructive the future may look. It is, after all, a
time of our rebirth, and birth is full of struggle.

We may need to examine the fact that some of our reluctance to let go may have little or nothing to do with missing
our children, but rather, with our terrible fears about living
with ourselves. At such a moment we tend to see ourselves as
having lost something, of being bereft.

In truth, anything that enriches one's understanding and deepens one's sensitivity is the nourishment one needs for future endeavors. Parenthood is in no sense something you do until it's over; it is something that offers you profound experiences that you take with you and use in whatever you do next.

Work is certainly the issue in that "next." Some of us go on doing what we've been doing all along, only more so. Others are faced with a dramatic shift in roles. There is no general "good solution"—each of us has to seek our own individualized answers. One "answer" that tends to at least postpone decisionmaking is not at all uncommon—the "career" that keeps cropping up for middle-aged women is that very late "accident child," who really is no accident at all! For some women the challenge of the empty nest is too frightening, and there is a tremendous desire to prolong the role of motherhood, and having a late baby in such cases is one way to avoid facing a new time of life. It may be a financial and emotional burden to a father who is ready for a period of time in which there will be fewer distractions from pursuing his work. When having another child represents an evasion, it is likely to present serious problems for the whole family. On the other hand, many parents have assured me that a late child is the most fun of all. Parents tend to be more relaxed—they've been through it all already. There are older brothers and sisters who are more like aunts and uncles and baby-sitters, and the late baby tends to have plenty of grownup attention and love. For some families the extended period of childraising may well be a very special middle-aged experience, to which one brings new understanding and maturity; it may be a more enjoyed parenthood than ever before. But it surely makes a difference whether or not it is an affirmation of one's deepest needs or a flight from facing change.

Sometimes our fears of change play funny tricks on us. A

man who had been a well-paid successful business executive for many years was fired at the age of fifty-eight. The shock was overwhelming and he could not understand what had happened. He was told that his work had been declining for a long while, that he had just not had his old enthusiasm and drive; maybe a change of scene, a new challenge would help. He chose another job very similar to the first one, told himself and everyone else things were just fine, and then was fired again at the end of another year. Since he was well trained for this particular work and had never had work problems before, he was truly shattered now and very frightened and decided to see a therapist. When the therapist asked, "Could there by any reason why you might *want* to get fired?" he looked very startled and then said, "I've raised three kids who all wanted to 'do their own thing.' I guess they stirred me up—I'm jealous—I want what they've got." He had got into the world of business simply by acquiescing to his father's expectations, and because he was a bright and charming man, he'd succeeded very well. But he had really wanted to teach high school English, and he had found himself longing to get out of the business world all during the high school years of his children. Now they were living away from home, and unconsciously he had been sabotaging himself. It became clear that he was too ashamed to quit, too frightened to give himself a new chance, and in what was really quite a healthy impulse, was forcing himself to face a real change by subtly failing. He and his wife moved to smaller quarters, told the college-age child he'd have to earn most of his tuition, and father went back to school to get certification as a teacher, supported by his wife's job.

It can be a source of enormous gratification to either partner to be the person who is making it possible for the spouse to pursue a new field of interest. Often this begins before the children have left home; I know of one father who took over all the evening chores with his children three nights a week so that his wife could go to night school and begin her preparation for going back to work full-time.

It isn't that the opportunities don't exist, it is that we have all kinds of resistances to change! We say "I can't" long before we really have evidence that this is the case. It doesn't seem possible we could live on half the income we've got; where in the world can you find a cheap apartment? Isn't it criminal to throw away the pension, the health insurance, the years of seniority you've got? The answer is: it can be done, it should be done if we don't wake up looking forward to each day, if we have a sense of hopelessness and despair about our lives. When we want it badly enough it *can* be done. The problem is to examine one's fears and see what they mean.

One of the most characteristic kinds of work-identity crises was described to me recently by a friend. She said, "I'd been working in this nursery school for about five years, loving every minute of it. But my children were both in high school by this time, and I began to feel it was all too easy and unchallenging; I was getting bored, even though I loved being with children. One day at school I looked at myself in the mirror and said, 'What in hell are you doing here?' I knew five years at the same job was enough, but I just didn't have the courage to do anything about it. Several months later a man I knew, who was the head of an adult-education program at our community college, called and asked if I'd be interested in teaching child-development courses to parents and teachers. He knew I'd been doing a lot of that in the nursery school. I knew that what he offered me excited me more than anything I'd ever done professionally, but I was terrified; suppose I was no good at it? I could talk to a few teachers or parents that I knew well, and I was good at it, but could I be interesting to a whole class? It seemed impossible. I finally went to talk it over with my minister. He listened, and then he said, 'Well, if you think you can't do it, don't do it.' That made me mad! When I told him he wasn't being at all helpful, he smiled and said, 'Just a minute. *I* have faith that you can do it, but that isn't going to do *you* any good.' He asked me what was the worst possible thing that could happen if I took the risk. Well, the worst was that I could fail. And suddenly it all became easy; failure isn't so serious! If you do the best you can and you fail, well, where's the crime? As soon as I could accept the idea of failure, I knew I just had to try. As you know, it's been the best job, the happiest time of my life. But I'm beginning to wonder what will happen if I look in the mirror again sometime and say, 'What in hell are you doing *here?*' I hope what I'll do is take the next risk."

There is no doubt that it is helpful if we have begun to think about our middle and later years—our changing roles—in our thirties, at a time when gradually and sensibly we can begin to develop an awareness of some of the things we would like to do with the rest of our lives, what we may want to develop more fully a little later on. One high school graduate arranged with a local junior college to take two credits each term until her youngest child was in high school; then she would become a full-time student. Another woman, who gave up a budding career in social work while her children were young, gave two mornings a week as a volunteer in a community mental-health clinic. Her talents were so special that she was given more responsibility as her children grew, and by the time they were all in college, she was able to take some refresher courses, and then became a paid staff member. Women who give their time to such child-centered activities as Scouts, the PTA, the local Community Chest, are also providing themselves with the kinds of experiences that enrich and that may give them a clearer idea of what they like to do and what they do well for those years when there will be more time to dig in.

It is also becoming increasingly possible to work at part-time paid jobs during the years one is not quite ready to take the plunge into full-time employment. It used to be that employers were very reluctant to hire part-time staff, but this has been changing. The most common reason for this was expressed by the director of a social agency who told me, "We used to have a hard-and-fast rule that all our staff had to be full-time. Most of our staff were young, recent graduates—bright and full of energy, but often lacking in maturity and understanding. Anyway, most of the women were soon off to parenthood themselves. We found we had a much wider and richer field to choose from when we began allowing for part-time workers. They tended to be far more conscientious. When a young girl got the sniffles, she stayed home; when we hired a mother, with two little kids, she was so anxious to prove that she could handle the job that we had to beg her to stay home when she had the flu!"

It is often difficult during a period of growing and changing to find a necessary balance between planning and spontaneity. If we appreciate the fact that our present is all we've really got, and it's terribly important to us, then how can we plan so far ahead as to go back to school for several or many years, in order to prepare for a career that we might enjoy a lot, but can't work at for a long time?

I know one woman who, at fifty-six, is starting her first year at law school. She had a wonderful job and could have stayed where she was for as long as she liked, but her children were grown, she'd been widowed for many years, and a long-ago dream could at last be realized. The reaction of many people on hearing her decision was, "But it takes so *long* to become a lawyer—it's such hard work—and after all, how many years will you have left for practicing law?" If we stop to think about it these become foolish, meaningless questions. If you are doing something you have wanted to do all your life and you are enjoying every minute of *the process*, what else matters? A young man of twenty-two could start law school and get run over by a car a year later! Should that possibility stop him from the pursuit of his life? There are no guarantees of any kind at any age, and in making decisions about work the central criteria we ought to use is "Do I want this experience for myself, right now, whether or not I ever achieve any long-range goals?" It is one thing to feel, "I am going through all this because of the good job and the good pay it can lead to," and quite another to feel, "Whether I ever get that degree or not, I'm sure having a ball right now!"

It has become quite clear to college administrators that mature students often have more going for them than younger students. The middle-aged have a sharper sense of their own goals, they have learned to appreciate the process, not just the end result, and bring a great deal more experience to their new discoveries. Young people are by nature oriented toward the future. In middle age you're *in* your future, and you want to enjoy it and make the most of it.

Going back to college *is* planning for the future, but it can also be an end in itself; the moment *must* count. If we are going to be miserable in the process, then it may well be time to think of some alternative possibilities. A fortyish friend told me recently, "The happiest day of my life was the day I decided that I'd rather die then spend the next two years of my life getting a Master's Degree!" This was a goal that she had had in mind for ten or fifteen years. She thought that all that was stopping her was lack of money and time. Then her father died leaving her a bequest that could quite comfortably see her through graduate school. For a while she was thrilled; she went through all the necessary procedures of finding the school that would suit her best and arranging her classes so she could still work part-time. But just as the day for making the first tuition payment came due, she began to have awful abdominal pains. After an array of unpleasant tests, her wise doctor said, "There's nothing wrong with your stomach, but there's a lot wrong with your head—that's where the pains are coming from. You better find out why." It took only two or three counseling sessions for her to realize that this unfulfilled dream was not at all what she really wanted.

At the same time that middle age may be a very appropriate time to contemplate change, the ability to reexamine change that one thinks one wants is very important. Despite momentary thoughts of other ways of living, and the ordinary annoyances and frustrations that exist in every kind of work, in many cases we really don't want to be doing anything else. A social worker told me, "I was getting more and more heartsick at what was happening in the Welfare Department. I could see that we were doing less and less for more and more people—the red tape, the politics, the almost unendurable inhumanity made me so exhausted and depressed that I could hardly live with myself, to say nothing of what I was doing to my husband and kids. I began to do a lot of talking and thinking about getting out of the social-work field altogether. I'd always been interested in interior decorating, and I thought, 'I'll have my big identity crisis right now, I'll start all over.' But I never actually did anything about it, and I began to feel guilty. What kind of a coward was I? I was a great believer in people starting over, it would be awful to find out that I didn't have the courage to go on growing and changing. I finally went back to my old analyst who straightened me out in short order. We know each other very well—she just said, 'Oh stop this nonsense about growing and changing. You know perfectly well you couldn't bear to leave those poor benighted people, no matter *what* goes on; they need you more than ever and you were born to be just where you are, no matter how miserable it makes you! Just take longer vacations!' I felt a great sense of relief. It was suddenly clear to me that I had mistaken frustration for a loss of interest in my field. I really *don't* belong anywhere else—I'll go on taking human suffering home with me for the rest of my life, and my family will just have to put up with it."

We have to be careful when we begin to think about new opportunities and possibilities for fulfillment that we don't trap ourselves in the priorities, the value system imposed from the outside, where some kinds of work are valued more than others. Making money is usually at the top of the list in our culture; then come "the do-gooder people"; then perhaps the artists; and at the very bottom of the heap today, the home-maker. We need to do our own individual thinking about what it means for us to be creative, inside ourselves, and to remind ourselves constantly that that is the only criterion of any merit in making new choices. Psychologist Abraham Maslow summed this up succinctly by saying, "A first-rate soup is better than a second-rate poem." It seems to me that too often the middle-aged set work goals which have nothing to do with inner needs, but rather, with social status; middle age is a good time to quit that silly game. If one happens to be a first-rate soupmaker, and if the satisfactions in this ac-complishment are deeply fulfilling, then to aspire to writing poetry *only because that's supposed to be more worthwhile* is self-destructive. To feel like writing poetry—whether first-, second- or third-rate being immaterial—because it gives one pleasure is another matter entirely.

Of course most people have to earn money, and we happen to have become middle-aged in the midst of what seems to be the most unacknowledged Depression in history. Our chil-dren, some with graduate degrees, can't get jobs. How can we? There is no doubt that this is a frightening situation; it is more than likely to be the reason we use for not making a change even when we want to very much. It may be a legiti-mate reason not to make a change, at least for a while. But it is not hopeless. Even if we have to stick with a job we've got, we can be taking evening courses, or we can work as a vol-

unteer once or twice a week in the field we think we'd like
to go into some day.

It would be foolish to deny that as we get older we naturally become more concerned with pensions, retirement
plans, security for our old age. We are terrified of becoming
dependent on our children—assuming most of them ever
get around to being self-supporting! I suppose the best that
one can do concerning the reality-fears about retirement and
old age is to try to strike some sort of balance about priorities. The person who is always saving everything for the future never really lives at all because he has no "now."
Equally, the person who absolutely refuses to face any future
necessities is usually caught in a perfectly awful mess when
that future is suddenly the present. In trying to strike some
balance, I must admit that, given the choice, I would rather
err on the side of making hay while the sun shines than to belong to that dead-in-life group at the other extreme who have
never traveled, never bought anything they wanted on impulse, never bought orchestra seats in a theater, never gave a
really extravagant present to anybody, never indulged in a
wild binge just because they felt like it—but whose only
pleasure in life is the perusal of Savings Bank Books and the
contents of a bank vault.

Facing retirement presents another whole new area of
planning and adjustment. In our generation, men and women
still feel differently about work and retirement. Many men
tend to feel that when they stop working at a job, that's the
end of who they are, while women, who may lose the childraising function, still see themselves as homemakers and therefore still "employed." Attitudes are changing gradually, but
among a great part of our generation there is also still the
feeling that men *must* work in order to be "real persons" and
that women *may* work in order to "keep busy."

The degree to which marriage partners are really able to
take a candid and careful look at who they are and where

they have been seems to be the degree to which they are able to make satisfactory decisions about future work arrangements. In one family, the wife was a brilliant professor of history, but had never worked full-time while her children were young. She had felt frustrated. She'd turned down some wonderful full-time jobs and had not been able to work on a book she wanted to write, which many of her colleagues had told her was sorely needed. Her husband had been a salesman for a book publisher. He was never much good as a salesman, and was not really a very ambitious man. He loved being with his children, he loved his home, and most of all, he had an inordinate pride in his wife's accomplishments. When their youngest went away to college, the wife took her first full-time job and began working on her book, while her husband gave up his job and became a full-time homemaker. He loves cooking, shopping, and cleaning and is genuinely delighted that his wife is just as successful as he always knew she could be. Neither feels threatened by their reversal of roles. The wife told me, "We're just a couple of young revolutionists for Women's Liberation! I confess there are times when I feel very peculiar when Harry talks about my messing up 'his kitchen,' and I miss some of it—but not enough to want to go back there. And Harry is happier than I've ever seen him."

There are other adjustments possible when a husband retires and his wife continues to work full-time. One man told me, "Lil has a wonderful job which keeps her in the city, so at first I felt very resentful because I wanted to travel, now that I was footloose. We finally realized that it was time for each of us to do our own thing, and not try to make constant adjustments to the other person, as we had always done. I've been taking lots of trips by myself. Lil joins me on her vacations. And believe it or not, at sixty-six, I'm taking up mountain climbing!"

There is often a real problem about doing volunteer work. In a society that is as money-oriented as ours, it is very hard for anyone to feel that he is of value if he isn't getting paid for his work. Typical of these reactions was the man who told me, "I was a salesman for a hardware firm for thirty years. My company had automatic retirement at sixty-five, when I didn't feel the least bit ready for it. Everybody kept telling me I could do such interesting and valuable things, but I didn't believe a word of it. A man is worth what he gets paid, as far as I was concerned. But I couldn't stand staying at home all the time; I was restless and depressed. My wife was working in a drugstore, and I felt I'd been permanently put on the shelf. Life was over. My wife is a terrible nag, though, and she kept after me until I finally went to an organization that coordinates all the volunteer jobs in our town, and even gives training courses. There was a community center in a very poor neighborhood where they needed a shop teacher every afternoon, and I knew I could do it; after working for a hardware company for thirty years, if I didn't know tools and what you could do or not to with them who should? I've been there two years now. I have never had a better time in my life; I feel I'm doing some real good and I love the kids I work with. If I get a cold and can't get to work, I feel terrible. They need me and I need them more than was ever true in my former job."

We need to work at getting over our hang-ups about money, and we also need to behave in ways that will give more status and prestige to volunteer work. A woman who uses many volunteers in the social agency in which she works told me, "We are ready to prepare volunteers for very important kinds of work, but we can't do it unless the volunteer takes it as seriously as we do. Because there's no pay, they often feel that they can take time off whenever they want, show up late, come when it is most convenient, and only stay so long as the work is pleasant all the time. Such people are no help at all."

The quality of volunteer work has changed tremendously

since we were growing up. I am old enough to remember when "charity" meant carrying the Thanksgiving baskets to "the poor families." We also all know that there are some organizations which want you on their Boards of Directors for only one reason: to help them raise money. Some people are great at this, and for them it is meaningful work. For the vast majority, working for an organization must have other avenues of self-expression and gratification.

Volunteer work can now offer more challenge and fulfillment than ever before. It's a sad irony that the middle-aged should benefit from the fact that we have terrible social problems facing us, in poverty, racial tensions, problems of ecology and the increasingly hair-raising and heartbreaking complexities of international relations. One might well say that volunteer work for the middle-aged gets better and better in quality and challenge as the world gets more and more awful!

We have been discovering as a nation what a lot of us have known privately, that in most of the "helping professions" school-learning is not the only crucial factor; tender, compassionate, sensitive people can learn very quickly, and they can often make a greater contribution to a nursery school, a hospital ward, a tutoring department in a school than someone with advanced degrees but less feeling for people. I simply cannot imagine anyone who is reasonably mature, who has had relatively rich experiences in living, who has an attitude of flexibility, adventurousness and kindness, who couldn't, within one week, find a volunteer job in any city in this country that wouldn't challenge and inspire and give new meaning to one's life.

Play is as important as work at every stage of life. The trouble is that children know instinctively how much they need it for growing, while the middle-aged are inclined to treat it as "childish" and a waste of time. But often it is more vital than work to growing. Each of us has his own unique and special ways for refreshing himself, for creating a sense of renewal and replenishing the reservoirs of energy and creativity. One grandmother told me that hers came very unexpectedly (the best kind!) when she had to go to the optician to have a new prescription for glasses filled. She had always got perfectly ordinary middle-aged frames, but this time she found herself looking longingly at some of the great big silly glasses that the young people were wearing. She told me, "There was a new, younger optician there. The man who'd been making my glasses for twenty-five years wasn't in. This young man saw me looking at those crazy frames, and he began to give me the business! I should get out of my rut, I should get with it. Well, it didn't take much urging. I bought some frames—bright blue—that covered half my face. All the next week I regretted what I had done; I thought I'd been an idiot, and that I'd have to go and ask the older optician to change them for me. But when I went to pick them up, I had to admit I looked good! You know, I'd been feeling depressed and tired and out of sorts for weeks, but just getting those glasses gave me such a lift!" Expressions of playfulness need to change as we change. "I spent every Saturday afternoon ice skating," a lady told me, "until I was fifty-three. Then I decided I just couldn't take the cold anymore, so I joined a Y and learned how to swim in a heated pool! At sixty-two, I realized I wasn't so crazy about that, anymore —I was tired when I got home. So then I discovered cooking. A Saturday afternoon with Julia Child, cooking things whose names I can't even pronounce, suits me fine right now. Haven't decided what I'll take up next."

For some, inner refreshment may take the form of suddenly deciding to go to a museum, or taking a walk in the park and feeding the squirrels; for some it may be having a good talk with one's African violets—giving them some extra food—or suddenly deciding to buy a camera and take pictures of children in the playground. Or putting the telephone in the closet and muffling it with three or four coats, and just reading a book all afternoon. Whether it's a picnic at a nearby beach or taking a trip to Kenya, what we are doing in the search for inner refreshment is trying to get centered inside ourselves.

Refreshment of the spirit is really that more than anything else—a kind of exercise in centeredness, in focusing all one's attention into oneself. It is detaching oneself from peripheral stimuli that keep us from being in touch with our most profound feelings, sensations, thoughts. Daydreaming is a wonderful source of refreshment. Children understand this naturally, but grownups do everything possible to discourage this wonderful source of renewal; we call it "doing nothing" and sooner or later most of us give it up. It is a vital part of being in touch with what is most human in ourselves, and this may be the time for us to relearn what was once a natural part of our daily lives. We can teach ourselves to focus our full attention on a seashell or a flower or a leaf, or the rain hitting the windowpane; we can consciously allow our thoughts to focus, and then to wander into daydreams. Or we can give ourselves tasks that begin to reactivate our imagination; one technique is to close your eyes and visualize a movie screen, and then allow inner pictures to form on the screen. Another method is to give oneself a beginning for a story and then let it wander where it will. "I am on my way through the forest," or "I am going to build a perfect house," or "I am snorkeling along a coral reef."

Another way of getting in touch with oneself is simply to lie down on the floor, listening to music, and just try to become more conscious of the different parts of the body—to be aware of breathing, of what happens when you move an arm or a leg, or turn your head. Or one may want to be somewhat more disciplined and direct in learning techniques for inner contemplation by taking a course in Yoga or some other form of meditation. There is enormous interest in this area right now in all parts of the country, for we are beginning to understand that one of the most severe problems in modern life is the degree to which each of us has become disconnected from ourselves. From childhood we have been taught to forget about our bodies and feelings and just to think. We are heads, disconnected from our bodies. The new interest in meditation and sensory awareness are attempts to reconnect the head bone to the rest of the body, so that there can be the natural, instinctive flow with which we were born but were soon trained to give up.

Often a frenetic pace of running-and-doing becomes a running away from oneself, from an inner sense of emptiness. At the same time that one can look forward with pleasurable anticipation to *doing*, it is equally important to learn to *be;* to have a deep inner sense of aliveness and contentment in just being with oneself. There is really only one companion that one can count on all through one's life—oneself; that needs to be a meaningful and satisfying friendship.

One of our problems in facing retirement is that our concept of meaningful work is usually doing something for other people or being very busy all the time. The one characteristic of our teenage children that has probably driven us up the wall more than any other is that they have no such views on the nature and value of work, and while theirs may be an exaggerated attitude, so is ours. We need to have more respect for the "work" of learning more about oneself, learning to contemplate, to center and focus one's consciousness so that one is more deeply in touch with oneself.

A man who is about to retire told me, "The one thing that terrifies or infuriates every person I talk to, who asks what I'm going to do now, is to tell them I want to do absolutely nothing at all for a while. Right away they tell me that's a terribly negative attitude, that maybe I should see a psychiatrist, and I can see long, woeful looks directed at my wife. It's really quite simple; I'm sixty-five years old and for thirty years I have worked hard at a job that I did not enjoy very much. It was an excellent living, but not much else. I have watched my wife and my two sons 'find themselves' over all these years that I have been working; they have been going to school and getting training to do work that they love. I figure it's time for me to contemplate my navel for awhile. I want to wake up in the morning and say to myself, 'Fred, nobody needs you to do anything for them, today; do something just for you.' For the first time in my life I want to think about who I am and what I want to do with the years ahead of me. As the kids say, I'm going to get my head together. If that kind of growing is so important to young people, and leads to a more meaningful and fulfilling life, I can't see why I should be denied a privilege I've worked so hard for; our kids get it for nothing."

We think too much about being busy and too little about the life of the spirit. Because we grew up in a time when work was still presented to us as a matter of necessity for human survival, we are almost as uneasy with leisure as our parents were and are. Thousands of years of terrible struggle, with almost total concentration on providing food, clothing, and shelter and having little or no time for anything else, has been changed dramatically in less than a century; the industrial revolution, the advances in modern technology have created a society in which the concept of work has undergone staggering changes, and we are reeling with it all. It is very hard for us to believe that anyone of any age who isn't working at least eight hours a day, five days a week at a paid job can really be a worthwhile person.

There is a retired couple who live across the road from us on the Jersey shore. Their house faces a bay and some wetlands that have not yet been destroyed by man's greed. Many species of gulls nest there, along with blue and white herons and beautiful statuesque egrets. In the spring and fall all sorts of fascinating birds make a stop in the wetlands on their way north and south; one of the most exciting times is when flocks of Canada geese visit briefly. My neighbor sits for hours almost every day with her fieldglasses, marveling at the birds, at the sunsets, at the sailboats and the fishermen. She once told me that in the five years she's lived here, no two sunsets have ever been similar, and that each day she looks forward with excitement to the new drama before her.

Her husband loves to keep his house in first-rate shape, to fish for his dinner and to help his neighbors. Children and grandchildren come and go, there is a weekly trip to the supermarket, lots of friendly talk along the shore—and as far as I can see, that's just about it. I have never met people who seemed to me to be more fulfilled and contented. They are doing just exactly what gives them the most pleasure they could possibly have. In the winter they work on various committees for good causes, but the essence of their daily lives is simply being at home in a natural world that they love.

At the same time that we ought to encourage people to go back to school or change jobs or do volunteer work, if they need to be busy and active in those ways, we also ought to remember—just in case this happens to be who *we* are— that many people find their deepest sense of being alive in the simplest kind of environment and where one cannot really measure what they are "doing" because so much of it is going on inside of them and doesn't show.

One of the things that makes the word "renaissance" stick in the throats of the middle-aged is our fear of widowhood during these years. It is a real fear, and cannot be dismissed lightly. The possibility of losing a relationship upon which one has become very dependent, the specter of being alone for the first time is a shattering and terrifying idea. There is no alternative—one simply has to accept it as one of the possibilities that exist in life. But that is only the beginning; after acceptance, there are *lots* of things one can do about it.

Women worry most, with good cause, since it is the middle-aged man who is more vulnerable to early death. But we have mountains of evidence that many of these deaths might well have been avoided, that they tend quite often to be the result of unbearable tension or profound despair over one's life. The heart attack may be symptomatic of unreleased tensions and angers—the man on the treadmill. When we see somebody driven to success, when work becomes a kind of total obsession, but without joy, when there are too many unsaid hurts and furies, we all know enough now to know there are ways in which we can prevent catastrophe. If the truth be known, very few husbands and wives are *truly* surprised when a spouse dies; those who are closest know, deep-down, there were physical and psychological wounds and handicaps with a long history, for with rare exception, dying in middle life is not so mysterious and accidental; it has profound implications for the life one has been living.

A forty-eight-year-old man is watching television at nine o'clock at night. He gets a look of pain, starts to get up—drops dead of a heart attack. Everyone (on the outside!) is shocked, horrified. How could this happen to such a young man? It could happen; was he the man who has so little inner life that he has been working eighteen hours a day? Was he the man who hasn't loved his wife for ten years, but stays because of the children? Was he the man who has hated his job since the day he left school, but can't ever get out of debt or far enough ahead to take the chance of doing something else? Was he the man who never lost his temper? Was he the man who played the role of perfect son and father and husband without ever once allowing himself to find out who he really wanted to be, for himself?

I have had a rare and remarkable opportunity to understand the hidden agenda of middle-aged deaths. For fifteen years my husband worked on a research project raising the question of whether or not there might be psychosomatic aspects in the etiology of cancer. At the present time there are many physicians, psychiatrists, and psychologists all over the world who share my personal conviction that in at least half of the terminal cancers, deep and utter despair about one's life plays a major role. This was certainly the conclusion my husband and his colleagues came to; it was a position shared completely with the dying patients with whom he worked. This is not the place to go into all the research findings, or the results of intensive psychotherapy with terminal patients. What I want to relate here is what I learned about the "unexpected" middle-age death. It is almost never so unexpected. The typical story, repeated over and over again, goes something like this: A woman of forty-six with "everything to live for" is dying of cancer of the stomach. It is an unbelievable tragedy. She has two children, a handsome and successful husband, loving parents, money, a beautiful home; God is cruel and vengeful to take such a woman. When she faces her own death with a psychotherapist, who has suggested there may be an alternative if she can begin to examine her life, she says, "I have no reason to get better; I am dead already." It turns out that she has been the good little girl, always doing what was expected of her, never doing what she wanted to do. The truth is, she always had a secret dream of becoming a news photographer and traveling all over the world on dangerous and exciting adventures. She likes her husband, but she doesn't know what people are talking about when they describe falling in love, feelings of passion. She has never had a strong feeling for or about anything or anyone, except for the one happy year in her life when she studied in France during her third year of college. She didn't really want to marry or have children, but she was so used to pleasing her parents that she had no drive, no reason to oppose their wishes. She'd never felt her life belonged to her. A year before she became sick, she told her husband she had made the decision to go back to school to study photography. Her husband was very upset, but she went ahead with it. She joined a camera club, and when the group planned a trip to Africa, she longed to go—even asked her parents and husband if they would let her go and take over care of the children. They were shocked. A widower, a member of the camera club, twenty years older than she, had urged her to come along, and she found herself very attracted to him. They had a sudden and, to her, shocking affair, after which she was devastated by guilt, ending the relationship quickly. She began to have trouble eating. . . .

There are private agonies in every life; if we want to live we have to have the courage to look at them. It all depends on how much one wants to live. Some people told my husband very openly and frankly that death was preferable to facing the anguish of living. A woman said, "I would have to leave my husband and hurt him terribly. I can't do it." Another said, "I am fifty-six years old; every decision I've made has been a mistake since I was twenty-two. I don't have the courage or the will to begin again."

Both husbands and wives must keep in touch with themselves and each other; they must often force wounds to stay open that they might like to forget about. If we want to stay alive we need to keep the body very much connected to the head, to feelings, which influence our physical well-being to an absolutely staggering degree.

By stressing the fact that profound psychological problems play an important part in longevity, I don't mean to deny for a moment the importance of physical well-being and the degree to which we can take responsibility for an active and intelligent battle against the inevitable process of aging.

When I was about thirty, I went to a three-day educational conference held at a lovely country estate. After the meetings were over for the day, a group of us would head for the local beer and pizza joint, where (oh youthful power!) we would sing and talk and dance until 3:00 A.M. and still show up for breakfast at eight the next morning, ready for the day's work. One night we were joined by a colleague who must have been about fifty or fifty-five at that time. She ordered tea and toast, and asked if someone could drive her back to our headquarters at about 11:30. As a callow youth, just about to leap into middle-age, I told her she was chicken; the pizzas were divine, how could she pass them up? She just looked at me and smiled, and said, "Ten years from tonight, I want you to remember what you said. Wait!" It didn't take ten years for me to reach the point where a pizza at midnight could damn near kill me! There *are* concessions that one must make to aging; it seems to me that for me to deny this takes up too much energy that I need for other things. Yes, the body does begin to "depreciate," and we are stuck with that reality. But in the very process of accepting this fact and trying to do intelligent and creative things about it, we can open ourselves up to all kinds of new experiences that may be even more rewarding.

Despite the realities of physical aging, most of us are very well preserved! We may get indigestion more easily and out of breath walking up several flights of stairs, and be more prone to insomnia, but it seems to me that most of my contemporaries are in very fine shape, physically—often better than ever before because they are so much more aware of the importance of respecting and caring for the only body one's got. It seems to me that most of us are getting more exercise now than we ever did during our twenties and thirties; we ride bicycles, walk, do exercises every day, jog, and tend to be far more careful and sensible about our diet.

One friend told me, "I can't recall ever thinking it was awful that I sat at a desk all day, until I was forty-five years old. I just took my body for granted. Now I do fifteen minutes of exercises every day before going to work, walk back and forth (about four miles) in all weather, and do all my own housework instead of having a cleaning woman in once a week. I save money and I save my muscles at the same time."

Expectations seem to have a great deal to do with how

young and healthy we feel. For example, I had a hard time finding a woman who would complain bitterly and hopelessly about the problems of menopause. In the first place, medical science has made the process far easier, and in the second, even those who have "hot flashes" or other discomforts seem more often than not to see this not as a sign that life is almost over, but rather, as an indication that the day is almost upon them when they can enjoy sex without worrying about pregnancy! When you expect to remain young physically, when science tells you it is perfectly possible, you live up to these expectations.

It seems to me there is a vast difference between doing everything one can through diet, exercise, and preventive medical checkups to keep oneself in optimal physical condition, and a mad panic to remain young and gorgeous forever. We are a generation very much caught in the youth cult of our times, and the strain can be considerable. We are victims of a well-organized conspiracy to make us believe that external appearances count for everything.

Somebody recently said, "There is plenty of room in the world for women who *look* beautiful, sexy, and exciting. There is much less room for women who *are*." It is hard for both men and women to see middle age as "a Renaissance" when they find themselves caught in a social climate that places so much value on youthfulness and outward appearances. Even if you feel young and vigorous and just about as sensual as you have ever felt, it is almost impossible not to react with feelings of inferiority when Madison Avenue has managed to create a nightmare world in which hands are forever soft and white, armpits and genitalia are always perfumed, hair is never gray, faces never lined, bowels are always regular, teeth are always white, breath is minty fresh, and men and women of sixty are still supposed to have the figures of eighteen-year-olds.

The American economy, with its dependence on luxury

spending, has created a monster in advertising, an environment in which what people look like is far more important than what they really are—where, for example, a Hugh Hefner Bunny-type, with a full bosom and a provocative behind, is considered more sexy than a seasoned woman of forty, who got her wrinkles and bulges in the course of many years of sensual appetites being thoroughly explored. The young boy on horseback or skis who exhales cigarette smoke in a sexy way is considered the perfect image of the masculine male, while the man of fifty who has devoted many years to the careful study of how to make a woman feel wonderful is judged to be old.

In moving toward an active commitment to live our lives as fully as we can, it is essential that we come to terms with the myths of our times; that we exorcise the phantoms of the brainwashing each of us has experienced constantly all of our adult lives, which make us feel less than we really are.

On the other hand, to look as young as one feels seems to be a perfectly reasonable goal. A grandma of forty-five told me, "Now look—I'm going to *college*, and if you think I'm going to let myself look like a dried-up granny, with white hair, you're crazy! I dye my hair and diet, not to prove anything—just to make the most of myself. I don't *feel* old, so why should I *look* old?" This is a very different orientation to aging from the woman who said, as she looked sadly at the new wrinkles in the mirror, "It's the most terrible thing in the world to see yourself growing older, and to know that nothing good will ever happen to you again."

It seems to me that we have at hand an excellent antidote to the youth cult that has been imposed upon us by Madison Avenue, and that is our children! They are surely a generation that has reacted—perhaps even overreacted—to advertising, and if there is one statement they seem to be making, it is that people ought not to be judged by outward appearances, and they should be free to be comfortable.

In order to *feel* young, and to *be* as healthy as possible, we need to wear comfortable clothes and not worry all the time about whether or not our coiffure is perfect. We need to be able to move easily, if we are going to get the exercise we need.

I don't think that wanting to be comfortable, to free oneself to move easily, necessarily means becoming a slob, or never caring about one's appearance. It means making choices at specific times. If we are hung-up about never looking more than thirty-five, if our life is devoted to trying to be ready for the cover of *Vogue* at all times, we are never going to have the sense of relaxation and ease that helps us to feel healthy and vigorous. The strange part of it is that, in many ways, middle-aged couples become more attractive to each other as they become more relaxed about how they look, more focused on *what makes them feel good*. As we began to try to please ourselves, to search out what it meant to be our "real selves," my husband and I began to choose clothing the like of which we would not have dared to wear five or ten years ago. What happens is that when one looks for what is true and right for oneself, a marvelous flair develops, and something terribly exciting happens. You see the person you love, not for what he wears, but what the wearing does for *him*. This year the big thing with my husband is an almost ankle-length British Air Raid Warden's coat, created during the Second World War, and meant of course to keep one warm whatever the temperature. It has brass buttons and epaulettes, and he *does* resemble a hotel doorman—but I think he looks divine in it. I am also utterly overcome by the crazy guru shirts he wears, for what I see is that he is expressing his deepest sense of himself, and that is such a good thing to be doing that it shines through in a beautiful glow.

No matter how sensitive we may be to psychological tensions, no matter how sensible we may be about our physical well-being, death is still inevitable—and it may come in middle age. Widowhood is a fact of married life, for outside of a suicide contract to leap off a high cliff together at eighty-five, or a plane or car accident that kills both, there is bound, sooner or later, to be a "survivor." Whether any of us can survive well depends on whether we have made the most we could of our time together, and whether or not we have prepared ourselves, at least to some degree, to the idea of living alone. This involves working very hard long beforehand, at seeing to it that when one *is* alone one still has a very good companion—oneself. There is nothing harder for most of us, who have been so oversocialized since early childhood. Every time we tried to nourish that inner companion, we were told to stop daydreaming, stop doing nothing, get busy and do something or "go play" with others. Most of us feel utterly cut off from human life when we are alone, and it is a terrifying experience. Rediscovering the only person we are really with from birth to death is a serious and necessary task if we would quell the terrors of being alone. There are different ways of finding one's inner companion: some do it through meditation exercises; many through psychotherapy; some through various kinds of religious experiences; some through the hard work of providing time for isolation and contemplation, learning to take long walks alone in the woods, going on a hiking trip alone, taking a trip by car or boat or plane, alone.

In addition to cultivating one's inner life, it seems to me also very wise to see to it that the central relationship in one's life never becomes all-consuming and utterly dependent. I know one couple, married thirty-two years, who have never spent a single night apart, except for the two times the wife was in the hospital having a baby. I am horrified to contemplate what will happen to the survivor when one of them dies—the dependency is so pervasive. The fear of widowhood ought really to help a happily married couple move away from each other in many real and important ways, rather than encouraging them to cling even more closely, which only increases the fear of separation. The only relief from the terror, for me at least, has been the degree to which I have been able to cherish the closeness, and at the same time do everything possible to nurture my own life, my own inner self. I feel, after years and years of working hard at it, that now I could live alone if I had to; that my inner companion would be a comfort to me. But how hard it is to get to like oneself that much!

"This might have been a time for me to find new ways of expressing myself," one middle-aged lady said. "My children are grown, and I still feel fine, but have you any idea how much time and energy can be consumed by taking care of aged parents?" Probably no other single factor interferes more with the possibility of a "Renaissance." Children, spouses, jobs—all cause worry, frustration and pain some of the time, but they are also the sources of satisfaction and fulfillment. I found as I talked to many of my contemporaries that relationships with elderly parents seemed strong on frustration and weak on gratification. Of the very considerable numbers of people with whom I discussed this problem, only two or three were able to say that their parents were having a good and happy old age, were a pleasure to be with and had made sensible and adequate plans for continuing to be independent and well cared for until their death. "Even if you love your parents very much, and have always had a good relationship with them," one man told me, "it is very difficult to watch them age when you yourself are middle-aged and already have many anxieties about your own old age. I often wonder what it would have been like if my parents had died when I was much younger—say in my twenties or thirties. Old age and death were very remote and unreal for me then. I never would have connected myself with it. Now I see the helplessness beginning, the preoccupation with bodily functions, the loss of physical well-being. I see that gradually I must become the parent and they my children, and I can't bear it. I want to remember them differently, but even more than that, they are a constant reminder of what will happen to me in a few years, and I'm depressed and frightened."

"Medical progress is causing more heartbreak than happiness," another man told me. His father had started a retail furniture business more than fifty years ago. Now two sons ran the firm, "He's almost eighty, his sight is failing, he simply has no understanding at all of how to carry on a business in these times, and yet he will not retire. He clings to his daily routine as if it were life itself—and of course, that's what it is. How can you make a man give up something that he created? And yet, he is making life a living hell for my brother and myself; he just cannot let us take over, and his decisions are all wrong. His presence there also means that at a time in our lives when we feel most capable of really being innovative and creative ourselves, our hands are tied. I love my father—he breaks my heart—and I know I'll be old someday, but I also can't help but resent him for depriving me of the pleasure and success I feel I could now be experiencing."

Almost everyone I spoke to about this subject expressed feelings of guilt and frustration. Just as our parents were never in any way prepared for the fact of living a long life, so we are in many ways a first generation to have living parents when we are well into middle age ourselves. A sixty-five-year-old woman said, "I am sure that when I am eighty or eighty-five, I will struggle for my own life, and want every bit of it that I can have, but from where I sit now, I sometimes feel it's unnatural for so many people to be living so long. The death of one's parents is a terrible crisis in one's life, but it is also a kind of release from childhood; from that time on I would imagine that if there has been a good and satisfying parent-child relationship, the child finally comes to a fullness of his own being. He is really 'on his own' and I keep feeling that is an important and natural step in maturing. I'm sixty-five, both my parents are still alive, and their demands on me are tremendous. I constantly have the feeling that I am a bad child because I can't make them young and happy again."

"The worst thing of all," a friend told me, "is not the financial burden, or having to spend so much time with them, or play God making arrangements for their living. It's watching the deterioration. I adored Bob's parents. When we got married they really became my parents, and I've admired them all of the thirty years we've been married. Now they are both old and sick and miserable. Pop is senile and Mom is a complete invalid. We have a housekeeper living with them, but we know we will soon have to put them in a nursing home, and that they will feel we are murderers. But the worst of all is that they *really* loved each other—we used to kid them about being such lovebirds—but because of the miseries of being old they snap at each other, they can't wait until we visit so that each can complain privately about the other, they can't stand the sight of each other. I can't bear it. I want to remember how they used to hold hands in the movies, and give each other that bedroom look when they were leaving on a vacation. Bob and his brothers are being torn apart by what they see now."

Most of the middle-aged I talked with felt that in their parents' generation there tended to be a considerable amount of unexpressed feelings, unresolved problems. A fifty-four-year-old man said, "Our parents never had the kind of help and understanding we have had. Hates and fears were buried deep, and while they were busy and active and healthy, it was possible to delay facing many things about themselves and their lives. Now they see that life is drawing to a close, and all those unexpressed feelings have surfaced. Unconsciously, I think, my father is seething with fury because he couldn't have the education he provided for all his children;

my mother feels both pride and pain to see her daughters involved in successful careers when she never had that choice. They never learned to communicate about their feelings when they were younger, and now all the negative feelings come out. For example, when I visited my parents last week they were having a really bitter fight about a trip to Europe they took thirty-two years ago. My mother was saying, 'You are a mean and thoughtless person; the worse my feet hurt, the faster you walked, until you just left me alone in that hotel room. I want you to know I cried for four hours.' That was thirty-two years ago, their first time in Paris—and now she's telling him how she felt!''

A great many aged parents unconsciously want their middle-aged children to make them feel healthy and young again. They want respect, attention, constant reassurances of love. We the middle-aged resent many of their claims on us, and yet—making everything only more heartbreaking— there is great love and caring on both sides. We find ourselves caught in an agonizing web of human feelings and frailty, and we are profoundly frustrated by our helplessness. The most common and typical comment I've heard these last few months has been, "I love them but I can't save them from old age and dying—and so I feel like a monster."

None of us is going to find simple or satisfactory solutions to the problem of aging parents, but there are some ways in which this crisis of living can also be for learning and growing.

For one thing, and much to my surprise and gratification, I could not find a middle-aged person who was attempting to deny the painful problems. We have already taken an important first step by talking about how we feel, and we are saving ourselves a great deal of psychic exhaustion. We say we feel guilty, but we are not too guilty to talk to each other about our sense of feeling burdened, frustrated, unable to cope. Loving feelings surface so much more easily when one can express the anger too. A friend put it so well when she said, "All the way home from visiting my parents in the city, I rave and rant about how awful they are, and how I can't stand all the complaining and criticism and interference, and blaming—and then, by the time we turn into our driveway, I'm weeping with love and tenderness and compassion, and remembering how much I loved them and how good they were to me when I was little."

But many middle-aged *don't* remember a happy childhood, and that can make this a much more difficult relationship. A man told me, "I finally went to see a psychiatrist about my feelings about my parents. It seemed crazy at this point in my life—I'm almost sixty—but I found myself really getting sick every time I had to do something for my parents. I could hardly talk to them, and I couldn't sleep for weeks before I took them to an old-age home. I had a car accident on the way to visiting them one day, and I knew it was because I just could not stand the idea of being with them even for a couple of hours. I found out that I was just filled with resentment, that I had never stopped blaming them for all the hurts and miseries of my childhood. I resented every single thing I had to do for them, and it made the burden ten times heavier. I got a lot of help in just a couple of months of therapy. I can see them now as two sad old people, who just never had a chance, who hardly lived at all, and I can't make up for what they missed in life. They did the best they could for me and my brother, and I can accept their shortcomings now. I'm sorry for them, deeply sorry, but I also understand that I must not let them drag me down anymore. I do what I feel I must do for them, but now I've got my own priorities, and I'm clear about giving what I can, not what they feel I owe." This was an important resolution; if I have learned anything from talking with others, and from my own observations, it is surely this: no human being can ever satisfy the needs and demands of those who are unhappy inside themselves.

In the face of the dependence and petulance that often express the anguish of aging, we have to remind ourselves of the truer human person that lies buried beneath. "My mother is horribly crippled with rheumatoid arthritis," one woman told me. "Every time I go to see her, she pours out a poisonous monologue about what a good mother she always was, how horrible her children are for not taking care of her at home, how heartless and cruel and selfish we are. I can hardly bear to listen or look. I see such pain in her twisted, tortured face, I feel so guilty because I know I could not have her in my home for one day without wanting to kill myself. She's just 'not there' anymore, not my mother. And so I finally learned to tell myself that the things she says come from her pain and her age, not from the person she was; that somewhere inside her there is still a courageous and loving person who wants me to take good care of my children and husband and fulfill myself as a person. I hear her pain on one level, and on another I listen to an inner voice that tells me she is really saying, 'Don't listen to these terrible things I'm saying; if you love me, go have a good life, and remember me as I used to be.' "

We need to recognize that this is a time in human history when life has been greatly prolonged but few seem to know what to do with it, and we will have to make difficult and painful decisions. There is no reason we have to feel impelled to do this all alone, without help. There are beginning to be more and better social agencies that can help us make the crucial decisions about housing, and medical and financial care. We need to acknowledge our sense of frustration and anger, and we may need to get help in facing our own unfinished business of childhood, which may be adding to our difficulties. Some form of counseling or psychotherapy for ourselves, at this time, may be a constructive and creative way of allowing the very best of our good feelings to come to the surface even while we may be facing staggering responsibilities and frustrations.

There will be no easy solutions, but if we can bring tenderness, strength, and mature nurturing to our relationship with elderly parents, good kinds of growing must inevitably come to us. If we fear our own aging, this may be a confrontation through which we can begin to assess and affirm the ways in which we can plan for a different kind of experiencing of the last few years of life for ourselves. If we accept our own imperfect attempts to do the best we can, we come close to sharing with our parents just how they felt when they were raising us; we need only do the best we can, just as they did.

Sometimes older parents may try to seduce a child into taking over, long before this is appropriate or necessary. Many people reported that their parents often said, "Tell us what to do," about retirement, investments, savings plans, the choice of a place to live after retirement. We ought to be sensitive to the hazards of infantilizing our parents before this is appropriate or necessary—and it isn't always at their urging, but may come from our own needs. We need to take a good hard look at our own motivations. Have we been looking forward to the time when the tables would be turned and we would have the power to control? Is there a sense of satisfaction in mothering or fathering someone who has been good to us? Whether out of anger or affection, the tendency to take over and run our parents lives, too soon, too quickly, is often the source of unnecessary problems. A regretful woman told me, "I overreacted terribly when I saw my parents beginning to show their age. I know now it scared me out of my mind, and to avoid looking at my fears, I just took over and became an efficient administrator. I talked my father into retiring. I found them an apartment in Florida, I hired a part-time cleaning woman, I went around like a social director, finding friends for them, I moved them—and a year later my father had a stroke. I know he blames me; he hated quitting work, he hated Florida, he hated being with my mother twenty-four hours a day. Who was I to play God?"

It seems to me that we need to set some clear limits about

how much help we can give and we also need to recognize that our parents are persons who have lived a long life and have a right to the dignity of making their own decisions whether these seem wise or foolish to us. When they become incapacitated there will be time enough to make decisions —quite enough of a responsibility for someone else's life.

It is not only that we see our own problems of aging in our parents, but that we also find ourselves frightened by having to see our parents in a new role. A woman told me, "My father has always been like the Rock of Gibraltar to me; always getting me out of trouble, always making me feel secure and safe. Now, gradually over the past ten years, I see this pattern shifting. He is beginning to depend on me. It's crazy; I'm fifty-three years old, and yet I'm frightened by this shift in roles."

On the other hand, the fact that our parents live well into our middle age, also means that *we* feel infantilized. In our forties and fifties we are still being told to comb our hair, clean our fingernails, go on a diet, stop staying up so late, and wear our rubbers! Almost every middle-aged person with living parents reported how easy it was to get "sucked into thinking you're seven years old" when with their parents. In order to make the best relationship possible, it seems to me to be just as important to set limits on the infantilizing one will allow, as to curb one's own tendency to do this to parents. One woman told me, "I tell my mother if she'll stop nagging me about how long I can keep meat in the freezer, then I won't nag her about drinking too much coffee!"

Very few of the people I've talked with felt that much could be gained by the kind of open confrontation that they find may be effective in better human relations with their children or contemporaries. As one man told me, "I have been to several encounter groups, and I thought it would be growth-enhancing for my mother if I tried to develop greater authenticity in our relationship. Very gently, I began to say we ought to speak the truth to each other more clearly, tell each other what we are really thinking and feeling. It was disastrous! She completely misinterpreted everything I said, and felt terribly threatened and rejected. It took me six months to undue my clumsy do-it-yourself therapy, and I don't think I'll ever really hear the last of it. Every once in a while when she's angry at me, she'll say something like, 'Maybe you want to tell me again about what a terrible person I am.' Open and frank confrontations sometimes may work well for younger people, but as far as I can see, it's a bust with older people."

"Some of the things we have to do seem so terribly *cruel*," a friend said. "My mother was living alone in an apartment in Brooklyn, where she'd lived for thirty-five years. All her memories of my father were tied up with her life in that neighborhood, and she loved to go shopping and to cook for visiting children or grandchildren. But it was a third-floor walk-up apartment, in a neighborhood that was getting worse every day. In one week there were three robberies in her building. She was mugged once on the street in broad daylight. All her old friends were moving away, all her old stores were disappearing. We just couldn't let her go on living there. We tried to find another apartment. We couldn't find anything that wouldn't cost four or five times as much as she was paying. In any event, there was no place else she wanted to be. I saw her aging right in front of my eyes, all the months we talked about it. After a while, she seemed to just give up. She gave up wanting to shop or cook or take care of herself, and finally we had to put her in a nursing home, where she has to share a room with two other women. I couldn't have her come and live with me—my working hours are very long and Ed would have gone crazy, he needs his quiet and privacy. There are no decent, human alternatives anymore. If her neighborhood hadn't changed, she could have lived in her own apartment for another ten, fifteen years, with her dignity and independence. But what could I do?"

One man told me that for his own pleasure, and to help his aged father to reaffirm his unique individuality, he makes a great effort to get his father to talk about the past. This can be a source of real communication, and gives both parent and child a sense of perspective on the ongoing cycle of human life. He told me, "As soon as my father starts giving me all the details about the peculiarities of his digestive system, I begin to ask him questions about his childhood in Austria. His face lights up, and we are really together again."

By beginning to examine some of the ways we can prepare for our own old age we can also discover what our parents may need most from us. If we can speak to their deepest needs, neither we nor they will feel as much sense of distress. And those deepest needs, just like our own, are to be helped to feel that their lives have had meaning, that they are persons who matter—and are loved.

Middle age is also likely to be one's first experience with the death of a parent. Psychologist Dr. Abraham Maslow once told me, "I'm glad you're attacking education for being too fact-oriented. The most important learnings are internal, intrinsic; one learns more from the death of a parent than from all the academic subjects one studies."

I didn't fully understand what he meant until the death of my mother, when I experienced new depths of pain and growing I never imagined possible. This can be a time of profound growth and change, if one allows oneself truly to experience all the rich variety of mournful, ambivalent, guilty feelings, as well as the new awareness of how deeply one has been influenced by one's parents, and how much they are part of oneself—often more in death than even in life.

The death of a parent opens up new avenues of insight and perception about dependency, mortality—and immortality—the meaning of love and acceptance, the importance of remembering human frailty as well as strength—the meaning of "family"—how that includes memories and relationships that suddenly take on new and deeper significance. The inner work of accepting and using such a separation for one's own maturation may add greatly to one's stature in middle age. Discovering that it is terrible to be a motherless child even at the age of fifty teaches you some important lessons about the human condition.

There are, of course, the painful practical realities of a totally changed relationship with the surviving parent. In most cases our parents did not have separate lives and identities. In talking with my contemporaries, we have been shocked to realize that in most cases, where our parents were married for from forty to sixty years, it is hard to add up twenty to thirty days when they were separated. Can someone in their seventies or eighties make an adjustment to being alone after such an intensity of shared living?

The answer, of course, has to be, some can, some can't. It will depend partly on the courage and inner resources of the surviving parent—but also of equal importance will be whether or not children are able to strike a balance between genuine compassion and dangerous infantilization. A friend asks, "How do you let your mother know you really understand her loss and care about her, without taking over her life and never giving her the opportunity to discover her own strengths? I think we have to show faith and encourage self-respect—but sometimes that may look like coldness or insensitivity."

New issues arise; the surviving parent may become very dependent—wanting the children to take over all the roles once fulfilled by the spouse. A wife survives who has never in her life made out a check or made a major decision; a husband survives who has never boiled an egg or taken a shirt to the laundry. The question of a parent coming to live with his or her children may have to be considered. It's a good rule of thumb for no one in a bereaved family to make any major decisions for at least six months. In the first moments of grief and shock, gestures are sometimes made that cannot be fulfilled without great conflict and eventual misery for everyone.

There are surely no simple answers for such problems as breaking up a family home with the acquisitions of a lifetime; helping a parent find new avenues of fulfillment; helping in decisions about retirement, illness, a new place to live. As I begin to fumble my own way through the anguish of this time in my relationship with my father, the only thing that seems certain to me is that I must not be impatient but must allow for time and change, and that I must not allow my compassion to lead me into any dishonesty. As time goes by, we will talk about future plans and necessities, but what I think I must do most of all is encourage a relationship in which all of the family is open about feelings and needs and where we don't try to force anything to be done before we are all ready, together.

Even the death of a parent can become part of one's middle-aged Renaissance if one allows the experience full scope, if we ride out all the feelings we are having and if we use the intensity of our awareness of how precious life is for being more loving and honest with ourselves and those we care most about.

Finally, anybody who can't have "a Renaissance" in his "Middle Ages" just isn't trying hard enough! I think I began to appreciate the good fortune of being middle-aged today, despite the problems of life, when I saw an old movie on television one night. It was *Strange Interlude*, Eugene O'Neil's play made into a movie in 1932, starring Norma Shearer and Clark Gable. In the course of the story they are called upon to age considerably; in fact at the end of the movie they look ready for the mortician, gray, wrinkled, palsied, tottering, quavering, barely able to walk. But then I began to figure out how old they were supposed to be. At the end of the film, they have a son who can't possibly be more than twenty-two or twenty-three years old, since he's still in college, and in those days you didn't drop out after high school, to go and find your identity for a few years! But even to stretch the point, let's say he was twenty-five. He had been born when his parents were certainly well under thirty, so the most they could possibly be was somewhere between forty-five and fifty-five. I almost fell off my chair when I figured this out, and took another look at them; by today's standards they looked at least one hundred and seven! They looked that way because aging did come more rapidly then, but a significant factor was that they *expected* to look that way, back in the "olden days" of 1932! I guess most people in their fifties thought life was pretty much over, that you were supposed to be gracefully readying yourself for death. Expectations seem to have an awful lot to do with how you feel, and because we expect to have another twenty or thirty really good years, it is almost impossible to find any fifty-year-olds who even vaguely resemble the doddering, feeble wrecks I saw in the film.

Not only are parents looking better all the time, but grandparents have become a special brand of "swingers"! The director of a nursery school told me, "I can almost never tell, when a child is brought to visit the school, whether he's with his mother or the rich grandma who's going to pay the tuition—they look the same age."

Grandparenthood can surely be a kind of "Renaissance" experience in middle age; it certainly has to do with a sense of renewal, of life beginning again. And yet, an inordinately large number of grandparents don't seem to be having much fun with it. One young mother told me that among her contemporaries, her own parents, who love to babysit, are considered a rare exception. She said, "All my friends keep telling me how lucky I am. They thought their parents would be crazy about their grandchildren, and bug the hell out of them to be with them, but much to their surprise—and very hurt feelings—the parents hardly ever come around. And if they do, they stay for a half-hour and leave, and never offer to babysit. They're too busy with their own lives, I guess."

Grandparenthood has certainly changed radically. When our parents were young—and to a less extent in our time as children—grandparents were the teachers, advisers, counselors; out of the wisdom of their experience, they could tell their children the best ways to raise their grandchildren. Freud and Dr. Spock changed all that! Within less than half of this past century, grandparents were robbed completely of this role as childraising experts; we were learning all kinds of new things about child development and psychology, and a whole new breed of cat was developing: the child expert. The loss of status for grandparents was very serious, very hard to take. I suppose our parents were the generation that took the full brunt of this revolution in family life, for when our children were young, we were not about to listen to our own parents' ideas. We were too busy checking with Dr. Spock, the school guidance counselor, our friendly family therapist, the pediatrician, or our next-door neighbor who majored in psychology at college! It seems likely that in the course of this profound change, grandparents got turned off about there being much possibility for pleasure in grandparenting, when you have no control, no prestige, no power of any kind. As I talked with some of my contemporaries who had become grandparents, many of course reported this was positively the most delightful experience they'd ever had. However, there were also many who responded in this way: "You know, I don't feel like babysitting very often. I love the baby, but when my daughter leaves him here for a weekend, my husband and I are so nervous, we're so worried about doing something my daughter and son-in-law won't approve of, that we just can't enjoy ourselves and be natural." Other grandparents told me that they find themselves on the defensive, feeling stupid, because every suggestion, every observation is greeted with derision or anger, they feel they are being patronized. One grandfather said, "Somehow or other my wife and I managed to raise two children, but now they treat us as if we never warmed a bottle or changed a diaper. You have to be so goddamned careful what you say—they're so touchy about criticism—that it doesn't seem worth the effort." This seems to be changing; parents in their early twenties are much more natural and relaxed with their children, and grandparents are reaping the benefits.

But aside from grandparents who feel turned off by their children's criticisms, it is also true that grandparents *do* have full and active lives of their own and are not as available for babysitting. They work longer and play harder. Many more middle-aged women have full-time jobs.

During my childhood, not only grandparents tended to be more available. There were also maiden aunts or widowed uncles or live-in maids who could help to raise the children. Now young couples often feel isolated and cut off from those much-needed extra hands; and I suspect that, as in most things, the pendulum has swung from one extreme to the other, and is now coming back to a middle-of-the-road position. Today's younger parents don't really care whether or not Grandma has a Ph.D. in child development from the Yale Child Study Center; they know she can be an important and useful person in their and their children's lives. With the advent of the isolated nuclear family, grandparents are very much needed to help out in emergencies and for some relief from child care. We have been learning that possibly the most important functions grandparents can play have nothing whatever to do with how much child psychology they know.

Grandparents are usually the only people a child will ever know in his whole life who can give him unconditional love. Not being responsible for the development of character, as parents are, they don't have to be disciplinarians. I think that is the greatest discovery of the century for today's grandparents! When they felt responsible for teaching childraising methods, grandparents were naturally involved in trying to set standards. When parents were no longer willing to listen, this got pretty sticky; there was Grandpa, with his clear, concise, and unequivocal theories about the proper punishment for lying—but nobody wanted to pay any attention to him.

For a while parents and grandparents tuned each other out: what was the fun if you couldn't run the show, at least some of the time? But parents missed that precious time off once a week, or one weekend a month—and not so strangely, as grandparents began to practice a hands-off policy in the discipline department (since no one was listening anyway) it dawned on grandchildren that maybe grandparents could be allies instead of just another set of grownups.

I think grandparents are for spoiling children; that this has always been to some degree, and ought only to become more so, their chief role. The demands, the expectations, the conditions we set for young children are an unrelieved and awful burden—somewhere, somehow, there ought to be emotional relief from all the frustrations and restrictions our children live with. Grandparents are the perfect choice. They ought to let their grandchildren stay up later, eat more junk, bounce on the furniture, say dirty words, and get toys they don't need. I am not recommending utter anarchy; I am only saying that children are smarter than anybody; they know perfectly well that parents are the people who have to try to make them be good. That's their job, and you can't hold it against them. But parents and teachers are enough, already; you don't need any more grownups working on improving your character. What you need is someone who loves you crazily, blindly, and without reservation.

This means we have to learn to be different kinds of grandmas and grandpas from those of any previous generation! We have to learn to let go of all our own theories about childraising, and have genuine faith in our children to do it their own way. If we have any confidence at all in our childraising methods, how bad can they be at the job?

Once our children know we are not going to tell them, "Nobody ever got away with *that* in *my* house" or, "Of course it's none of my business, but that child is suffering from malnutrition"; once we stop saying things like, "Eat it for me—make Grandma happy" or, "I'll be so proud if you get an A in arithmetic," we can relax and enjoy ourselves and be enjoyed by our children and grandchildren. It seems to me that if I'm going to look forward to being a grandmother, I want my daughter to understand that I'm not going to tell her what to do—but then when I'm babysitting, she can't tell *me* what to do either! She isn't going to destroy my grandchild by her procedures, and I am not going to ruin her methods when I use my own once a week or once a month. Any kid in our family is going to be smart enough to know that mothers and grandmothers are not alike, and that you learn to behave differently with each one. I want to feel that when I come to visit or when he or she comes to see me, we are *going to have a ball!* I'm going to regress, I'm going to bask in child's play. I'm going to make mud pies, or eat four hotdogs at the amusement park, and buy something ridiculously expensive at F. A. O. Schwarz. I'm not going to lecture on good study habits, or warn of the consequences of not drinking enough milk, or how you might go blind from reading without a good light, or how selfishness can lead to loneliness; that's Mama's and Papa's job, not mine. I'm for laughs, for fun, for loving—nothing else. It seems to me this is the route to making grandparenthood a better deal than it's ever been for any generation yet. Parents have felt defensive because they were using new methods their own parents neither understood nor approved of; grandparents have felt demeaned, worthless, without dignity or respect. Children felt badgered by two older generations.

We middle-aged have a chance to change all that. I've done enough studying of the supposedly "right" and "wrong" childraising methods; I used too many of them on my poor child. Now it is my chance to be spontaneous, human—childlike—loving just for love's sake only. I can hardly wait!

Our children will not have to feel threatened by our interference. One hopes they will tolerate our indulgence as they see it isn't really destroying their children's moral fiber. (Loving for loving's sake is so rare, it can't possibly hurt a child.) And for the first time, grandchildren can be unambivalent about a grandparent's visit, because it isn't going to be an equal portion of too many toys and candy and the price one pays for that, of long lectures about who is starving in the world (and would love to eat your vegetables), and how it's not nice not to say Thank you.

We taught our children to behave better in front of their grandparents than they did when they were home alone. There were words you could say in front of friends, or us, but never when the grandparents were visiting. We didn't tell Grandma and Grandpa about failing geography, or the day you played hooky and got caught, or the time you almost got busted for being at a party where marijuana was being smoked. Many of us protected both our children and our parents from each other. I'd like to see that reversed. I'd like to feel that my grandchild could let me know about the fallible human side of things; the imperfections, the impulses, the less-than-lovely thoughts. Parents are for building character; I would rather just be a friend at court!

I think more parents will want help, more grandparents will enjoy giving it, and more grandchildren will be the hospitable and happy recipients when the main thing about Grandma and Grandpa is that they love blindly and too well.

A young mother told me, "My mother is the perfect grandmother; she is absolutely incapable of seeing anything wrong with my children; they are perfect, beautiful, and geniuses, of course. Jason is two, and someone stepped on his foot in a supermarket, and he yelled, 'You Dummy!' My mother's reaction was classic. She didn't tell him he was bad, she didn't hit him—she looked at him in wonder and adoration and said, 'Jason, I didn't know you knew that word! What a smart boy you are!'"

That's the kind of Grandma I want to be. I hope I'll be able to communicate to my daughter and her husband (I *think* she's planning marriage before motherhood, but either way) that what I propose to do and be is in no way a challenge to their role as parents. Just a supplementary emotional vitamin, to be taken often enough to make the realities of the everyday world more endurable for my grandchild.

"Silly girl," I can hear some of you muttering to yourselves, "these days when do grandparents ever live near enough to their grandchildren to see them more than once or twice a year, if that much?" How true; the most significant of all changes in "cross-generational emotional fertilization" is distance, the mobility of families. But I'm not a silly girl, for as far as I am concerned, any children whom I like and who like me are my grandchildren. I only wish I could befriend more than I have already, and as time goes by and I get too feeble in the fingers and the head to write any more books, I would hope to find more children to be grandmother to in any way I can. At the moment I am the Jewish Grandmother to the Italian children who live next door, and to the three children of a young Methodist minister and his wife, my theory being that whatever maligning there may be of Jewish mothers, I still think children ought to have a Jewish grandmother.

My daughter understood grandmotherhood in its larger and more important sense far better than I did. One year at

Christmastime, feeling that we were much too self-indulgent and surfeited with gifts, I sent some money—enough for one month's care—to one of the foster children's associations, in my daughter's name, as part of her gifts. I could well have given more without suffering at all. The following summer my daughter worked as a waitress in a "Dunkin' Doughnuts" on the night shift in order to earn extra spending money for clothes for college and for whatever other extras she might decide to get herself. But our anniversary came around in August, and quite suddenly she changed her mind; almost everything she had earned was spent on getting us our own foster child and paying the full load for a year. Nam Soo Kim, a nine-year-old Korean is another of my "grandchildren," who gets packages with such things as racing cars, lollipops, a flashlight, and Hostess Cup Cakes (because I can't bear the idea of a child growing up without cupcakes, recalling what "Dugan's Cream-filled" used to mean in my young life!). Grandparenthood is as much a state of mind as anything else, and there is no time in the foreseeable future when any of us would have to look very far to find a child who needs us.

I started this chapter by telling about my California friend and our sense of bereavement about never having seen each other with a baby. Now let me tell you what we did about it. We went next door, where my young neighbor was beside herself with the exhaustion of sleepless nights and harried days with a colicky baby of four weeks, and a three- and a four-year-old also underfoot. We asked if we could borrow the baby for the afternoon. She looked as if she had been praying for just such a miracle, and God had heard her! Soon we were loaded down with all the necessary paraphernalia, including the baby, and went triumphantly back to my house, like two kids who had stolen a chocolate layer cake from the kitchen window and were going off to a secret hiding place to enjoy their spoils. We bathed the baby in the kitchen sink, we bottled and burped him, we rocked and jig-gled and tickled and sang and cuddled him out of his mind; we theorized about the state of his digestive track, as we handed him back and forth, while the poor kid tried desper-ately to get a nap in. By the time his father came to get him, the three of us were exhausted; but I will never forget the soft, tender, quiet way in which my friend held that baby —the melting look of her, the circle of that nurturing embrace—and I know that if I had seen her with her own babies, when I was young, I could not possibly have had the wisdom or perception to understand the beauty of it all.

To accept and to relish what is past gives color to the pre-sent; to become preoccupied with the past, and to cling to it, robs one of new frontiers. There is a vast difference between a normal and natural nostalgia for what has been; it is human to feel disappointment over one's failures, some guilt over one's mistakes. But we need to accept our human fallibility and move on. Most of us did the best we could. If we resign ourselves to quiet despair over the life we have already lived, we will rob ourselves of the life we might yet live.

We were standing in the entrance hall of a small Swedish restaurant on Cape Cod, waiting to be seated for lunch. A middle-aged woman and her aged mother were talking to the proprietor, who happened to be telling them about a party he was going to be running the next day, for which he was going to close the restaurant to the general public. We heard him saying, "Thank you, I'm so glad you like our dishes. As a matter of fact, we have many, many people who have been coming to us for twenty, thirty years. To-morrow we are going to have a birthday party for two ladies, who will be ninety-four and ninety-seven! They are first cousins, and their relatives are going to surprise them. They are remarkable women—still vigorous and active—and they were among our very first fans when we started this restaurant in 1938." As he spoke, all those in earshot joined his pleasure in thinking about these old ladies, until we heard the elderly woman, walking with difficulty and pain, holding on to her daughter's arm, say, "I don't know that I think they are so lucky to have lived so long, but I hope you all have a good time."

There was a moment of silence as we all took in the meaning of her words. Then I think we all shared a sudden and frightening sense of shock—and we all did what the restaurant owner did—we ignored the meaning of her poignant, ironic message. He flushed, looked uneasy, and then said, "Yes, I know it will be a wonderful party."

As we made our way to our table, I suddenly felt a cold chill of anxiety—one that I become more familiar with as I get older—that momentary perception that I will someday be old and will die.

I remembered that just that morning when I woke up, my elbows and fingers were very stiff and painful, and I had had a sense of physical aging and deterioration which terrified me. Part of me thinks of old age as a total disaster, and I am horrified by it.

The most painful and difficult part of being middle-aged is that old age and dying are no longer ridiculous abstractions. Each of us reaches that moment of truth, at some point in the forties or fifties, when the terror lives with us, for moments at a time, at least.

For me it has happened when I am walking on the street and I see a maid or a nurse helping an old woman learn to use a walker, or I see an old man being wheeled into the park by a daughter or a son—the final reversal; once this same man moved proudly and strongly, wheeling a baby carriage, carrying a new life, totally dependent on *him*. Now *he* is in a wheelchair, totally dependent on that life he once created. What I see is not a living person, but the shell of a human being, without dignity, without purpose, a burden to himself and everyone around him. I am terrified at the specter of myself becoming such a creature, a bag of misery, of wasted flesh and bones, unable to care for myself, unable to live with dignity and self-respect, a wasted child with no present except pain and helplessness—and certainly no future.

To look toward illness and death in our times is to live with some degree of horror. Too many of the old are isolated from the life of the world. They are no longer the venerated elders, sharing the living sounds of a household in which they remain persons who matter. Most of us, when we allow ourselves to think about it at all, are frightened and horrified at becoming helpless and dependent, and ghettoized in a home for the aged or a nursing home, when our relatives will be counting the days for blessed relief from watching us move toward unliving. I once visited such a place with a friend, and the sight of ancient men and women being fed and cajoled like infants, who were incontinent and senile, was almost more than I could bear. One's first reaction is the fervent prayer that life will never be that long for oneself, and yet we cling to life with tenacity even then. If one respects and reveres the human person, it is unbearable to face the possibility for oneself—or for anyone else—of a time when nothing is really left of the full person who was once there.

What bothers me most as I look into the empty, hopeless, helpless faces of the men and women sitting on the steps of the nursing homes in my neighborhood is that they are no longer in charge of their lives, they do not will their own existence—and to me this seems the ultimate loss of one's dignity and identity as a human being.

One recent example of this loss of selfhood, the eighty-four-year-old mother of a friend: For thirty-seven years of widowhood she had lived alone in her own apartment in the Bronx, quite self-sufficient, never so sick or feeble that she could not visit her children and grandchildren on the subway, on her own. Her neighborhood began to change radically within the last ten years, to the point where it was impossible for her to go out alone; she had been mugged four times before she accepted her imprisonment. She finally gave up, after an arm was broken when someone took her shopping bag and knocked her down, and the elbow would not heal. She became a recluse, and soon thereafter developed cancer of the stomach. In spite of this, she still maintained some independence and free will; *she* decided if and when she wanted to visit relatives and friends, and *she* paid for the special taxi she hired that picked her up at her apartment-house door. But the illness eventually made her too weak, and finally she had to be hospitalized. She knew how sick she was, and there was little question that her own choice would have been quietly to starve to death, her dignity as a human being still intact; but the medical profession, being what it is—rarely related to the real needs and wishes of individuals—insisted to her relatives that, if they really cared for her, she must have an operation. Eighty-four years old, with an advanced metastasis, they insisted her "only hope" was an operation, which was performed, which was unsuccessful, which left her dying an agonizing, slow death, attached to all kinds of machines that sustained her poor dead life for weeks, even months, during which she became each day more and more a living vegetable. A woman who went to work at thirteen, raised a family of eight children, and prided herself on serving the needs of those she loved—and never knew any other way to be in the world.

The story seems to me to represent so much that is real in our fears of old age. The changing social order, which makes the old feel useless and unwanted, the living in surroundings that become less and less familiar and more and more dangerous as the erosion and death of all of our major cities continues.

And there is the hypocrisy of the way in which our society responds to aging; on the one hand, isolating the aged, and letting them know we don't want them and need them, and then at the same time, in the name of medical progress, prolonging their lives beyond the point at which life continues to have any meaning to them. There is an underlying anguish in the black humor of the joke in which a little boy asks his father, "But Daddy, what are we saving Grandfather *for?*" We discard and waste all our natural resources—including our elderly. We are a nation of youth worshipers, and anybody who isn't scared of getting old in this society, just doesn't understand the situation!

But at the same time that I freely confess my anxiety and fear, I also know, just as truly, that old age and dying need not be thus; that despite the difficulties in aging that are imposed on us by society, there is still free choice, free will, about the ways in which we react to the problems that face us.

I know this in a special way; through my own work and partly through my husband's work as a psychotherapist with dying patients. In the early 1960s, while working as Director of Education at the Manhattan Society for Mental Health, I was part of a research team on a special project in which we were trying to develop mental-health education programs for the aged.* These are some of the things I learned: wherever and whenever the elderly are genuinely treated as persons, their physical well-being improves. For example, when a day center was provided in a neighborhood, and the older people had a place to gather, to talk, to develop new interests and activities—including political action for better social services to the aged—there was a 70 percent decline in visits to the nearby medical center. In England a remarkable nurse by the name of Cecily Saunders decided that she did not like the kind of impersonal, dehumanizing care dying patients were receiving. She went back to school and got herself an M.D. and a degree in social work, and started her own hospital, St. Christopher's Hospice, in London. The hospital was to accommodate 50 percent regular patients and 50 percent terminal patients. There was only one problem which soon became apparent, and that was that the terminal patients just weren't dying off at the normal rate, and so fewer new patients could be admitted. In a hospital designed to meet the

* Klein, LeShan, and Furman, *Promoting Mental Health of Older People through Group Methods*, Mental Health Materials Center, 419 Park Ave. S., New York, N.Y. 10016 ($4.50).

human, individual needs of patients who were respected, who were talked to honestly about their condition, who were allowed the kind of free-will choices they had a right to make as adults with dignity and self-respect (one old gentleman had his glass of schnapps before bedtime each night!) they began to recover, to will themselves back into life.

In our discussion groups with the aged in all kinds of neighborhoods—in a Harlem health center, in an upper-middle-class surburban recreational club, in nursing homes —we found that no matter what the psychological climate might have been before these discussion groups were formed, there was clear and recognizable improvement. We found that the very people whom we *thought* looked helpless and hopeless—and who usually described themselves in just that way—were hungry for involvement, had a passionate desire *not* to give up hope, a wish to rediscover their sense of personal identity. They *were* capable of growing and changing and taking hold of their own lives again, and *this was irrespective of their physical condition.*

It has also been my experience that those who adjust best to the later years not only have enjoyed their lives more, but have liked themselves better. Typical of those who seem to lie down and get ready to die too soon was a man who said, "I can't stand myself; I nag my grandchildren, I complain to my children, I don't make friends easily, I can't stand to live with myself." At the other end of the scale, I remember a darling birdlike creature I met at a YWCA meeting, who said, "Why should I get mad at myself because sometimes I feel old and cranky? I have a right! All my life I have said to myself, 'You're not the best person in the world—and you're certainly not the worst!' "

I well remember the reaction of some psychiatrists and psychologists when my husband first started doing psychotherapy with dying patients, some time in the early 1950s.

They were horrified. One psychiatrist kept asking my husband why in the world he would choose to work in such a hopeless cause, and when my husband told him that human beings had a right to the fullest life until the moment of death, his response was, "I think what you are doing is obscene." In the early years of the psychiatric revolution of the past half-century, there seemed to be a hidden expectation that the therapist was to be rewarded for his efforts by seeing his patients live a long and happy life after the therapy was over. Most people who became therapists seemed to have this expectation without even really being conscious of it, but it became quite clear as a few brave souls began to work in the area of geriatric psychology. The atmosphere has changed considerably in recent years. Having discovered through many research projects how full and active and meaningful life can be for the aged who are encouraged to find new ways of affirming their selfhood, this field of endeavor has become increasingly respectable and widespread.

One of the earliest studies, which shook up a lot of old theories, was done during the Second World War. A social scientist was very distressed by all the old people who sat each day on the benches in the middle of upper Broadway. They were mostly retired, widowed, semi-invalided people, living alone, with nothing to do with themselves all day. He began to talk to them, and found that they were bitter, unhappy, and despairing. They felt useless, they had no pride and most of them said they wished they could die. He got in touch with the War Manpower Commission—there was a great shortage of labor for the defense plants—and recruited many of these elderly people for jobs. At first they were sure they could not handle the work, but within a short period of time their physical and mental condition had improved markedly. One of the most interesting findings in this project was how many people reported an improvement in their ability to remember. The absentmindedness of older people seems to have far more to do with one's perception of oneself than with physical deterioration.

One of the things we are constantly learning more about is that there need not be intellectual deterioration during aging. One imaginative university, in danger of having to close for financial reasons, developed some innovative programs, among which was a call to retired professors and trustees to volunteer their services as consultant specialists in many different departments. It was soon discovered that they brought a wealth of wisdom and expertise to their guest lectureships, and the program was continued after the financial crisis had passed. Another example has been the use of retired businessmen to serve as advisers and counselors in ghetto communities where the government is sponsoring the development of small businesses by local residents. Given an opportunity to use one's mind and maturity in creative ways, the elderly come through with flying colors.

One of the things that seems to be most closely related to the rapid deterioration of intellectual and physical functioning is retirement from the roles that gave one purpose and status—a reason for being. In one study, seven men retired from the post office; during the first year five of them died. None of them had been known to be sick at the time of retirement. If we are frightened by the unhappiness of the elderly we now know, we ought to remember that they are usually people whose sense of identity derived not from who they were, but what they did. They are mostly people who went to work or married and raised a family without having had the kind of search for oneself that our children insist on now, and that we have an opportunity to explore in our middle age. In the discussion groups that I led, I found that regardless of whether an old man had been a tailor, a butcher or a doctor, he saw himself as *being* that role; he did not consider himself a man who earned a living at some specific job.

He and the job were one and the same. Under such circumstances, I constantly heard such people say, "Now that I am no longer 'Sam, the Tailor,' I am nothing."

It is possible for us to experience our retirement and old age quite differently. We need *not* be identified by what we *do*, but by what we *are*—if we make it our business to believe that *now*. One of the fascinating things I discovered in my work at the Manhattan Society for Mental Health was that when I assumed that there simply were no such things as "nothing people" in my groups, all kinds of new and beautiful things began to happen. For example, one of the roles which many older people tended to make little of was being a grandparent. They felt that their children did not want them to interfere in their childraising ideas, that their grandchildren could not really understand their world, their experiences and values—and there was a great deal of hostility expressed about "today's spoiled brats." I suggested that it was time they learned a little about why childraising practices had changed; it was time for them to benefit from all the new things we had learned about child development and child psychology. I began to give lectures on this subject, and the response was fantastic; I have never met with a group of young parents who were as eager, as hungry, for new knowledge, new understanding as these old people. Once it was indicated to them that I expected them to move on, move forward, in their own growth and development, there was no further talk of being useless, sick, helpless, and unwanted.

In one of the centers where a colleague was working, she made an arrangement with the local public school to have a special afternoon workshop where the members of her group went into the school as "everybody's Grandma and Grandpa." Some told the children stories, some had a woodworking class, others did some tutoring. I have no doubt whatsoever that the life expectancy in that Senior Citizens' Club was changed markedly; but what was more significant was that its members were finding pleasure and meaning in the present, in each day's possibilities, and were no longer merely preoccupied with the horrors of being old.

One might suppose, on the face of it, that it would be normal and natural for older people to be preoccupied with their own deaths because this is an imminent reality. But there are too many elderly who are *not* so preoccupied, and so we are forced to look for a different explanation. There seems to be a universal consensus among those who work in the geriatric field that an obsession with death is almost always related to a fear of not living one's life, of having all kinds of regrets for never having truly discovered and fulfilled one's own destiny and identity.

I have never yet met anyone who was constantly concerned about dying, who was not also full of self-hatred and unfulfilled dreams. I have never met anyone who hardly ever thought about dying, who was not also happy to be who they were and pretty contented with what they'd done with their lives. There must be a connection. I know a woman who is one hundred and one years old, and while it does concern her that she can no longer travel around the city alone on buses to get to all the good causes she works for, she does not seem to be at all concerned with the idea of her own death. We have all heard of people like the man who has had a heart condition for fifteen years, is only seventy now, and lives in terror that each breath will be his last. One finds oneself wondering why he carries on so; if his life is unbearable, why should death be so awful? He is preoccupied with dying *because* his life is so unfulfilling.

A second factor which seems to play an important part in the fear of dying is really a fear of loneliness, of being cut off and alone at the very moment in one's life when one needs most to be close to those one loves. This is a very real and understandable anxiety. Most doctors, nurses and relatives are themselves so afraid of the subject of death that they simply cannot bear to face it with someone who is dying. The patient himself wants desperately to talk about what he feels —anyone who has encouraged such discussions knows this —but the dying are too kindhearted to force the living to confront something that fills them with horror. We rationalize by telling ourselves that the patient doesn't want to talk about it, but it just isn't true. There *is* a terrible loneliness in dying, when the people you care about the most can't even say a decent goodbye, but stand around your bed discussing the elections, the baseball scores, or Aunt Joan's pregnancy. The sounds of life and living are important too, but the loneliness of denial is *dreadful*. There was a lovely and important television play about this on "The Bold Ones" (January 24, 1971) in which a doctor tries to help a friend (also a doctor) meet the challenge of his approaching death. It told of a hospital in which a genuine effort is made to help the patient and his family learn to communicate with each other during the crisis of dying. After the friend's death, the doctor goes home and is talking to his wife about his own fears—not of dying, but of being isolated and alone. His wife says, "*I pledge you an absence of loneliness.*" If each of us could make this pledge to our own aged relatives—and if we could exact this much courage and respect from our children—there would be a considerable reduction in the fears we may now experience.

Another realistic contributing factor to an obsessive fear of dying is the fear of becoming helpless, of having the kind of dependency needs we once had as infants, of having to be cared for by others, with no control over our own lives and destiny. This raises the important medical-social issue that simply must be wrestled with by society as we develop more and more technological miracles for keeping people alive when they really would not choose to be alive anymore. Thus far there has certainly been little if any help or leadership on the part of the medical community about this. For example, the attitude in every hospital that I have ever heard of is that addiction to pain-killing drugs must never be tolerated. A family will plead with the doctors to give more morphine to a seventy-nine-year-old woman dying in agony from cancer, and the answer will be, "But she'll become *addicted!*" There are any number of specialists concerned with the problems of old age and dying who say—and without being facetious—that once it is clear that a patient cannot possibly recover, that the deterioration of health and the increase in pain are inevitable by all possible medical standards, the patient ought to be given heroin or LSD in whatever quantities might be necessary to let him die in a blaze of forgetful, dazed glory! These procedures are in use in some hospitals in England and a few research centers in the United States, and the fact that they are not encouraged is a testament to our puritanism, not to any compassion.

I honestly wish that there were some way in which we middle-aged could prepare ourselves for such an eventuality —by stashing away some kinds of drugs, right now, that could end our misery and degradation at the moment *we* want it, to go with our pride and our humanity still intact. But who would bring such a cache to us in the hospital— and will we be able to judge when the right moment is upon us? All one can do, I suppose, is now, while one is mentally competent, make it absolutely clear to our children that we do *not* want our lives prolonged for one minute beyond the point at which our living is a death-in-life.

Beyond these kinds of realities, I think it is important for us to remember, as we try to gain some perspective about our own later years, that much of the misery we see among the aged has far less to do with age than with previous conditions of servitude! As with people of any age, the elderly are just as prone to use illness and loss of optimum functioning as a way to handle unsolved problems that have existed for all or most of their lives. Old failures, old regrets, old feelings of worthlessness, life-time neuroses, simply come into fuller bloom—and these are problems we can avoid to a very considerable extent by what we do with our lives now, while we are still in full control of ourselves.

Several years ago, my husband and I visited a relative in a luxurious resort retirement community. I had the feeling that I was in a cemetery, where the dead just did not lie down. As I listened to the conversations of the people sitting around the pool, in the sunshine, I was overwhelmed with a sense of horror. The talk was so meaningless, so superficial; there was so much anger, so much petulance, such preoccupation with bodily functions, so much wallowing in one's aches and pains. Life *was* over for these people, and the focus of their attention—full-time—seemed to be on how to get through the next ten or fifteen or twenty years as untouched by life as possible.

The large majority of those who are now in their late seventies and eighties, and who are able to retire in relative comfort, are people who went to work, married and raised their families, almost never having had time to think about what they really wanted to do with their lives. Few among their numbers truly chose a source of income; few even truly chose their own spouses. There were things which they were expected to do, and they did them. When they were the age of their grandchildren, life was a serious matter of basic survival; there was no time to sit and think, "Who am I? What do I want to do with my life?" It was understood that you went to school and went to work, and the opportunity to choose that work was limited to those few with very special talents, the energy to work full-time while going to college, or the accidental good fortune of finding themselves in a father's business that truly challenged their own unique gifts and interests. Caught in a web of their own making—a life of struggle, the attainment of material wealth and security—they now find themselves faced with a sense of, "What was it all for?" and anger is often the only tool at their disposal to handle their discontent.

There were certainly some exceptions to the pattern of living we saw there. One was a spry and charming man who took one look at the people in his apartment building, and marched himself to a nearby hospital to offer his services as a volunteer. He was a man who had always enjoyed his life and, with no unfinished business of regrets and self-abasement, was able to find new ways of feeling useful to others and to himself. Another man told us he felt more alive than he had ever felt before. He was well aware that he had always hated the work by which he had earned his living, and saw retirement as an opportunity to do something that would give him pleasure. He had had a secret yearning to go to sea as a young boy, but in all his years in business, he had never had time to get on a boat. He set himself up in a boat-charter business at the age of seventy-four, and is having the time of his life. Another exception we came across was a woman who had recently been widowed, and was sure that her life was now over. She was terrified of being alone, especially since she, not her husband, had been the invalid for many years, having had a heart condition for some twenty years. Urged on by her children, and by a heart specialist of remarkable talent and vision, she had, with great reluctance, forced herself to look for something to do "to kill the time," to "get through" the days of unspeakable dread and loneliness. It had taken more courage than she had ever thought she had, but she had found two jobs for herself at the age of seventy-three; she modeled "mature fashions" part-time in a department store and worked several days a week as a receptionist in the offices of a charity that interested her. Much to her own amazement, she found herself in better physical shape than she had been in for thirty years, and looking forward to each day with zest and pleasure as she found herself participating more fully in the world around her.

In working with older people, I discovered that the greatest handicap they faced was not the aging process itself, but their attitudes toward it. Many of them felt overwhelmed by feelings of inferiority, they did not trust their own capacity to change, to try new ways of living and learning. Feelings of isolation from the mainstream of life, feelings of loss of identity when work and childraising were over, the sense that others saw them as useless, ideas about their not being able to think so well anymore, the fact of having to be less active than before, had all been interpreted by them as meaning life was over. As soon as they found themselves in a group in which it was assumed that this was simply a crossroads at which they had to make some new choices, they were able to deal effectively and courageously with even the most challenging and difficult problems of physical handicaps, inadequate housing, prejudices against them in the job market, financial limitations and the pressures created by a Youth Cult.

What I think I have learned through my husband's and my work and observations is that if one has insupportable anguish in old age, it is usually an indication that one has *always* had trouble with *all* the ages and stages of life, but because old age does have its own special infirmities and difficulties, the maladjustment is more accentuated. Typical of this was the man who was at first told that he had terminal cancer, but was then unexpectedly cured by some of the new chemo-therapy procedures. He told his doctor, "You may not be aware of it, but my biggest problem was not that I was going to die. It's what I will do with my life, now that I must live."

Those who have the most misery in old age tend to be those who have had the least pleasure in being themselves. One woman, trying to "find herself" at the age of seventy-four, trying to search out what would give her pleasure in being alive, told her counselor, "I always lived as if there was only yesterday and tomorrow; today didn't exist." For those of us who are making a real effort to get in touch with ourselves, and to cherish the "moment of being," right now, it is unlikely that we will not know how to use our moments later on.

A beautiful and touching French film, *The Shameless Old Lady*, tells the story of a woman who has spent seventy years doing what she had to do, taking care of her family, never questioning whether or not this was what she wanted to do with her life. After her husband's death she begins to explore the world; she takes a ride in a carriage, she spends whole days walking through department stores, she dares to go for a walk along the waterfront, alone at night. She refuses to live with her grown children, who are horrified by her behavior but unable to force her back into her former role of dutiful acquiescence. With her small means, she befriends a young prostitute and a group of young leftist intellectuals. She buys a car and goes off on a long holiday trip with her new friends, and finally, she helps a young shoemaker to buy his own store. She eats when she is hungry and sleeps when she is tired; she looks and listens, smells and tastes and touches, with new delight in all the wonders of life. She has a special rapport with a young grandson who is having a difficult struggle in trying to find himself. For eighteen glorious months "the shameless old lady" is truly and deeply herself—and out of the wellsprings of her own joy she comes to care more deeply than ever for others. Out of her sense of final fulfillment when she is dying she leaves a package of photographs for her grandson; they are a pictorial chronicle of this last period of her life, and they are meant to convey a message to him about his own life: to continue the courageous struggle to find himself, that that is the most important adventure *at any age.*

I don't mean to play Pollyanna or to suggest that old age and dying are something to look forward to with glee! That's nonsense. All one can say for old age is that the alternative is less appealing. But it is possible to accept the inevitable and then make the most of it. The more we think about it now, the more we prepare ourselves for it, the more chance there will be for continuing fulfillment and joy in living when we get there.

One form of preparation that seems essential to me is to try to do something to forestall the kind of guilt in our children that many of us feel now about our own aged relatives. If this book serves no other purpose than to bear witness to my daughter, that when I was still of sound mind, I did not ever want her to feel responsible or guilty because of the problems and discomforts of my old age, it will suffice. There is some sort of undeclared, unconscious claim on the part of many older people that we, their juniors, are capable of making them feel better or happier if only we were more understanding, patient, forbearing, sensitive, and wise. Almost all the middle-aged whom I have talked to, while writing this book, have described this feeling. They say, "All I can tell you is that my parents make me feel guilty—I feel I'm responsible because they are old." One says,"My mother sighs deeply, while she tells me about her indigestion—and I swear, I feel as if I deliberately gave her gallstones." Or another, "I had lunch with my father the other day, and we talked about his retirement—how useless he feels. He looked so sad—and I couldn't help myself—by the time I walked out of the restaurant, I felt that *I* had done something terrible to him."

I doubt that our children will experience this sensation as much as we do; the idea that children should give pleasure (and therefore, it follows, take away pain) to their parents is fading. But maybe there is something about aging itself which brings about such feelings of despair and anger that life is almost over, that one can't help but appear to be blaming— hating—younger people simply because they are not old. If this is the case, I hereby serve notice to my daughter: *Wendy, don't pay any attention!* Only nature can be blamed for my mortality, and I am stuck with it. I do not ever want to be allowed to victimize those who are younger, and to the degree that it is humanly possible, I here and now implore my daughter not to allow misguided love or guilt to force her into letting the medical profession prolong my life when *she* judges that if I could see what had happened to myself, with middle-aged eyes, I would wish to be allowed to die.

From all that I have learned about old age, I am convinced that nobody should retire from work that he loves until it is impossible to go on, and he has no choice. I don't really know what the solution is. It is good to have turnover, new, younger people, with fresh ideas, but this putting people out to pasture at sixty-five is no solution. The statistics on life expectancy drop alarmingly when people retire. I suppose part of the solution is to begin to give social approval and support to recognizing all the ways in which older people can still be of service. There are such rich resources of experience and expertise among older people; if only we could find ways to connect loving older people to unloved children, or to using the experience and wisdom of retired professionals in our schools and apprenticeship programs. It would certainly improve the mental and physical well-being of all retired people if they were *required by law* to volunteer some of their time to a community service of some kind!

Harry was a shoe buyer for an exclusive and fashionable department store. In his heyday, in the 1920s and 1930s, he led a glamorous life that all his family and friends envied. He traveled to Europe two or three times a year on the biggest and fanciest boats, he wore elegant clothes, he was The Expert in the trade. At sixty-five there was automatic retirement. He might have stayed on for five more years, as a consultant, but the truth was that he was slowing up and his ideas seemed old-fashioned to younger people coming into the field. Harry had always kept himself in great physical form—he was a real nut about exercising. He followed several baseball teams with religious ferocity, was very active in his church, and loved little children. When he retired from his job, he *really* retired; he quit his calisthenics, he stopped going to baseball games, he resigned from his church commit-tee work. Then, for a while it looked as though he were going to have a new job. He was hired by two very young men just starting their own shoe-designing business. He really knew the ropes, knew the contacts; he could be their guide. Within two months of being reemployed he was speaking of his employers as "two young whippersnappers, who don't know beans about shoes." He soon antagonized the small staff with his long stories of past successes and his unwillingness to make any concessions to the new rules and regulations of a union he had never had to deal with before. When he lost the job in six months, he commented, "I thought God had found a niche for me, but I guess I was wrong." Whatever one's personal convictions about God, I have never heard anyone suggest that He is now in the employment business. The Harrys of the world, are people who cannot change, cannot redesign themselves to fit new niches, and they are doomed to failure.

Early "retirement" seems like a great idea if you have hated what you are doing, at worst, or at best have been bored by it. Under such conditions what one is experiencing is not retirement at all, but the freedom one has earned to have a new beginning. Viewed in such a light—again as an opportunity, not a disaster—it is possible to begin a whole new life.

A widow who adored babies, but had found raising three children a great strain and had felt quite imprisoned by her life—too early to be saved by Woman's Lib—took her husband's not too substantial insurance policies and gambled on them. She said, "My lawyer told me that if I lived very simply, Dave's money would take care of me the rest of my life. Well, his money had been taking care of me all my adult life, and yet I felt I had hardly lived. I decided it was time for me." She opened a small infant's-wear store in a shopping center. It was in an area where there were many retired people, and she advertised for "The Grandma Trade." Among her ads in the local newspaper, which she wrote herself, were: "At your time of life why should you go blind, knitting, when I can sell you a sweater even your daughter-in-law won't know you didn't make yourself?" . . . "In a couple of years your grandson will be dirty, fresh, too busy to talk to you. So now, while he's cute, and he'll hug you, buy him a Donald Duck jacket." She capitalized on what she knew about the feelings of grandmothers, and her store is a wild success. "Now it won't be Dave's money that takes care of me," she says, "but Edna's money—that's me!"

An acquaintance told me recently about his sister. She was unmarried, had hated her work, retired as early as possible —but then did nothing. "She behaves like a spoiled child who is going to punish the world for making her do work she hated, by now doing nothing at all. Each year she's more insulated, more withdrawn—*and such a bore!* By having nothing to talk about she is cutting herself off from everyone. Only someone who really hated herself *could do such a cruel thing to herself!*"

And speaking of retirement, one of the most important changes taking place in attitudes toward old age is the contribution made in recent years by such sex experts as Kinsey, and Johnson and Masters, who have been assuring us that sexual functioning can continue just as long as an individual assumes it is natural and good for it to continue; that much inhibition of sexuality in the later years has been due to social taboos and psychological guilt. I must say I have found it a source of comfort and hope to know a twice-widowed lady of seventy-four who is having her first affair (with a gay Lothario of seventy-seven), and I recall with equal pleasure a conversation I had with a friend several years ago. She sounded a little vague and far-away when I called, and she finally explained, "You'll have to excuse me—I'm in something of a state of shock. I've been talking to Grandma on the phone—she's eighty-three—and she's terribly upset because she's having a dinner party for sixteen people tonight, after which she and her forty-eight-year-old boyfriend are taking all the guests to the opera. She says she feels awful— she can't wear the gold lamé evening dress she wants to, because it's too tight for bending down to get her roast out of the oven." I could see why my friend sounded shook-up; but even if her grandma was something of a unique marvel, she certainly *did* provide a worthwhile goal for one to work toward!

I know of no other single factor that is more terrible in our self-destruction in old age than spending all our time thinking about ourselves. Loving is necessary to living, and concern for others is the kind of loving that seems to lead one to new fulfillment in the later years. Mrs. Ernest Hemingway was quoted some time ago as saying, "All my friends have their faces lifted, but it's five grand, and I'd rather give it to charity. Any time I think of spending that much on myself, when I could give it to the Legal Defense Fund of the NAACP— so I'll go around with the same old wrinkles this year, anyway."

One of the most exciting things that has been happening to older people in the past few years—sometimes as a result of discussion groups in centers for older people—has been a reawakening of a sense that one is a citizen as long as one lives, and that old age may well be the time for full concentration on trying to improve the lives of all age groups in this country. Participation in social change is a wonderful antidote to the danger of infantilization of the elderly. And there's nothing like a good cause to make the juices flow in one's veins again! There was a sound truck on Madison Avenue and 86th Street in New York some years ago, with two ladies making impassioned speeches for Robert Kennedy's nomination for president. One was ninety-four, the other was her "little sister," eighty-nine. Another example of the possibilities for social action was something that happened in a large nursing home, where a new director began to impose all kinds of regulations that seemed arbitrary and unfair to the residents. A social worker on the staff told me, "By being a lousy director, Richard did that place a world of good! Before he came, most of the people were listless, constantly complaining about their aches and pains, unwilling to try anything new. He made them so furious that they began forming committees, and finally they planned a strike! It was marvelous to behold. I never saw so many people 'at death's door' recover their strength so fast!"

Slowly but surely one begins to see less stereotyping of older people, and a greater willingness to allow them to participate in the life of the world. For example, more and more government-sponsored housing projects are making provisions for a mixed population in terms of age. Feeling that the young need the old as much as the old need the young, apartments are beginning to be designed to serve the needs of all ages.

One example of the changing attitudes toward the social importance of older people was an imaginative project in Rochester, New York, where nursery schools were being set up for two purposes: (1) to meet the needs of children of working mothers in low income areas, and (2) to offer training and jobs to people who were unemployed. A course was given in child development and nursery education for people who were considered unemployables by the State Employment Service. This included adult illiterates, alcoholics, the aged, and the handicapped. One man who had been on welfare for twenty-two years, and spent at least a few nights every month in jail, sleeping off a big drunk, was asked if he'd like to participate. He was seventy-seven years old, crippled with arthritis and almost illiterate. In one of the nursery schools they set up a special room called "Grandpa's Room." In it they put a rocking chair, a child's cot and a few books and toys. Any time a child seemed overtired, or homesick, or coming down with something, he was asked if he'd like to spend some quiet time with Grandpa, who would take him on his lap and rock him, or gently rub his back. For many of the children who did not have any fathers at home, this was a first positive experience with a man—and Grandpa stayed sober almost all the time, missing only four days during the first six months of his new job.

That is to me the epitome of a society concerned with using all of its human resources, not discarding them. But until there are thousands of such government-sponsored projects, it is up to us as individuals to prepare for a time when we will have to make some crucial decisions for ourselves.

We need to keep in mind that life has meaning for us only so long as there is loving and some kind of serving the needs of others. No matter how old or decrepit we may get, there will never be a time when someone won't need us more than we need them. I sometimes try to imagine a fate that scares me to death—such as that I'm living alone in an apartment, semi-invalided, unable to go out without help, or cook or go shopping. I hope that I would call a social agency in the neighborhood and say that I needed someone to help me, and I wanted to find someone whom I could help in return. Was there a youngster, about fifteen years old, who could come and see me every afternoon, go shopping for me, and do a little cleaning? In return I would pay a small salary, and also do some tutoring or coaching of a student having a hard time getting through high school. It might not work out at all the first five times, but I wouldn't give up. However, I'm not going to wait until then; when I get to that stage of life, I'm going to have a long list of things I can do, that I like to do, that will help me feel needed.

Middle age is a very good time to begin to make plans for

one's old age, and in a society in which financial independence is so inextricably tied to personal dignity, this seems to me to be an important area of planning. I never gave it a thought until forty-five, but I'm giving it a lot of thought now. Some middle-agers I know are actually shopping around for retirement homes, nursing homes, and beginning to make financial contributions in return for a "reservation, date still open."

A wish to be independent doesn't mean that I don't believe children have some responsibility for elderly parents; in a loving and giving family relationship, there ought to be genuine reciprocity of love and caring. The problem is that if an aged parent lives with his children or is totally dependent on them, the danger of infantilization becomes greater; one's children begin to take over, to run things, and the reversal of the earlier roles naturally causes anxiety and then anger in one who isn't about to give up his adult status, no matter how old or infirm he may be.

For myself, I would like to be relatively independent, but if I can't be, I hope my daughter will not invest a lot in my care. I will do my damnedest to live so hard and well, right now, that if I have to go into a Welfare Home for the Aged, at some point, it really won't matter; I will have had more fun than any one person has a right to expect, and assuming no one tries to prolong my *existence* when my *life* is over, I won't mind being alone with my rich and beautiful memories, even in the least aesthetic of surroundings.

Two women whom I know, sisters, aged eighty-four and seventy-three, both still capable of living in their own apartment and taking care of themselves, have spent the last few years doing two things; from January to April they take a freighter to all the romantic, exotic parts of the world they haven't yet seen. From May to December, they shop around for a retirement community that they can move into now, while the choice is still clearly theirs to make. The requirements for this housing are that in addition to good medical care, ir should be near a university, have public transportation or a good taxi service, and that it be a large enough community for there to be social problems to which they can address their attention.

I know of one old man who finally conceded that he could no longer live alone, did not want to live with his daughters, and went to visit a nursing home. He walked into a large lobby in which there were chairs and couches, and absolute silence. Old people sat about, not reading, not talking, just staring into space. At ninety-three, he looked around, and said, "Well, one thing's for sure; if I come here, we are going to have to turn this *waiting* room into a *living* room!"

One of the newer approaches being tried in housing for older people has been foster-home placement. It has been very successful on the whole, and makes excellent sense. Rather than being a denial of the love and compassion that exists between parents and children, it seems to me that the frequent difficulties in their trying to live together really proves how much they care; they are too emotionally involved. I know that some families have carried this off very well, and there are situations in which the needs of both children and elderly parents can really be met adequately by their sharing a home, but not for me, thank you! There are too many old patterns, old roles, too many emotional habits that would inevitably lead to my inability to mind my own business, and I would become defensive and anxious about the fact that in trying to be solicitous and caring, my daughter might encourage me to give up my independence and autonomy long before I needed to.

The classic story in this connection was a conversation I had with a friend some years ago. She was forty, her mother was sixty-five, and her grandmother was eighty-seven. She had spoken to her mother on the phone that morning, and her mother had started to give her some advice about how she should be raising her children. My friend, growing angry, started to say she wasn't exactly a baby anymore, when her mother laughed and said, "Okay, okay, I know how you feel. Grandma has just been nagging *me* about going out without a sweater!"

If one lives with somebody else's family, one still has to make compromises, of course, but they are not so emotionally charged. In this way it is possible to be among young people or not as one pleases—there is choice and selection in the household one chooses. And if one wants to be where there are children, and to feel needed by them, I would imagine there would be less competition between parents and a foster grandparent because they haven't shared an experience of childhood with each other.

On the other hand, if both children and elderly parents genuinely and eagerly want to live together, I don't think the difficulties that often occur should stop them. The idea is *not ever* to live by other people's expectations and attitudes, but to develop one's own.

In all the new experimentation with communal living, it has occurred to me that one aspect of these new life-styles might very well be a solution to the housing for older people. It might just be the kind of setting in which an older person could feel useful and needed.

Another problem for us to think about now is the geography and logistics of where we live when we are old. At one time, it made sense to me that one should stay where one's roots were, where one felt most at home. I recall one grandma in one of our suburban discussion groups who was miserable. She had been moved by her loving children from a tenement in Brooklyn to a garden apartment in Great Neck, Long Island. She told me, "I'm like a prisoner here; if I want to go ten blocks to a movie, I have to call a cab or one of my children to come drive me; everything is too far for me to walk, and oh, how I miss the women in my old building! We knew each other for thirty-five years! I miss the butcher and the tailor—I'm so lonely here." I remember at that time, perhaps fifteen years ago, I thought it was a terrible mistake to uproot someone from a life she loved, and that a child's guilt was an unfair weapon to use against the true wishes of the elderly person. It also seemed to me then that city living was far more ideal for many older people; there were buses, stores right nearby, excitement and chatter of children in the streets, parks for sitting and streets for strolling. All this has changed as our cities wither and die; there is no longer much question that old men and women are the easiest targets for drug addicts and that it has become more and more dangerous for them to live alone in the cities. It is a heartbreaking but real fact of life. The only solution I can think of is that now, while we are younger, we ought to be knocking ourselves out to save the cities, to insist on decent preventive and rehabilitative drug programs, housing projects—more social services of all kinds to save our cities—so that it will again be possible to enjoy the rich resources of city life, if that is what we prefer when we are old.

For myself, I try to think in terms of a small city, or perhaps a college town. At one time the thought of living away from New York would have destroyed me—I loved the excitement, the feeling of being at the hub of the world's activities. I seem to need that less and less as I get older, and the isolation or greater immobility of country living no longer bothers me. I think it is important for us to begin to think about the alternatives, the possibilities for where and how we will live when we are old. But the truth of the matter is, that if we are busily cultivating our inner lives right now, we will be able to live almost any place and not feel lonely or bored.

All the experts on aging talk at great length about the importance of developing hobbies, of having recreational interests, so that one will have these interests for fulfillment when work and family-raising are over. That's all right as far as it goes, but it seems to me that it has led too many people to work too hard at having fun! There are too many people telling us what we *ought* to enjoy doing, what we *should* do, and we often end up being just as serious and intense about leisure as we may be about our work.

One example of this: I recently bought my husband one of the silliest-looking boats any fifty-one-year-old man ever went to sea in. It is an inflatable rubber canoe, like a kayak, with a double paddle. It holds two people—one comfortably—and you sort of lie down and float along. We have had a strange experience with the boat. Every time we go out in it—just bobbing about aimlessly, or bird-watching in the wetlands of the bay—we pass all sorts of very expensive motor and sailboats. Invariably—and the more elaborate and luxurious the boat, the more surely it happens—the middle-aged or elderly people on the fancy boats will smile or burst out laughing, and then say, "Boy, that's *really* the life!" or, "Now *that's* what I call living!" We were very puzzled about it, but I think I finally figured it out; our boat is for *playing;* we are like a couple of kids who don't need anything elaborate for their games, but their own imagination, inventiveness and most of all their childlike capacity for playfulness. We began to see that the response to our boat was a kind of sudden recollection of a time when play was natural, not organized and prescribed, expensive and complicated.

If you want to relax today, you are *supposed* to want to play golf, or you are *supposed* to want to go fishing; maybe what you really feel like doing is lying in a hammock drinking iced tea or watching the wild ducks skiing into the water in their clumsy, comical way—or making a raft and going down the Mississippi River with a pal! What we need to re-cultivate before we are old is the rich capacity we once had to do whatever gives us pleasure in a given moment. I don't think my husband and I have ever walked over a viaduct on a country road, with any kind of stream underneath it, without stopping to make a few tiny boats out of pieces of wood that we set to sailing from one side of the road to the other. I hope we never will. It is just something you feel like doing, because it is fun, whether you are six or sixty.

There was an item in the Talk of the Town in *The New Yorker* about an artist who passed a certain bank each day when he went out for a walk. In the window of the bank was a poster that showed a plump, elderly man sitting outdoors, painting at an easel. The text at the bottom was, "Do Something Now So You Can Do Nothing Later." The artist's acid response was that he supposed from a banker's point of view, sitting at an easel all day might be doing nothing, but from an artist's point of view, doing nothing at all would be sitting at a desk figuring out debentures, checking interest rates, and foreclosing mortgages. He went on to point out that bankers work from nine to five, while artists are working all the time; if they're not painting or sculpting they're thinking about their work. The beautiful point of this piece was, who is supposed to decide what is "something" and what is "nothing" in a human being's life? Each of us must seek out our own inner needs and pleasures, and to hell with how they look to someone else. I recall one Senior Citizen center where I arrived for our weekly discussion while a crafts class was still going on. A charming man of about eighty was making a leather purse for his granddaughter. He looked up, smiled, and said, "I suppose this looks like just keeping an old man busy, doing nothing. I want to tell you something; I never had more pleasure in my life! I used to be a geometry teacher in a high school, but all my life, I really wanted to work with my hands. When I was a boy, being a carpenter or a plumber was looked down on by my family, so I became a teacher. Sitting here, with this little piece of leather, I am having a wonderful time—and my granddaughter's pleasure, in addition, is almost too much!"

The most important influence on the quality of life in old age has to do with whether or not one has been able to learn —and really believe—that every stage of life can be viewed as a developmental opportunity. The challenge is to accept whatever realistic limitations may exist, and then to move on to the new possibilities available. For example, the handsome former juvenile actor who, seeing the wrinkles and the gray hairs, and realizing his hero days are numbered, begins to study the problems of film direction, a whole new and fascinating career opening up for him. Or the woman who can no longer leave her wheelchair, but who says, "In the rush and activity of my life, I never had time to listen to music, or watch a butterfly. Now I can do both, any summer day I want to." Or the man who says, "I was so busy *doing* that I never had time for *thinking*. Now I think all the time!"

Old age is a time for inner development, a time to think and to feel, to contemplate, to become more aware. It is a time to treat oneself to new pleasures. In some ways, the times we live in are getting better and better for older people, as there are more and more people who are active and vigorous after sixty-five or seventy. Almost every university now offers a program of continuing education for those who want to go on learning; there are more and more well-planned programs for retirees to work as volunteers; there are travel agencies that specialize in planning trips for older people; there are more middle-income retirement communities of more varied kinds.

But the real issue for each of us is to begin to think about the inner life of the mind and the heart, the inner world of our own thoughts and feelings. To a considerable degree this involves our capacity to be alone—the enjoyment of being alone; not just tolerating it, but seeking it out as one of the best experiences of life. I do not recommend this lightly; it is something that I have struggled with for many, many years. I grew up in a fairly traditional middle-class environment where husbands and wives spent almost all their nonworking time together. In the early years of marriage, I was devastated by the separations that were caused by my husband's military service; I envisioned that after the war we would never be separated. But that was not the kind of man I married, I have discovered over the years. I sometimes think that what he has done is spend the years of our marriage preparing me for widowhood!

Time came, as we both developed and changed, when it became clear that we were each separate people, with lives and interests of our own. This recognition was harder for me, and at first I fought it. The other day I took a look at my 1970–71 calendar and added up the times we had been separated, as each of us pursued our own work and needs. It was shocking to discover that where, ten years ago, I was devastated if my husband went away for three weeks, the accumulated separations of this past year add up to several months.

One of the positive aspects of my psychotherapy, which I did not mention earlier, was that as I came to value myself more and more, as I was able to express myself in more creative ways, I became more interesting to myself to be with! Further, as I became more mature emotionally, I could mother myself more effectively. I could feel safer and more secure in my own company; I knew that there was someone present who could take care of me—*me*. My husband came to this earlier—and when he would take off on his own necessary pilgrimages (an early one was to walk from Athens to Delphi, for example), I would spend most of my days and nights lonely, miserable, feeling sorry for myself —deserted and rejected. Then, about five years ago, I felt ready to find out what would happen if *I* took off—not to go to a professional convention, not to visit a friend, not to do a television show, but just to be alone. I spent a week in April on an island off the New Jersey shore; I think I only saw four or five people all the time I was there (it was mostly a summertime place). The first three days were just about the worst days of my life; I seemed to sink into a black abyss of nothingness, I ceased to feel my own existence. But as time went by, I discovered that I was getting in touch with myself, that I was searching out what would give me pleasure. I began to look and listen with an awareness I'd never experienced before—to such a degree that when I now go back to the same beach and the same dunes, there is an impact, an intensity of connection I have never experienced anywhere else. What I have developed in these intervening years is an inner companion with whom I am at home in the world. I have begun to learn the lesson we all need to learn, that ultimately and forever, each of us is alone, inside our own skins, no matter how close we may be to other people. We are born alone and we die alone; and if there is one single thing we need in order to face our later years, it is to find pleasure in that companionship.

Each of us needs to search out our own natural and unique ways of being alone; for me the best place is the seashore—a place where I can be a birdwatcher, a surf-listener. For someone else it may be walking in the woods or sitting in front of a fire, or lying in the sun, or walking across the park, or going off to paint a picture, or staying alone in the kitchen, trying out a new recipe. It seems to me that if one can begin in middle age to get a clear sense that each partner in a marriage is a complete and separate person, it should mean that during middle age each will become the most he can be, with no restraints, and, in that becoming, will be most fulfilled and most prepared for any enforced isolation or separation later on.

I consider it an essential preparation for old age, not to have any regrets! Long ago my husband taught me that we rarely if ever regret the things we *do*—we only regret the things we *don't* do. If you make a mistake, you don't have to regret it because you learn from it; even if your mistake hurts other people, it still means that from that point on, you can bring greater sensitivity and compassion to your relationships with others.

At one point a number of years ago, a young niece whom we hardly knew at all came to stay with us during a college vacation. She had been badly burned by her life with rigid and "up-tight" relatives, and didn't expect much of us. Her face clouded over with ready hostility and defensiveness when my husband said, "Now, there are a few words of advice I'd like to give you," but it was love forever after, when he added, "Always try everything twice." That's sound advice at any age!

I have tried hard to accept this philosophy—it didn't come to me easily!—and I can report that it is very sound counsel. As I look back, it was almost always when I was being careful, sensible, realistic, and cautious that I truly lived to regret my actions! One of the worst aspects of old age for too many people is a longing for the "might-have-beens." I am going to try to have as few of those as possible!

As we get older, we have to work harder and harder at mobilizing the life-force within each of us—and what that seems to mean is being as clear as we can be about who we are. One's unique identity as a human being is the force, the vitality that makes life worth living. Until my last breath, I would like to go on trying to figure out *who I am*. I would like to continue to have a sense of the sacredness of life, and to go kicking and screaming with exultant joy at being alive —right into the jaws of my own death. I assert my inalienable right to *be myself* for just as long as I can, and then to choose to die. I *will* that my life end in a blaze of glory, not in the whimpering cries of a senile old woman in pain.

Death is final for me, a total ending. When that finality arrives, I want to feel that I gave everything there was to give, everything that was in me, to my living. I want to save nothing, spend everything, of my energy, my ideas, my loving; I want to use it all up before I die. That means never living in fear of dying, and thinking, "If I take it easy today, if I stay home in bed, I'll save my strength for tomorrow." Not for me! There will be no counting on tomorrow when I am old. I'll take the day I've got.

In *Report to Greco*, Nikos Kazantzakis writes, "For this was my greatest ambition; to leave nothing for death to take —nothing but a few bones." That seems to me to be the only antidote to our terrors.

TODAY IS
THE FIRST DAY
OF THE REST
OF OUR LIVES

Chapter 10

This is the beginning of the day when I will complete the task of writing this book. It has taken almost two years, and I am now fifty. Now there will (hopefully!) be the time for rest and renewal—and another beginning. I'm eager to discover what I will do with my todays, as they come. I couldn't really be any more middle-aged than I am right now. How does it feel? I was surprised by my lack of depression on reaching the half-century mark. But life is so exciting and still so full of promise! I feel more truly myself than I have ever felt before. I am far better able to live in this moment that I have, without unnecessary preoccupation with the past or insistent demands on the future. Each "this moment" becomes far more precious and valued than ever before. When you have learned it's all you can count on, you are not prepared to squander or ignore it; life takes on a vividness rarely experienced before.

One day recently I was standing in a traffic island in Times Square waiting for the light to change, when a taxi screamed by at a frightening speed, seeming to avoid crashing into me by a hair's breadth. As the light changed and I continued on my way across the street, I was reminded, as one is frequently, living in the frightening technological jungle most of us inhabit, that our lives are tenuous and uncertain every moment.

It wasn't an especially nice day. If anything, it was for me a time of stress, uncertainty and pain, and yet, as I walked down the street I had the clear and exultant sense that if I had been hit by a taxi, and if I had died, there would have been more than enough living to satisfy any one person.

I was reminded of another episode about five or six years ago, when I was returning from a magazine assignment in Florida. The plane arrived over La Guardia Airport at about dusk on a spring evening, and it was breathtakingly beautiful, a fairy-tale scene of lights and colors. But something had gone wrong with the wheels; they weren't lowering properly, we later learned, and after a while we began to realize that we were circling around and around. I guess there was about a half-hour of suspense before we did finally make a somewhat wobbly landing, and during that time I surprised myself more than I ever had before. I had always assumed that I would become hysterical under such circumstances, that I would be the biggest coward on the plane and that the idea of dying in a plane crash would be the most terrible moment of my life. It wasn't. Instead I found myself thinking of how much I had lived, how many good things had happened to me. It seemed to me that, all things considered, I had done just about everything I ever had really wanted to do with my life. It was shortly after my first book had been published, and at that time I felt that I had truly written my personal "letter to the world." Although it was no perfect storybook romance, I could not imagine having been married to anyone but my husband, and I had had the infinitely satisfying experience of watching my child grow, of seeing in her every indication of becoming a lovely young woman. I had been greatly loved as a child, and I had had every opportunity to sing my own song, beat out my own music, professionally. I had been loved by many and I had loved. The only sense of panic or regret was that there was no way that I could let my parents, my husband and daughter, know what I was feeling. It seemed a shame that anyone might think that my life had been cut off too soon, when I felt so satisfied.

I was in a state of shock when we landed; not because of the near miss but because of the totally unpredictable quality of my reactions. I had always been a complainer, a screamer; I had always been greedy for more, never content with what was; I seemed to have more than my fair share of "divine discontent." It was a source of wonder and delight to discover that underneath the constant push toward more and more living, there was a deep and quiet pool of contentment.

Since then I have discovered that there were dreams and hopes I never even knew I had at that time—new and greater pleasures and fulfillments than I could have imagined were possible. There have also been times—many of them —when I have looked back with nostalgia, and wished that the plane had crashed, so that I could have missed out on some of the agonies I've known since then. But essentially, I still feel the way I did then. Life has really been wonderful, and whatever more is left is just so much gravy.

That is the beginning of where I go from here, in middle life. No regrets, no bitterness. But there is far more to it than that. What that does is make it possible for me to take chances, to live dangerously! I don't have to hold back, because whatever happens, I'm already ahead of the game. I want to take chances, I want to gamble on whatever creative powers I can find within myself, I want to challenge myself to try new fields of endeavor, conquer unknown countries within myself. It's far from over, but feeling good about what's past, will, I hope, give me the courage to make a continued "quest for maladjustment"! I don't want to settle for being ordinary, and in some ways middle age seems, after all is said and done, to be the very best time of life because I feel I have earned the right to be an eccentric!

My husband has been a great help in that department. He

was an advanced eccentric when I was hardly out of first grade. I have tended for most of my life to worry a great deal about what other people think of me and to try to please other people before pleasing myself. But I'm learning. A couple of summers ago we were taking a walk in Central Park on a terribly hot summer day; it must have been 95° accompanied by the usual, world-famous New York humidity. We passed a playground in which there was a marvelous fountain spray for the young children to play in. We were both fully dressed. My husband began very methodically to take off his watch and shoes, instructed me to do likewise, took my hand, and started marching me toward the fountain. I reacted as usual, "What will people *think?*" and then it just seemed to me that that was too damn silly to worry about. We ran right through the center of the fountain several times, until we were soaked to the skin. It was marvelous! I must say I had some second thoughts when we appeared in the lobby of our apartment building, dripping wet, especially since a few people looked as though they might be about to call Bellevue to send an ambulance for us. But the truth is that the elevator men in our building are just crazy about us, and I think our arrival that day, with the calm observation, "It's lovely in the Park," won their undying admiration. If there are, among you in the New York area, some brave middle-aged souls who would like to organize for future fountain refreshment on a summer afternoon, we are ready to join any such movement.

There are times when I still get terribly chicken about being the eccentric I want to be. A case in point is ankle socks. If you are a middle-aged woman, I don't really have to explain any further; all of us know that bobby socks and saddle shoes were *the* most comfortable combination for walking ever invented. Ankle socks are absolutely wonderful for walking in any kind of comfortable walking shoes, but just try to buy socks, today, even if you had the courage of your convictions and would wear them! You can buy white socks because it is still considered appropriate to wear socks with sneakers, but you can take it from me that in the city of New York there are no navy, brown, wine, green, or black ankle socks. And any woman seen walking in the streets, wearing socks, is assumed to be one hundred and ten years old and in need of immediate embalming.

I get madder and madder as I think about it; why should we let changing fashions dictate to us on comfort? I've tried —God how I've tried! Those little "Peds" roll up; talcum powder keeps your feet from chafing, but only for about half an hour, and stockings or pantyhose are unbearable in the summer. I love to walk, and I need the exercise—and every day, winter and summer, I have this battle with myself; shall I be comfortable and enjoy my walking, or must I concede to the dictates of a fashion I do not understand and that I abhor because it has cut me off from so much pleasure? If any middle-aged ladies would care to form an organization dedicated to reintroducing The Sock to American Fashion, that's another movement I want to join. Until then, I will persist in trying to overcome my cowardice; if you can't look like an eccentric (much less be one) in middle age, when can you?

I am being facetious about eccentricity, but it has a deeper meaning for me. It involves, really, the right to be different, and therefore to be creative. I recently saw a poster on the subject of creativity:

> The man who follows the crowd will usually get no further than the crowd. The man who walks alone is likely to find himself in places no one has ever been before.
>
> Creativity in living is not without its attendant difficulties, for peculiarity breeds contempt. And the unfortunate thing about being ahead of your time is that when people finally realize you were right, they'll say it was obvious all along. You have two choices in life; you can dissolve into the mainstream,

or you can be distinct. To be distinct, you must be different.
To be different, you must strive to be what no one else but
you can be. . . .*

Middle age is the time to start pleasing ourselves. The more
we do it, the happier we will be, and the happier we are, the
nicer we will be to other people. This is a simple idea but it
has caught the attention of many social scientists, and there is
even a very fancy name for it.

The late and brilliant anthropologist, Ruth Benedict, developed a theory about what she called "synergistic societies."
She observed that in cultures that were peaceful and constructive, where people got along well and lived most con-
tentedly, there was always a very specific factor operating,
namely, a philosophy underlying all the behavior of the members of the society. They all believed that when they did
what was good and right for themselves, as individuals, it
could only be good and right for everyone. She wrote: "Societies where nonaggression is conspicuous have social orders
in which the individual by the same act and at the same time
serves his own advantage and that of the group." That is a
most profound and important idea. Most of the miseries of
modern life seem to me to be rooted in individual discontents;
we only tear at each other, try to destroy each other, find
reasons to hate each other, when we feel unfulfilled as persons, ourselves. When a painter is painting his heart out,
when a poet is singing his songs, when a cook is making the
greatest pastries he can make, when a mother is nursing the
child she has longed for, when lovers make love—they
don't want to hurt anybody. Quite the contrary: people who
are using their own unique talents in living want everybody
else to have the same chance.

I try to keep on my middle-aged toes by repeating a ques-

* By Alan Ashley-Pitt (Aardvarque Enterprises, 116 W. Arrellaga Street,
Santa Barbara, California 93104).

tion to myself, every six months or so: "What would I do, right now, if I found out I had six months to live?" If I can't answer myself by saying, "I'd go on doing exactly what I'm doing now," I figure I may be in trouble. It is time for me to be living my life *now*. No pie in the sky tomorrow.

But it is more complicated than that. It is necessary to begin to relinquish some old pleasures as well—to relinquish what one cannot hang onto without paying a price. I cannot hang onto the role of mothering to the degree that I could live it when my daughter was three or seven or eleven; but I *can* discover and experience motherhood as a deep companionship with a young woman I love; and I even dare, sometimes, to dwell on the possibilities of grandmotherhood! There are times, I admit, when there is painful nostalgia for the breathless ardor of falling in love as a young woman, but I soon recover as I consciously remind myself of the far more profound wonders of loving that has behind it twenty-eight years of growing and changing and deepening.

Sometimes I think I have more trouble relinquishing the nonessentials than the really important things. For example, I'm struggling right now with the problem of swimming in cold water! All during the years of my childhood, I was a fish—never happier than when swimming for five or six hours a day. I remember my derision, my exultant superiority when I would watch my parents and other adults getting into the water, splashing a little water on here and there, dunking a limb at a time, looking pained, then swimming for a minute or two and returning to the shore, chilled to the bone.

About ten years ago, I began to notice that while I still could get into the water with reasonable grace, I really was no longer inclined to make a day of it; five or ten minutes seemed to be quite sufficient. By now of course—I know you can all anticipate me!—getting into a New England lake, or the ocean anywhere but in Florida, San Diego or the Caribbean, is simply unmitigated torture. I sprinkle a few drops of the icy water here and there, knowing full well that in spite of inching my way along, the final plunge is still going to be awful.

What I am trying to work toward is a total relinquishment of my image of myself as a cold-water fish, about eight or nine years old, immersed in the Saugatuck River in Westport, Connecticut, and to face the fact that I am now a fifty-year-old lady, at the Jersey shore, hating that plunge into the icy ocean! Whenever we have stayed at a motel with a heated pool, we have had a wonderful time, and my husband, who always seems to get there first, glories in the fact that now he can have years and years of delightful swims in warm bath-water; for him there is no regret, no shame.

I try to remember that when I was of an age to race into the water and stay there all day, I really didn't have much else going for me. I hadn't yet read any great books, or fallen in love, or worked at a job I enjoyed, or listened to the world's store of glorious music—I was really nothing much. All things considered, I know, deep-down, I'd rather be the me who needs the heated pool.

Some relinquishments came without any ambivalence—dinner parties, for example! Most of us did a lot of going out and a lot of entertaining in our thirties. Sometimes I look back in amazement at the days devoted to competing with each other as hostesses to see who could make the best Hindu curry or quiche Lorraine. Almost every Saturday night there was a gathering, and while we really did like each other, and they were all nice people, it began to be a drag. What happened to most of us is that we got to be middle-aged, discovered we were not going to live forever and had limited time, and we began to get pretty choosy about how we spent it. In your forties you begin to retrench; you get much more selective about your friends. And you suddenly discover that because you are making your own life count for more, you have far richer experiences with a selected few than you ever had when you were a social butterfly.

Beyond relinquishment, I think one of the most important keys to a full and happy middle age has to do with trusting oneself. That is why throughout the pages of this book I have placed so much stress on the developmental task—the opportunity one has and ought to take in middle life—to discover who one is and what one wants to be. The better we know our real selves, the more we can let life happen to us, the more we can trust our perceptions, our wishes, our sensitivities, our courage to meet life with an open heart without needing to have life programmed for us.

Trusting ourselves also brings into focus the fact that we must take responsibility for our own lives. No one else is responsible for what we do with our lives, and the sooner we understand that, the better off we will be. And so will everyone we love. For example, about four years ago I decided that if I didn't have an escape hatch, a place I could run to, to get away from the city, I would never survive. It was I who decided to make the commitment to buy a cottage at the seashore. My husband and daughter went along with the gag, neither having any inclination in this direction at all. A few weeks ago, after I had spent about ten days there all by myself and was getting a little lonely and stir-crazy, I heard myself complaining to both husband and daughter on the telephone. At one point I said, "I'm going to sell this damned house. It's insane to keep it just for me to rattle around in all by myself." My daughter suddenly sounded very contrite on the phone. She said, "I'm sorry, Mommy, we would have come to see you more, but you know we had to work, and then we had to find an apartment . . ." but before she'd said any more, I was ashamed of myself. *I* wanted to spend *my* time at the seashore; nobody stopped me, or interfered with my decision—even though it was impulsive and extravagant, and has been a heavy and unrealistic financial burden. I did it—and the minute I hold anyone else responsible for making me happy, I am in deep trouble with myself. It is time for me to accept the burden of having trusted my own needs.

A woman I know was suffering greatly; her life was in turmoil and she was in the agonizing throes of the possible ending of a marriage that she valued deeply, while also having discovered herself to be in love with someone other than her husband. She said, "The pain of what I am living through is beyond describing, and yet, even now, I have the sense of something important and necessary happening. *I am present at my own life*—and that is so much better than feeling nothing." That too, seems to me to be an essential ingredient in our struggles with middle age; to seek the goal of always being present at one's own life, no matter what the cost in pain, to feel the fullest sense of one's own aliveness.

To be present in one's moment of being doesn't mean that there is no sense of future. I recall someone once asking a research scientist what he would do when the current project he was working on, was finished to his satisfaction. He smiled and said, "There's always another windmill." In order to savor the current moment fully, there needs to be, in that savoring, an abiding belief in the possibility of future moments just as precious—a world of future moments with many windmills.

In her autobiography,* English novelist and playwright Enid Bagnold (whose most recent play was written at seventy-five) wrote, "I shall continue to explore—the astonishment of living." That seems to me to encompass the sense of both the present and the future, for to "continue to explore" and to savor one's astonishment is to be in both the present and the future simultaneously.

* *Enid Bagnold's Autobiography*, Atlantic-Little Brown, 1970.

In the spirit of that continuum, where am I at this moment? This today that is the beginning of the rest of my life! About to experience a deep quiet of completion while I begin to contemplate the next windmill. Am I ready to try fiction? And what other triumphant joys and agonizing terrors will my next adventures bring? I wait breathlessly.

Index